Contract Law in the Netherlands

Contract Law in the Netherlands

Third Edition

M.M.C. van de Moosdijk

This book was originally published as a monograph in the International Encyclopaedia of Laws/Contracts.

Founding Editor: Roger Blanpain
General Editor: Frank Hendrickx
Volume Editor: Jacques Herbots

Wolters Kluwer

Published by:
Kluwer Law International B.V.
PO Box 316
2400 AH Alphen aan den Rijn
The Netherlands
E-mail: lrs-sales@wolterskluwer.com
Website: www.wolterskluwer.com/en/solutions/kluwerlawinternational

Sold and distributed by:
Wolters Kluwer Legal & Regulatory U.S.
920 Links Avenue
Landisville, PA 17538
United States of America
E-mail: customer.service@wolterskluwer.com

ISBN 978-94-035-3218-9

e-Book: ISBN 978-94-035-3228-8
web-PDF: ISBN 978-94-035-3238-7

The Author

Marloes van de Moosdijk (1987) completed the Research Master's Programme in Business and Law at Radboud University in Nijmegen in 2012. After taking her Master's, Marloes van de Moosdijk joined the Civil Law Section of Radboud University as a doctoral candidate and lecturer. In 2015, she worked for four months at the Max-Planck-Institut für ausländisches und internationales Privatrecht in Hamburg on a research scholarship granted by the Max-Planck-Institut. In 2017, she spent two months as a visiting researcher at Harris Manchester College (University of Oxford). From 1 March 2018, she has held a post as assistant professor of Civil Law at the Nijmegen Faculty of Law. Marloes defended her thesis on unjust enrichment in European law on 27 November 2018. As of 1 February 2019, she has been a law clerk at the Supreme Court of the Netherlands, working for both justices and advocate-generals. In her capacity as a researcher at the Research Centre Business and Law of the Radboud University Nijmegen, she has written several contributions on the law of obligations and the European influence on Dutch law.

The Author

Table of Contents

References

References in the footnotes have been restricted to decisions of the Supreme Court. The decisions are quoted by HR (short for 'Hoge Raad', Supreme Court), followed by the date of the decision, the volume of the NJ (short for 'Nederlandse Jurisprudentie', the Dutch periodical in which the court decisions are published) and the number under which they are published.

References

Preface to the First Edition (1995)

The present monograph deals with Dutch contract law as it has been enacted in 1992 as a part of the new Civil Code of the Netherlands. This code has been anticipated for a long time (work started as early as 1947) and represents a major update of Dutch patrimonial law. In the new Code, the system of patrimonial law has been improved, some parts of the law have been fundamentally changed, some parts have been slightly adapted, and a large part of the 'old law' has been revised and maintained. More information on the history and background of the new Civil Code will be found in paragraph 22.

Due to the fact that a new Code has recently come into effect, many references are made in the present monograph to the text and the system of the Code, whereas the number of references to legal doctrine and Supreme Court decisions is limited.

Articles of the new Code are quoted by indicating first the Book of the Code to which they belong, followed by a colon and the number of the article, e.g., Article 3:1 and Article 6:248. In order to provide a comprehensive overview of the system of the Code, the table of contents of Books 3 and 6 has been reproduced in Annexe I.

The legal English used in this monograph is, to a large extent, based on the English translation of the Code by P.P.C. Haanappel (Kluwer, 1990). In that translation, a deliberate attempt was made to use English civilian (as opposed to common law) terminology.

Some parts of the text are derived from earlier publications in English by the first author (*see* the bibliography in paragraph 37). Moreover, his treatise on the law of obligations ('Asser–serie, Part 4, Vols I–III') has served as the basis of a large part of this monograph.

Arthur S. Hartkamp
Marianne M.M. Tillema

Preface to the Second Edition

In the second edition, the number of references to Supreme Court decisions has been substantially enlarged. Moreover, new statutory regulations have been dealt with until 1 May 2003.

The legal English used in this monograph is, to a large extent, based on the revised English translation of the Code by P.P.C. Haanappel and E. Mackaay, Netherlands Business Legislation, looseleaf ed., Kluwer Law International.

The second edition of this book was written by Annemarie ter Heide and Arthur Hartkamp.

The Hague, May 2003
Arthur S. Hartkamp
Annemarie E.B. ter Heide

Preface to the Third Edition

In the third edition, I have restricted myself to updating the existing text. New legislation, case law of the Supreme Court and literature have been taken into consideration until 31 July 2008.

The Hague, August 2008
Arthur Hartkamp

Preface to the Fourth Edition

In the fourth edition, the existing text has been updated. New legislation, case law of the Supreme Court and literature have been taken into consideration until 1 August 2015

The Hague, 1 August 2015
Arthur Hartkamp

Preface to the Fifth Edition

In the fifth edition, the existing text has been updated. As such, it gratefully builds on the previous editions of this book by professor Arthur S. Hartkamp. New legislation, case law of the Supreme Court and literature have been taken into consideration until 1 February 2024.

Oss, February 2024
Marloes van de Moosdijk

General Introduction

Chapter 1. The General Background of the Country

§1. Some General Information

1. The Netherlands are located in the western part of Europe and cover an area of well over 41,000 km^2. On the northern and western side the country is surrounded by the North Sea, on the southern side by Belgium and on the eastern side by Germany. Apart from the mainland, several islands in the Wadden Sea belong to the Netherlands; five of them are inhabited. The Netherlands used to have more islands, but these have become a peninsula or are now surrounded by polder waters as a result of the so-called Zuider Zee and Delta works, which entailed, among other things, the drainage of substantial parts of the sea. Almost 40% of the country lies below sea level; the struggle against the sea has always been a Dutch concern, especially after the flood disaster of 1953, which hit parts of the provinces of Zuid-Holland, Zeeland and Noord-Brabant and caused the death of almost 2,000 people, the destruction of more than 40,000 houses and large economic damage, especially resulting from the fact that fertile soil became brackish.

The Netherlands are at present territorially subdivided into twelve provinces: Friesland, Groningen, Drenthe, Overijssel, Gelderland, Flevoland, Utrecht, Noord-Holland, Zuid-Holland, Zeeland, Noord-Brabant and Limburg.

The name 'the Netherlands' (the 'low countries') refers to the low-lying position of the country. Another common name for the Netherlands is 'Holland', which is a collective name for the provinces Noord- and Zuid-Holland (where the main cities are located and which has traditionally been the most important part of the country from an economic and political point of view), but serves as *pars pro toto* for the country as a whole. The official language is the Dutch language ('Nederlands'); the Frisian language, which is spoken in the northern province of Friesland, has a special status. There are also several dialects.

The currency is the euro; until 1 January 2002, it was the Dutch guilder or florin ('gulden'). The reigning king (the first king after three queens) of the Netherlands is Willem-Alexander; in 2013, he succeeded his mother, Beatrix. The Constitution states that the legal descendants of King William I, prince of Oranje-Nassau, are hereditarily entrusted with the monarchy.

The capital of the Netherlands is Amsterdam, but the government has its seat in The Hague. The population amounts to about 17.8 million inhabitants: the Netherlands are one of the most densely populated countries in the world. The western part especially is over-populated. As a consequence of the population density, the Dutch network of roads, waterways and railways is extensive.

The Netherlands boast one of the largest ports in the world, the port of Rotterdam. Dutch industry is highly developed, and agriculture is intensive and export-orientated. The Netherlands have a natural gas field in the province of Groningen, resulting in the country being the largest producer of natural gas in western Europe. However, the gas extraction has led to several earthquakes in that area, resulting in the necessary downscaling of the extraction.

The Dutch system of social security is elaborate and comprehensive. After a period of economic recovery in the years following the Second World War, the Netherlands have – in the period 1963–1980 – grown into a social welfare state, which intends to guarantee all members of society a certain level of prosperity. There is a large amount and variety of benefits, some intended for the population as a whole and some especially for employees. There are, for example, benefits for unemployed, invalid or incapacitated persons. There is a child allowance, a de facto national health service for the part of the population with lesser means and an old age pension for all inhabitants. Furthermore there is a system of minimum wages and a guaranteed minimum income for those who do not have the means to provide for the necessary costs of living. As a result, Dutch public expenditure is very high.

The Netherlands belong to several international organizations. Since 1944, there has been an economic and cultural association with Belgium and Luxembourg, the Benelux. Furthermore, the country has been a member of the European Union (EU) since its inception and also a member of the former Western European Union (WEU), the Council of Europe, the Occupational and Environmental Safety Office (OESO) and the North Atlantic Treaty Organization (NATO). The Netherlands were among the founders of the United Nations (UN) and took part in all specialized UN-organizations.

The Netherlands have a colonial past. Among the Dutch colonies were the Netherlands East Indies (now Indonesia), Surinam and the Netherlands Antilles. Indonesia became independent in 1949 – in the first period of independence, Indonesia and the Netherlands formed a Union, but this union was dissolved in 1954 as a result of irreconcilable conflicts between the two countries – and Surinam became independent in 1975 after internal autonomy had already been granted in 1954. According to the Charter for the Kingdom of the Netherlands, the six islands of the Netherlands Antilles still constitute together with the Netherlands the Kingdom of the Netherlands, consisting (since 2010) of four separate lands (the European part, Aruba, Curaçao, Sint Maarten) and three islands which form direct parts of the Netherlands (Bonaire, St. Eustatius and Saba). The Dutch Supreme Court ('Hoge Raad') is still the highest judicial body for the Antilles. On 1 January 2001, a new Civil Code for the Netherlands Antilles came into effect, which is largely based on the Dutch New Civil Code. A new civil code for Aruba followed on 1 January 2002 and has been adjusted in 2014 and 2016.

§2. The Dutch Political Order in Broad Outline

2. The Dutch polity may be defined as a constitutional, hereditary monarchy. In the Constitution of 1815, the constitutional monarchy was given its first shape. The first king was William I, who reigned as an autocratic ruler and did not grant substantial influence to the representatives of the people. Under the influence of liberal opposition, which became stronger during the reign of William II (1840–1849), a new constitution, prepared by a committee under the chairmanship of the important Dutch statesman Thorbecke, came into being in 1848. In this constitution some fundamental changes were introduced, like inviolability of the King, combined with full responsibility of the Ministers, extension of the powers of Parliament and direct elections for the Lower Chamber and the Provincial Councils. Although the constitution of 1848 was changed several times – it was reviewed in 1983, and some more changes were added in 1987 – it is still the foundation of Dutch polity. The last step towards a parliamentary system was taken in 1868. In that year, the – unwritten – rule that a Minister may be forced to resign if he loses the confidence of the Lower Chamber was actually put into practice for the first time. This event established the supremacy of Parliament. The final stage in the development was the realization of full democracy. In 1850, only 15% of Dutch men had the right to vote; in 1896, this percentage had risen to 50%. In 1917, universal suffrage for men was introduced, followed in 1919 by universal suffrage for women. Part of the process of democratization was the lowering of the age at which the right to vote was granted, from the age of 25 in 1917 to the age of 18 in 1972.

The most important organs of the state are the Parliament, Government, Judiciary and the Council of State.

The Dutch parliament ('Staten-Generaal') consists of two chambers. The Upper Chamber ('Eerste Kamer') has 75 members who are elected for a period of four years by the Provincial Councils; the Lower Chamber ('Tweede Kamer') has 150 members who are directly elected for a period of four years. The constitution grants the right to vote to Dutch citizens 18 years of age and older. Dutch citizens 18 years and older who have not lost their right to vote are eligible for parliament. There are quite a few political parties delegated in parliament. Traditionally, the largest were the Christian Democrats (CDA), the Socialists (PvdA), and the Liberals (VVD). More recent years saw significant changes, resulting, *inter alia*, in the VVD becoming the largest party, the CDA and the PvdA losing much of their support and several populist parties coming into being. The elections of 2023 marked a change in the political landscape: the Party for Freedom (PVV) became the largest party, followed by a new party, National Social Contract (NSC). Since 1917, the Lower Chamber has been elected on the basis of a system of proportional representation, which means – simply put – that a candidate is chosen if he has acquired at least as many votes as the total amount of votes divided by 150. Dutch governments are always coalition governments.

The government, sometimes referred to as the 'Crown', consists of the monarch and the responsible ministers. The ministers are heads of ministries, dealing (in 2023) respectively with General Affairs; Interior and Kingdom Relations; Foreign Affairs; Defence; Economic Affairs and Climate Policy; Finance; Infrastructure and Water Management; Justice and Security; Agriculture, Nature and Food Quality,

Education, Culture and Science; Social Affairs and Employment; and Health, Welfare and Sport. The number and composition of the ministries may vary, and in the past, there have also been ministers without portfolios.

Together, the ministers form the cabinet, which is presided over by the prime minister, who is charged with the task of policy coordination, among other things. The individual ministers are responsible for their own policy as well as for the policy of the cabinet as a whole.

The judiciary consists of independent judges who are appointed 'for life' by the King (they resign at 70 years of age, or, if they so choose, at any time from the age of 65 onwards). The organization of the judiciary is provided for in the Judicature Act, which was changed substantially by 1 January 2002. By this date, the subdistrict courts which dealt with minor civil and criminal cases, but also with employment cases and lease cases, were made part of the district courts, the number of which has been gradually reduced to eleven nationwide. The district courts are now the first instance in most legal disputes, notably in civil cases, criminal cases and most administrative cases. Appeal from judgments of the district courts may be lodged to one of the four courts of appeal. Finally there is in civil, tax and criminal cases the possibility of cassation by the Supreme Court ('Hoge Raad'). The Supreme Court does not re-assess the facts of a case but only checks if the disputed judgment exhibits misapplication of the law or non-compliance with procedural requirements.

The Council of State, the last of the above-mentioned organs of the state, is an advisory board for the government. The Council consists of two divisions. Advice by the Legislation Division of the Council of State is constitutionally prescribed with regard to proposed bills and regulations and the approval of international treaties. The Administrative Disputes Division of the Council of State gives decisions in administrative disputes in cases provided for by statute.

§3. The Legislative, Executive and Judicial Power

3. Departing from the classical doctrine of the separation of powers, legislative, executive and judicial power is vested in the above-mentioned state organs in the following way.

The legislative power is executed by the government and parliament together. A law that has come into being through cooperation between the government and parliament is a statute in the formal sense of the word. In a more material sense, 'a law' is defined as 'a general rule that is binding for the citizens'. Legislative power, in that sense, is also executed by government organs alone (delegation of legislative power to the Crown is a common phenomenon) and lower governmental bodies. The Netherlands are a territorially and functionally decentralized state. Provinces, municipalities and public bodies such as the water boards or the industry boards each have their own legislative and governmental power. Unity is guaranteed by a system of supervisory instruments.

The constitution assigns the executive power to the Crown, that is, the government (King and ministers). The executive power comprises all public activities, with the exception of legislature and jurisdiction. Parliament has the power to influence and control the governmental administration, especially through the budget right and the right of interpellation.

The judicial power is in the hands of the judiciary, as described above. The judges are obliged to apply statutes in the formal sense of the word, even if they consider a statute to be contrary to the Constitution. From time to time this prohibition of judicial review is subject to discussion. The discussion has been triggered by a remarkable judgment of the President of the District Court of the Hague, who held a statute contrary to the Charter for the Kingdom of the Netherlands of 1954. This Charter was intended to regulate the internal order between The Netherlands, Surinam and the Antilles and contains a set of basic rights that may also be found in the constitution. The judgment was quashed by the Supreme Court[1] after a leapfrog appeal, but the subject of constitutional review gained renewed attention (*see* further *infra*, paragraph 6). The practical importance of this subject, however, must not be overestimated. The Constitution may not permit judicial review (a constitutional court does not exist in the Netherlands), but it does provide for the review of statutes in light of international conventions. This has turned out to be a great source of development of the law, especially in the field of human rights.

§4. Legal System: Relation Legislation and Judge-Made Law

4. The Dutch legal system belongs to the civil law system. It is based on codification; primacy of legislation is one of its characteristics. Judge-made law is, however, very important as well. To find the answers to questions of private law, it is almost always necessary to examine both case law and the text of the Code. Due to considerations of legal security, equality before the law and unity of law, prior court decisions are generally observed by the courts. Especially decisions of the '*Hoge Raad*' (Supreme Court) have great authority, although there is no rule of *stare decisis.* Some fields of the law, for example, tort law, have been developed almost exclusively by court decisions. There is also a considerable body of case law on the concept of 'good faith' and 'reasonableness and fairness', mainly but not exclusively in the law of contracts.

The judiciary is generally cautious in its handling of statutory law. Texts are interpreted, gaps are filled, and law is developed, but the rules as laid down in the statutes – and nowadays, most of the legal problems are governed by statutes – are the basis for court decisions. For the interpretation of statutory law, not only the text of the law plays a part: the system of the law, its parliamentary history, the purpose of the law and the principles and intentions that lie at the basis of the law are as important, if not more important. If the literal text of the law is contrary to its purpose, the purpose will usually be decisive. Another argument that is sometimes used to reach a certain outcome is a 'reasonable interpretation of the statute'. It is not so that the courts fill all gaps in the legislation, however vast. Sometimes, problems could be solved in so many different ways that the Supreme Court hesitates to fill

1. HR 14-4-1989, ECLI:NL:HR:1989:AD5725, NJ 1989/469.

those gaps and explicitly leaves it to the legislature to do so. It then declares that solving the problem is beyond the 'law developing task of the judiciary'.

Decisions which are explicitly *contra legem* are very rare. An example of such a decision may be found in a Supreme Court decision of 1972,[2] in which the Court judged that two antiquated and obsolete articles of the Commercial Code with regard to fire insurance were no longer binding. An important argument to that effect was that in later special legislation, the legislature itself assumed the articles to have lost their force. Cases like this are rare; the constitutional position of the courts implies that they have to accept the authority of the legislature. However, the duty based on EU law to interpret national legislation in conformity with directives and other instruments of EU law sometimes compels the courts to stretch or restrict the text of national legal instruments to the verge of a *contra legem* decision.

§5. Vague Concepts in Statutory Law

5. Now and then, statutory law contains vague and undefined concepts (general clauses, blanket formulas). In such cases, it is the task of the judge to further substantiate these concepts. Sometimes, this is done in view of the specific case ('in this special case, the standards of reasonableness and fairness require'); sometimes, the vague concept is first defined in more detail by the development of a set of general subrules.

For example, in a famous decision of 1919,[3] the Supreme Court defined an unlawful act as an act or omission which violates another's right or conflicts with another's statutory duty or is contrary either to good morals or to the care which is due in society with regard to another's person or property.

This development of certain fields of law by the courts could take place because of the vagueness of the concepts and standards in question ('unlawful', 'good faith').

The present Code also contains regular references to open-ended concepts and standards, the most important of which in contract law are 'reasonableness and fairness' (*see* on the standards of reasonableness and fairness, *infra*, paragraphs 31 ff.). In this way, the judge is able to react adequately to the developments in society and do justice to the special circumstances of each individual case. Article 6:2, paragraph 2, even allows the judge to decide that a rule binding on the parties by virtue of law does not apply to the extent that, in the given circumstances, this would be unacceptable according to the standards of reasonableness and fairness. The use of the term 'unacceptable' already points out that the judge should show great restraint in this respect. *See* for a striking example of creative case law under the old Code *infra*, paragraphs 47–48 (natural obligation).

2. HR 3-3-1972, ECLI:NL:HR:1972:AB3597, NJ 1972/339.
3. HR 31-1-1919, ECLI:NL:HR:1919:AG1776, NJ 1919, p. 161.

§6. JUDICIAL REVIEW

6. Statutes are not subject to judicial review as far as the Constitution is concerned (which marks the supremacy of legislation over judge-made law). Article 120 of the Constitution contains a provision to that effect. The background of this provision is that the question as to whether statutory law is in accordance with the Constitution was primarily seen as political. Such questions could therefore best be answered by a political organ, the legislature, and not by the independent and non-political judiciary. This provision is, however, very much under discussion at the moment. There is an important movement in the Netherlands in favour of constitutional review, and the discussion on constitutional review is an important issue for the government and the judicial organizations in the Netherlands and Europe after the Dutch childcare benefits scandal in 2013–2019. A first draft bill proposing to introduce constitutional review was passed in both Houses of Parliament in 2008; the required second draft bill was withdrawn in 2018 due to procedural issues. In particular, the traditional view expressed by the Constitution seems to be entirely outdated where the review of national legislation in the light of fundamental rights is concerned.

The Constitution does not allow for judicial review of statutes with regard to the Constitution itself, but on the other hand, fortunately, the Constitution allows for judicial review with regard to self-executing rules of international treaties like the European Convention for the Protection of Human Rights and Fundamental Freedoms (ECRM) and the International Convention on Civil and Political Rights (ICCPR). The Dutch courts make more and more use of arguments derived from international treaties, especially the European Court of Human Rights (ECHR). If interpretation of Dutch law in conformity with the ECHR is not possible, the courts normally will set Dutch law aside, although it also occurs that a court establishes incompatibility but leaves it to the legislature to change the law. An example of a case in which the Supreme Court considered Dutch law to be incompatible with the ECHR (Article 8) and therefore did not apply the law can be found in a decision of 1988.[4] With regard to the recognition of a child by its natural father, Dutch law used to provide for an absolute right of veto for the mother of the child. The Supreme Court considered this incompatible with Article 8 ECHR and therefore introduced an exception to the rule. In December 2021 the Supreme Court held the systematic of the Dutch capital gains tax incompatible with the right to property (Article 1 FP ECHR) and the prohibition of discrimination (Article 14 ECHR). It is considered that a taxpayer can only be obligated to pay tax on the actual benefits gained on savings and not on a fixed return set by the authorities.[5]

4. HR 8-4-1988, ECLI:NL:HR:1988:AC0318, NJ 1989/170.
5. HR 24-12-2021, ECLI:NL:HR:2021:1963, NJB 2022/301.

Chapter 2. Distinction Between Public Law and Private Law

§1. Public Law and Private Law: Infringement of a Private Right by the Administration – Judicial Competence

7. The distinction between public law and private law is not clear and much discussed in the Netherlands. The boundaries between public law and private law are becoming more and more vague. One of the reasons for this is that the ordinary courts are (until recently on the basis of Article 2 of the '*Wet op de Rechterlijke Organisatie*' (Judicature Act) and presently on that of the Constitution itself) competent to judge (juridical) acts of the administration when the plaintiff claims that a private right has been infringed. The nature of the affected right is decisive, not the character of the legal relation (public or private).

However, if there is an administrative procedure (either before the district court or before a specialized administrative court) available which guarantees a due process, the ordinary courts withdraw.

There is no special procedure for actions based on torts committed by the administration. In principle, therefore, ordinary courts apply Article 6:162 of the Civil Code (the general provision on torts) to administrative acts.

§2. Position of the Administration in Tort Law and Contract Law: General Principles of Proper Administration

8. For a long time, the courts made a distinction between the position in which the administration is acting on equal footing with a private person and the position of the administration acting in the fulfilment of its public duty. In the first case, the administration was held liable in the same way as a private person; in the latter case, the courts judged by different standards. This distinction has lost much of its importance, not only because it is often unclear but also because it fails to acknowledge the fact that the administration, in all acts, purports to serve the public interest. For these reasons, there is a marked tendency nowadays to judge all acts of the administration by the same standards which prevail in the law of torts in general; within the framework of these standards, there is room for the necessary flexibility and discretion, taking into account the nature of the administration's task, the purport of the law from which the administration's authority to act is derived and the other circumstances of the case.

The principles set out above apply *mutatis mutandis* not only to the law of torts but also to other areas of the law, notably the law of contracts (*see also infra*, paragraphs 324 ff.), property law and the law of restitution.

As a consequence, all acts of the administration (in fact, of the central administration as well as those of the local authorities), which may be judged by the ordinary courts according to the criteria mentioned in paragraph 7 above, should comply with the 'general principles of proper administration', a set of judge-made (and now partly codified) legal standards which are applied within the framework of such generic concepts as good faith in the law of contracts (Article 6:2, 6:248 and 6:258) and 'rules of unwritten law pertaining to proper social conduct' in the law of torts

(Article 6:162). An example of a case in which the Supreme Court ruled that the administration is bound by the general principles of proper administration and the principle of equality (Article 3:14 BW) when selling property.[6]

§3. PUBLIC GOALS THROUGH PRIVATE LAW

9. In the Dutch system, the administration is, in principle, free to pursue its public goals through the means of both public and private law. The Supreme Court has formulated an important exception to this rule:[7] when the use of an instrument of private law thwarts a public regulation in an unacceptable way, the administration has to use the public way.

In accordance with the above-mentioned developments, the Supreme Court has repeatedly stated that if the administration chooses the way of private law, it has to abide by the 'general principles of proper administration' when exercising its powers based on a private legal relation (cf. Article 3:14).[8]

§4. PUBLIC CONTRACTS

10. Sometimes, administrative bodies enter into contracts with a genuine public law character, which can therefore be classified as public contracts. An example of this is the contract between two public bodies, based on the General Regulations Act of 1 April 1950, aimed at the promotion of their mutual interests.

The general rules of Book 3 of the Civil Code (such as the regulations on juridical acts, procuration and rights of action) or other rules of private law (such as the notion of reasonableness and fairness) may be applied *per analogiam* to these contracts (cf. Article 3:15). Moreover, the Supreme Court has decided that these contracts, too, are subject to the principle of good faith (reasonableness and fairness).[9]

6. HR 26-11-2021, ECLI:NL:HR:2021:1778, NJB 2021/3180.
7. HR 26-1-1990, ECLI:NL:HR:1990:AC0965, NJ 1991/393; HR 9-7-1990, ECLI:NL:HR:1990:AN1176, NJ 1991/394.
8. HR 27-3-1987, ECLI:NL:HR:1987:AG5565, NJ 1987/727; *see also* HR 26-11-2021, ECLI:NL:HR:2021:1778, NJB 2021/3180.
9. HR 10-4-1987, ECLI:NL:HR:1989:AD0834, NJ 1988/148.

Chapter 3. Distinction Between Civil Law and Commercial Law

§1. Incorporation of Commercial Law in the Civil Code

11. Commercial law partly is and will be further incorporated into the Civil Code. Book 2 concerns 'Legal Persons'; Books 7 ('Special contracts') and 8 ('Traffic and transport') are designed to contain the remainder of commercial law. For example, insurance law has been moved to Book 7; transport law has been moved to Book 8. The former Dutch Commercial Code dates, like the Civil Code, back to 1838. Its only predecessor was the French Code de Commerce (1811–1838).

Before the French Revolution, the distinction between civil and commercial law did not exist in the Dutch provinces. Hugo de Groot, in his '*Inleidinge*' ('*Introduction*', *see* paragraph 20 below), dealt with both branches of the law; so did other early Dutch authors.

Bringing together civil law and commercial law was also the logical outcome of a development which started in 1838. Article 1 of the Dutch Commercial Code provided that, apart from explicit deviations, the Civil Code applied to all subjects dealt with in the Commercial Code. Also, in 1838, the special courts of commerce, introduced in the Napoleonic era, were abolished. Subsequently, the law of bankruptcy was taken out of the Commercial Code and put into a special statute, no longer restricted to merchants (1893). Finally, in 1934, almost all differences between merchants and others were banned from private law.

Under these circumstances, it was no longer appropriate to arrange civil law and commercial law in separate codes.

Introduction to the Law of Contracts

Chapter 1. Definition of a Contract

§1. General Definition

12. A general definition of a contract is:

> A contract is a juridical act, established – in compliance with possible formalities, required by the law – by the corresponding and mutually interdependent expressions of intent of two or more parties, directed at the creation of juridical effects for the benefit of one of the parties and to the account of the other party, or for the benefit and to the account of both parties.

§2. Elements of the Definition

13. A contract is a species of the genus 'juridical act'. 'Juridical act' may be described as an act by which juridical effects are produced due to the expressed intention of one or more acting persons. Most multilateral juridical acts are contracts.

Normally, the most important characteristic of a contract is the mutual consent of the parties. Mutual consent is not the only characteristic, however; for the formation of a contract, it is necessary that the intention is expressed to the other party. Both requirements will be discussed later (*see infra*, paragraphs 37 ff.). On the other hand, it is possible that a valid contract is concluded without there being mutual consent; *see* paragraph 15 below (Reliance) and paragraph 40 below (Irrevocable Offer).

The corresponding expressions of consent must be interdependent. One party consents because or if the other party consents. Without this interdependence, there is no contract; for example, when in a meeting, a board of directors is chosen by general consent, this decision is a juridical act but not a contract because there is no mutual interdependence.

The intention of the parties must be aimed at the creation of juridical effects. There are a lot of agreements which bring about social or moral obligations, but no juridical effects. The appointment to go to the theatre does, in general, not create juridical effects, although this might be the case in special circumstances. The intention of the parties to create legal relations is decisive in these cases.

Finally, the juridical effects have to be produced for the benefit of one party and to the account of the other party or for the benefit or to the account of both parties.

It is a general rule of the Dutch law of contracts that parties can only create obligations towards each other, not towards third persons. The exceptions to this general rule and the other special problems concerning the position of third parties (whose position can be influenced by contracts of others in various ways) will be discussed *infra* in paragraphs 130 ff.

§3. Principles of Contract Law

14. Dutch contract law is based on several principles which explain the binding force of a contract or the necessary conditions for such binding force:

(a) The first principle relates to party autonomy (self-determination) on which the principle of *freedom of contract* is based. According to this principle, as a rule, anybody is free to enter into a contract with somebody of his choice,[10] to agree upon the contents of the contract, and to submit it to a form and application of a chosen law. The principle of freedom of contract is not expressly stated in any legal provision, but it is implied in Article 6:248. Another aspect of the principle of party autonomy is the principle of *consensualism*, that is, the principle that contracts are concluded by mutual consent of the parties without being subject to any requirements regarding their form. This rule is laid down in Article 3:37, paragraph 1, of the Civil Code: 'Unless otherwise provided, declarations, including communications, can be made in any form; declarations may be inferred from conduct.'

(b) The binding force of a contract cannot exclusively be explained by the principle of party autonomy and its corollary principles of freedom of contract and consensualism. These principles are necessarily coupled with the reliance principle. This principle implies that a party who exercises its autonomy by declaring its intention is responsible for the expectations created in the other party who receives that declaration. If the other party would not be protected in its reliance, it would be unjustifiably impeded in making use of its possibilities of self-determination. *See also* paragraphs 15 and 77. This principle of reliance is related to the principle that a man must stick to his promise.

(c) The extent to which a contract is binding is influenced by the status of the parties in society, which leads to the principle of societal justice. In case of a manifest disequilibrium between the parties, for example, relating to the possibility of choice or access to relevant information, the law provides mandatory norms to compensate for the disequilibrium and so to guarantee, to a certain extent, the societal justice of the contract. Mention may be made of the rules on defects of consent, consumer law provisions and good faith (reasonableness and fairness). A general principle of *iustum pretium* is not recognized in Dutch law (*see* paragraph 90 below).

---

10. *See* for an exception on this principle for specific organizations with a societal function, like suppliers of energy and water or banks, HR 5-11-2021, ECLI:NL:HR:2021:1652, NJ 2021/352.

(d) Our society is concerned with the protection of personality rights and fundamental values, with the maximization of personal freedom and with an efficient system of legal relations between the citizens among themselves and between them and the State. For a contract to be binding it must be in conformity with the basic values that govern the society as a whole. It may not undermine these values to an extent that is incompatible with the basic assumptions on which a society is founded. This principle of social conformity implies that a contract which violates those basic values is null and void or that it may be avoided in its entirety or partially.

See also paragraphs 16 ff. *infra* for some historical remarks on these principles.

§4. The Basis of Contractual Liability

15. On a more technical level, the principles referred to above should be distinguished from the problem of the basis of contractual liability; according to the will theory, it is the debtor's will (concurring with that of the creditor) which binds him; according to the theory of reliance, it is the fact that the debtor makes the creditor rely on his promise. The Civil Code does not solve this problem in a theoretical way but contains provisions which enable legal practice to adopt a solution suitable to the circumstances of the case. On the one hand, the Code provides that a juridical act requires an intention, manifested by a declaration, to produce a legal effect (Article 3:33).

On the other hand, it protects a party's reliance on declarations or conduct of the other party, even if they don't conform to that other party's actual intentions (Article 3:35). So the practical results are similar to the theory of reliance: a party may be bound beyond his will, if it is due to him that another, for good reasons, believes he has given his consent. In this case, there is a valid contract, in contrast to the German solution, which admits the annulment of the contract followed by an action of the relying party for its '*negatives Vertragsinteresse*'.

It follows from the principle of consensualism that, as a rule, the consent of the parties – or, in a given case, the reliance as to the existence of consent by the other party – suffices to establish a valid contract. This implies that normally, according to Dutch law, the formation of contracts is not subject to any requirement as to form. Contracts may be concluded orally or even tacitly by conduct of the parties from which the relevant intention can be inferred.

The preceding remarks already show that Dutch law favours a smooth and informal formation of the contract. This tendency is confirmed by the absence of other requirements, well known to many legal systems, viz. consideration and cause. *See* paragraphs 46 and 93.

Chapter 2. Historical Background of the Law of Contracts

§1. Introduction

16. As mentioned above in paragraph 14, among the basic principles of the law of contracts are consensualism, the binding force of contract and freedom of contract. The historical remarks in the next paragraphs pay special attention to these principles. In paragraphs 20–22, attention will be paid to the codification process in the Netherlands.

§2. Germanic Law, Roman Law and Canon Law

17. Originally, Germanic law hardly had a law of contract. Also, in later times, only real and formal contracts were recognized; contracts did not come into being by mere consensus.

The concept of contract has been strongly developed in Roman law. Roman law had four types of named contracts: *contractus verbis, litteris, re* and *consensus*. The *contractus ex consensu* were restricted to sale, lease (in a broad sense), partnership and mandate. Later on, the '*contractus re*' was enlarged to include the '*contractus innominati*'. The later Roman law still stuck to the condition that contracts – a few exceptions excluded – could only come into being in certain formal ways. Roman law did not have the general rule that mere consensus was binding. But there was a tendency towards more protection of the '*pacta nuda*' (unactionable pacts). This process has been delayed by the influence of the very formalistic Germanic law. Only in the late Middle Ages, had the rule '*nudus consensus obligat*' been accepted due to the influence of Canon law.

Canon law was especially important in the Middle Ages because of the fact that the ecclesiastical courts also had jurisdiction in certain secular matters. Under the influence of theological theories, the principle that mutual promises and agreements were binding in themselves was developed, and in approximately the thirteenth century, the principle '*nudus consensus obligat, pacta nuda servanda sunt*' was inserted in Canon law. It still took some centuries before this principle was also adopted by the '*ius civile*'.

§3. The Period after the French Revolution and the Nineteenth Century

18. The principle of freedom of contract, understood in the sense of freedom to contract what and with whom one wishes, existed in principle in Roman law and later in the Gallic countries. It was strongly supported by Canon law (but was restricted by the requirement of a '*causa*', a reasonable ground, and all kinds of medieval societal circumstances, institutions (guilds) and special provisions (like the ban on usury)). The principle reached its peak after the French Revolution.

Economists began to teach that one of the most important conditions for social order is freedom of the individual. Freedom could only be restricted by the own free will of the individual. Within the boundaries of the law (accepted by the individual by entering the '*contrat social*'), the own free will of the individual lies at the basis of all his rights and duties. The principle of freedom of contract was not explicitly laid down in the French Civil Code, but the principle permeated this Code and the authors of the Code were very much convinced of it. A contract entered into by free will was considered binding, but even the Civil Code – which came into being at a time in which almost limitless freedom was propagated – already made exceptions to this rule on the basis of justice, good morals and public order.

With some exaggeration, it may be said that at the beginning of the nineteenth century, people were still individuals fighting against each other in the struggle for survival. Since that time, there has been a dramatic change in societal structures and relations, which also had an effect on the principle of freedom of contract. Society became organized, collectivized and socialized. The individual became more and more a member of a group (workers, farmers, consumers). The power of these groups, after they had reached a certain degree of organization, resulted in restrictions on freedom of contract. For example labourers achieved that employment contracts were no longer unilaterally imposed and standard forms began to rule a substantial part of the economic life. Since the second part of the nineteenth century public interference has also increased, sometimes with the purpose to protect the economically weak, sometimes to protect the general interest. One of the most important examples in the Netherlands was the statutory regulation of the employment contract in 1907, which contained a large number of mandatory provisions. This way of restricting freedom of contract is still of utmost importance today.

§4. During and after the Second World War

19. During the Second World War and in the period thereafter, judicial matters were overall largely restricted and freedom of contract almost came to a standstill. The character of the restrictions varied; there were, for example, distribution and price regulations and the requirement for prior consent of the Ministry of Justice for virtually all juridical acts.

Since the war and after the restoration of a more or less normal situation, a tendency in doctrine and case law arose to expand the concepts of reasonableness and fairness, good morals and public order. One of the consequences of this expansion is that it imposes restrictions on the freedom of contract. Nevertheless, freedom of contract, although it is nowadays limited in various ways and by various means, remains a basic principle of Dutch contract law.

§5. Codification: The Situation Before 1809, the First Civil Code and the Code Napoleon

20. Before the introduction of the first Civil Code in the Netherlands in 1809, there was no unity in Dutch civil law. Provinces, towns and regions each might have their own laws. Two factors, however, had a unifying influence: Roman law, which had great authority throughout the country, and the description of Dutch law by

Hugo de Groot (Grotius) in his book '*Inleidinge tot de Hollandsche Rechtsgeleerdheid*' (Introduction to the Jurisprudence of Holland; 1631), which contained Roman law and indigenous law, arranged along the lines of Justinian's Institutiones.

At the end of the eighteenth century, influenced by the spirit of the Enlightenment, the first steps towards codification were taken. In 1806, however, a new situation was created because of the appointment of Louis Napoleon, brother of the emperor Napoleon, as king of the Netherlands. Louis Napoleon appointed a committee to adopt the French Code Napoleon for the Kingdom of Holland. This Code came into being in 1809. Together with the introduction of the Code, a Royal Decree was promulgated, by which Roman law and the local laws concerning civil law were abolished.

In 1811, after the incorporation of the Netherlands into the French Empire, this first Code was replaced by the Code Napoleon itself. The Code Napoleon served as the Dutch Code until 1838.

§6. The Code of 1838

21. In 1813, Dutch independence was restored, and the new Constitution demanded a new Code. Attempts to draft a national Code started immediately and were finally crowned with success in 1838. Apart from a number of more or less important subjects in the law of persons and family law, the law of successions and the law of property, this Code was largely, often *verbatim*, based upon the Code Napoleon. The system, however, differed on important points from the Code Napoleon. Since the Dutch Civil Code returned to the requirement of delivery for the transfer of ownership as known in Roman and Roman-Dutch law, a clear distinction was made between the law of property and the law of obligations; consequently, they were set out in the second and third Books, respectively. The law of successions was also included in the second Book. In addition, the 1838 Civil Code contained a fourth Book with provisions on the law of evidence and the law of prescription.

The system bears a striking resemblance to that of the *Institutiones* of Gaius and Justinian and also to the '*Inleidinge*' of Grotius. There are still other departures from the French system, for example a title with general provisions on the law of obligations.

The Code of 1838 has been in force in the Netherlands until recently; some (minor) parts of it still are. In the course of the years, some radical changes were made – in the Civil Code, as well as in the Commercial Code (which also dated back to 1838) and separate statutes – especially on a number of socially important subjects, like juvenile law, lease and hire, labour law, company law, etc. General and interdependent parts of the law, like the law of property and the law of obligations, were, however, not adapted to modern standards. Subsequently, the gap in the development of private law resulting from this situation was, for the greater part, filled by judge-made law. All this led to a situation in which the private law was inconveniently arranged, laid down in partially obsolete Codes, many special statutes and a great number of judicial decisions.

§7. TOWARDS A NEW CIVIL CODE

22. The recognition of the fact that the Civil Code contained gaps and defects in its wording and system and the growing conviction that this had resulted in an unfavourable situation led to a movement in favour of recodification.

In 1947, one of the Netherlands' most renowned legal scholars, Professor E.M. Meijers of Leiden University, who had insisted upon the need for recodification for a long time, was entrusted with the mandate to draft a new Civil Code. The goal of the revision programme was to replace the existing Civil and Commercial Codes with one 'consolidated' new Code, comprising civil law, commercial law, consumer law, much of the private law legislation enacted outside the Codes and codifying the results of an increasingly important body of judge-made law.

The new Code, as intended by Meijers, consisted of nine books, preceded by a preliminary title:

(1) law of persons and family law (including the law of matrimonial property);
(2) legal persons (general part, associations, corporations with limited liability, foundations);
(3) patrimonial law in general, that is, provisions applicable to all subsequent books;
(4) law of successions;
(5) property and real rights (rights in rem);
(6) general part of the law of obligations;
(7) special contracts;
(8) law of transport;
(9) law of products of the mind.

In 1954, the Preliminary Title and Books 1–4, together with the Explanatory Commentary, were published. After Meijers' death in 1954, the work was continued by a triumvirate – consisting of J. Drion, F.J. de Jong and J. Eggens, who was later replaced by G. de Groot – with the help of some assistants. The triumvirate published the draft of Book 5 in 1955 and the draft of Book 6 in 1961.

The draft of Book 7 – prepared by a number of specialized jurists and coordinated by a member of the triumvirate – was published in 1972. Book 8 was entrusted to a specialist in the field of maritime law, H. Schadee. Its first part, containing general provisions on the contract of transport, maritime law and the law of inland waterway navigation, was published in 1972, and its second part, transport by road, in 1976.

In the meantime deliberations in Parliament had started after the introduction to the Second Chamber of the Preliminary Title and Books 1–4 in 1954. (Each Book was submitted and discussed as a separate bill.) The draft of Book 5 was introduced in 1956, and the draft of Book 6 in 1964.

Book 1 was enacted in 1959, and Book 2 in 1960. Because of the amount of time needed for the deliberations about the other books, it was decided to put these two books in operation separately. Due to the fact that considerable time passed between the moment that the acts were adopted and their promulgation, the promulgation was prepared by another act, the '*Invoeringswet*' (Act to Put into Force), which contained:

(1) transitional law;
(2) necessary adaptation of the other Codes and Statutes; and
(3) changes which were made in the act already passed.

(This method was used with the other books as well.) Books 1 and 2 became operative in 1970 and 1976.

The Books 3, 5 and 6, which are closely interlinked, were enacted in 1979–1980. To put them into force, a complex legislative operation was required, which contained not only the three elements of the '*Invoeringswet*' mentioned above but also some new acts called for by the new Code (e.g., an act on public registers for registered immovable property); moreover it was felt indispensable to rewrite an entire book of the Code of Civil Procedure (law of seizure), and to enact four titles of Book 7 on Special Contracts, among which the important contract of sale. This huge complex of legislation, divided into approximately fifteen separate but interrelated acts, was passed in the Parliament between 1986 and 1990. The new rules were put into force in 1992.

Book 4, on the law of succession, was enacted in 1969 but entered into force only in January 2003. It has been the subject of intense debate for many years, mostly due to differing views on the subject of the position of the surviving spouse vis-à-vis the children.

Book 7 has partly been enacted and put into force simultaneously with Books 3, 5 and 6 on account of their close interrelationship. Other chapters have entered into force at a later stage, such as the contracts of donation, employment, lease (general, houses and land), contract for work and insurance. The recodification of some remaining contracts (both in the Civil Code and the former Commercial Code) is still under way.

Book 8 came into force on 1 April 1991. It contains general provisions, maritime law, inland navigation law and road transport law. Book 8 was not altogether complete when it entered into force. More provisions have been and will still be added over the years, for instance on aviation law and railway law.

It is uncertain whether Book 9 will be drafted. International developments have resulted in EU or Benelux Uniform Acts on quite a lot of subjects meant to be governed by Book 9, for example, patent law, law of trademark and law of designs and models. Because of these developments, it has been questioned whether the Civil Code still may be regarded as a suitable place to deal with these subjects. However, the interest in the idea of codifying at least a number of general provisions in a separate (ninth) Book of the Code was rekindled, and in 1994, a governmental expert was appointed to explore its feasibility. This work has come to nothing but the discussion on this topic is still going on.

Finally, outside the framework designed by Meijers, the decision was taken to codify Dutch private international law as part of the Civil Code. Book 10 has entered into force in 2012.

A part of the Code, originally planned and drafted but afterwards abandoned, is the Preliminary title. Its nine articles were divided into two groups. The first group of articles settled the order of importance of the various sources of law: statutory law, custom and equity. For instance, it laid down as a rule that a suppletive provision of law can be set aside by custom or equity, whereas a mandatory provision cannot. These rules have been harshly criticized and have been deleted, which leaves the issue to the courts. The second group was concerned with subjective rights, especially the doctrine of abuse of rights. These provisions have been transferred to the first title of Book 3. Consequently the whole preliminary title has been deleted.

Chapter 3. Classification of Contracts

§1. Classification of Contracts According to the Nature of the Branch of the Law to Which They Belong

23. Contracts may be classified according to the nature of the branch of the law to which they refer. On the basis of this criterion, we can distinguish:

(a) Contracts in the field of family law (marriage). Marriage is a contract in the above-mentioned sense. It is not an obligatory contract but a contract sui generis.
(b) Contracts in the field of property (in the sense of real rights). These are contracts aimed at the establishment or transfer of a right to a thing. This kind of contract is, in general, closely related to an obligatory contract. For example, in the case of a contract of sale, the intention of the parties is to create obligations but also to transfer ownership. In this example, a distinction must be made between the contract-creating obligations (e.g., the obligation to transfer ownership and the obligation to pay the price) and the contract directed at the actual transfer of ownership. In the Dutch system, mere consensus normally is not enough for the actual transfer of ownership, but a material act is also required. The provisions of the second title of Book 3 on juridical acts are applicable to this kind of contract. The provisions of Title 6.5 may be applied by analogy (Article 6:216).
(c) Contracts in the field of the law of procedure, especially of the law of evidence. By this kind of contract, the parties deviate from the legal rules on evidence. Such a contractual settlement is valid, provided that it does not infringe on rules of mandatory law. A contract in the field of the law of procedure/evidence is not an obligatory contract, but the provisions of Book 3, especially Title 3.2 and Title 6.5, may be applied *per analogiam.*
(d) Contracts in the field of public law. The public contract has already been mentioned *supra*, paragraph 10.
(e) Obligatory contracts. The obligatory contract is the most important of the contracts mentioned in this paragraph. The Civil Code contains special provisions on the obligatory contract in Title 5 of Book 6. Article 6:213, paragraph 1 gives a definition of the obligatory contract: 'A contract within the meaning of this title is a multilateral juridical act whereby one or more parties assume an obligation towards one or more other parties.' Within the class of obligatory contracts, further distinctions can be drawn.

§2. The Most Important Distinctions Within the Class of Obligatory Contracts

24. The most important distinctions are:

(1) *Contractus nominati* or *innominati* and mixed contracts. A contract is 'named' or 'unnamed' depending on whether the law contains special provisions on the contract in question. Mixed contracts are contracts, existing in practice (not regulated by the Code) which have characteristics of two or more named contracts.
(2) Consensual, real and formal contracts. In general, mere consensus suffices to create an obligatory contract. The Code contains a few contracts, however, where, apart from consensus, the transfer of a thing is necessary for the creation of obligations. These contracts are called real contracts. An example is the contract of gratuitous loans. For some contracts the Code makes a second exception to the rule of consensualism by requiring that the consensus is expressed in a certain form or is accompanied by a certain formality. Formal contracts are, however, rather rare (*see infra*, paragraph 54).
(3) Bilateral (reciprocal or synallagmatic) and unilateral contracts. A contract is bilateral if each of the parties assumes an obligation in order to obtain the prestation to which the other party, in exchange, binds itself towards him (Article 6:261, paragraph 1). The Civil Code contains in section 5 of Book 6 special provisions on bilateral contracts. In principle, only in bilateral contracts can non-performance give rise to the *exceptio non adimpleti contractus* and to the setting aside of the contract (*see infra*, paragraphs 190 ff.). Examples of bilateral contracts are sale, rent, labour contracts and insurance. A contract is unilateral if only one of the parties assumes one or more obligations towards the other party. Examples of unilateral contracts are the contracts of gift and suretyship.
(4) Contracts by gratuitous title and contracts by valuable title. A contract is a contract by valuable title if the obligation assumed by one of the parties is by law connected to a prestation of the other party (not consisting of the return of something that is obtained by virtue of the contract). Most contracts by valuable title will be bilateral, and most contracts by gratuitous title will be unilateral, but this is not always the case. For example, the contract by which someone assumes the obligation to pay a sum of money to another person if this person helps children with their studies is a unilateral contract by valuable title.
(5) Contracts that create passing obligations and contracts that create continuous obligations. The first-mentioned type of contract creates obligations which can be performed by a single prestation, for example, the delivery of a thing sold. Contrary to these contracts are the contracts that create obligations for one or both parties to continuous prestations. Between the parties exists a legal relationship that can be characterized as a permanent situation. Examples are rent, labour contracts and insurance.
(6) Main contracts and auxiliary contracts. Main contracts have an independent reason for existence. The characteristic of an auxiliary contract is that it depends on an external legal relationship, for example, a contract of suretyship that strengthens a contract of loan or a contract that changes the terms of another contract. A special kind of auxiliary contract is the agreement to enter into a contract (*pactum de contrahendo*). This type of contract will be discussed in paragraph 44 *infra*.

Chapter 4. Contract and Tort

§1. Relations Between Contract Law and Tort Law

25. Like many other civil law systems, Dutch law brings the law of contract and the law of unlawful acts (torts) under the heading of the law of obligations, together with some obligations from other sources, such as management of the affairs of another, undue payment and unjustified enrichment.

There is no fundamental difference between an unlawful act and a failure in the performance of a contractual obligation. Such a failure may be considered as a species of the genus unlawful act. For practical reasons, however, the law contains specific provisions on the juridical effects of a failure in the performance of an obligation (in Articles 6:74 ff.). This means that in cases of failure in the performance of a contractual obligation, normally only these provisions are applicable and not the provisions on unlawful acts (in Articles 6:162 ff.).

There are cases, however, in which acts that constitute a failure in the performance of an obligation are at the same time covered by Articles 6:162 ff. on unlawful acts. This will occur when the act would be considered to fall under Articles 6:162 ff. if the contract which made it possible were to be disregarded. An example is the case where a party to the contract receives a thing from the other party in order to repair it and then causes damage to the thing: the damaging of another's property without his consent is an unlawful act irrespective of the contract by virtue of which the debtor took power of the property.

Since the new Code came into force, the most important consequence of both unlawful acts and failure in the performance of an obligation, namely the obligation to repair damages, is regulated in a uniform way (Articles 6:95 ff.). Therefore, the question as to whether a claim can be based on an unlawful act as well as on failure in the performance of an obligation has become less important than it used to be under the old Code.

Still, the answer to this question can be of importance in some cases, for example, if the law limits contractual liability in a different way than non-contractual liability, if there is different regulation on juridical competence or if there is a different period of prescription.

§2. Torts Connected with Contracts

26. So far, the juridical relationship between contracting parties has been discussed. It is possible that a failure in the performance of a contractual obligation constitutes an unlawful act towards a third party who suffers damage as a consequence of that failure. Conversely, a third party can commit an unlawful act towards one of the contracting parties, for example, by profiting from the failure in the performance by the co-contracting party.

Chapter 5. Contracts and Quasi-Contracts

§1. 'QUASI-CONTRACTS'

27. The Dutch Code of 1838 did not adopt the French classification of the sources of obligations in '*contrats, quasi-contrats, delits, quasi-delits, loi*'. Article 1269 of the old Code stated that all obligations resulted from the contract or from the law. The obligations resulting from the law were divided into obligations resulting from the law only and obligations resulting from the acts of people (Article 1388). The acts of people could be lawful or unlawful (Article 1389). The quasi-contracts were therefore a part of the category 'lawful acts'.

Article 6:1 of the new Code states that obligations can arise only on the basis of the law. It should be added, however, that this does not mean that an obligation may only arise if the law refers to it in express terms. The Supreme Court ruled in 1959[11] that in cases which are not provided for expressly by the law, the court should adopt a solution which fits into the statutory legal system and is in line with rules already laid down for similar situations. Article 6:1 takes a similar view of the problem; the commentary indicates that the legislature intended to follow the decision of the Supreme Court.

The Code contains provisions on unlawful acts, contracts and three other sources of obligations, namely the management of the affairs of another ('*negotiorum gestio*'), undue payment ('*solutio indebiti*') and unjustified enrichment. *See* for these sources *infra*, paragraphs 325 ff.

11. HR 30-1-1959, ECLI:NL:HR:1959:AI1600, NJ 1959/548.

Chapter 6. Contract and Trust

§1. No Trusts in Dutch Law

28. The trust as a separate legal concept is not known to Dutch law. The Civil Code (Article 3:84, paragraph 3) even explicitly forbids the transfer of property with the intention to 'split' the right to the thing between the transferor and the transferee. Of course, some legal relations exist on the basis of which a person who is the owner of a certain property is under a contractual duty to manage and exploit this property on behalf of someone else. An example is the exploitation by BUMA (short for: office of music copyright) of copyright on music. But such legal relations only have the juridical effects provided for by the rules of regular Dutch law on property and obligations. On the one hand, there are juridical effects based on the ownership of the 'manager'; on the other hand, there are a number of obligations resulting from the obligatory contract between the parties.

Chapter 7. Contract and the Law of Property

§1. 'Relative' and 'Absolute' Rights

29. In Dutch law, there is a distinction between 'relative rights' and 'absolute rights'. A 'relative right' is a right directed at the prestation (performance) by a person; all rights to the performance of an obligation are relative rights. An absolute right, on the other hand, is a right to property that can be upheld against everyone. Rights like ownership or usufruct are absolute rights, together with copyright, patent, trademark, etc. There is, in principle, a closed system of property rights, whereas there is an open system of obligations.

§2. Intermediate Forms

30. Intermediate forms, however, also exist: legal relationships result from an obligatory contract with an absolute character. An example can be found in the provisions on 'qualitative' obligations in Article 6:252. (*See* on qualitative obligations also *infra*, paragraph 133.)

According to Article 6:252, a contract may stipulate that the obligation of one of the parties to suffer or refrain from something in respect of his registered property shall be transmitted to the persons who will acquire the property by particular title and that the stipulation may also bind those who will acquire a right to use the property from the titleholder. For this stipulation to have effect a notarial deed must be drawn up of the contract between the parties, followed by its entry in the public registers. (Even after registration, the stipulation does not always have effect. Article 6:252, paragraph 3 provides some exceptions.) Where, in exchange for the obligation, a counter-prestation has been agreed to, the right to that counter-prestation is also transferred upon transmission of the obligation to the extent that it pertains to the period following the transfer and that the stipulation with respect to the counter-prestation has also been entered in the public registers. Article 6:252 does not apply to obligations which limit a titleholder in his power to alienate or encumber the property.

The right of a creditor of a qualitative obligation can – under the above-mentioned circumstances – be upheld towards the successors of the debtor (in particular, a party who acquires the property from the debtor by means of a contract of sale followed by transfer of the property) and in that respect clearly has characteristics of an absolute right.

Another example of a relative right with absolute characteristics is the right of the lessee. According to the provisions on lease, the lessee cannot only maintain his right towards every successive owner of the leased property but also may claim protection and restoration against virtually everyone who violates his right (Article 7:226, *see also infra*, paragraph 281 and paragraph 283). (It should be noted that the right of the lessee differs in several aspects from an absolute right in the proper sense, the most important being that the right is not transferable without the consent of the lessor).

A final example of a right with both relative and absolute characteristics is the right of retention (*see* paragraph 192 *infra*). According to Article 3:291, the right of retention may also be invoked against: (i) third persons having acquired a right to the thing after the creditor's claim has arisen and the thing has come under his control, and (ii) against third persons with a prior right, if the creditor's claim results from a contract which the debtor had the power to enter into in respect of the thing, or if the creditor had no reason to doubt such power.

Chapter 8. Good Faith and Fair Dealing

§1. Good Faith ('Reasonableness and Fairness')

31. The concept of good faith permeates all branches of the Dutch law of obligations and contract law.

Article 6:2, paragraph 1 provides that both parties to an obligation should behave in their relationship according to what is reasonable and fair. Paragraph 2 states that a rule binding upon them by virtue of law, usage or a juridical act does not apply insofar as, in the given circumstances, this would be unacceptable according to the standards of reasonableness and fairness.

§2. The Three Functions of Good Faith Terminology

32. The principle of bona fides (expressed by the words 'reasonableness and fairness') has three functions in contract law.

In the first place all contracts must be interpreted according to good faith. Secondly, good faith has a 'supplementing' function; supplementary rights and duties not expressly provided for in the agreement may arise between the parties. Article 6:248, paragraph 1 provides that contracts not only have the effects expressly agreed upon but also those which, according to the nature of the contract, result from the law, usage or the requirements of reasonableness and fairness.

A test of bona fides in the performance of a contract is, of course, not a subjective one. In contract law, acting in good faith refers to the observance of reasonable commercial standards of fair dealing, or as the Dutch legislature has put it, acting in accordance with reasonableness and fairness. This is a purely objective test: if a party acts in an unreasonable and unfair way, it will not be a good defence to say that he honestly believed his conduct to be reasonable and fair. In the other sense, good faith refers to a test that originally was purely subjective, indicating a state of mind (lack of notice), for example, bona fides, as a requirement for the acquisition of moveable property, where the transferor is not the owner of the thing. Later on, this test was developed in such a way as to include an important objective element. In the present Dutch Code, this results from Article 3:11, where it is stated that good faith in this sense is not only absent if the party concerned *did know* the relevant state of affairs but also if he *ought to have known* it; this implies that he may be under a duty to investigate. In order to prevent the confusion resulting from the two concepts of good faith, the Dutch legislature has decided to use the term 'good faith' only in the second sense and describe the term in the first sense by the concept of 'reasonableness and fairness'. In this monograph, however, which is devoted to contract law, the term 'good faith' (or bona fides) can safely be used as a synonym for the concept of 'reasonableness and fairness'.

The third function of the principle of bona fides is its 'derogating' or 'restrictive' function. Under the old Code, which, like the French Code, merely provided that 'contracts must be performed in good faith', the Supreme Court has for a long time been very reluctant to admit the possibility of the extinction of a right expressly agreed upon by the requirements of bona fides, with the exception of cases where a party may lose his right because of his own conduct which is incompatible with his exercising that right in good faith. In a 1967 case[12] concerning an exemption clause, the Supreme Court took a different view, however, admitting the possibility that a debtor will not be allowed to rely on the clause which in the circumstances of the case turns out to be unreasonably onerous ('unconscionable') towards the creditor.

The present Code provides in Article 6:248, paragraph 2 (which formulates the principle of good faith in relation to contracts), that a rule, which would normally bind the parties as a result of a contract, does not apply to the extent that in the given circumstances, this would be unacceptable according to the standards of reasonableness and fairness. This provision clearly adopts the view that even express terms of a contract can be set aside where their enforcement would be grossly unjust in the circumstances. The term 'unacceptable' indicates that such a decision should be reserved for exceptional situations.

Subject to this restriction, the article operates with respect to *all* rules that are binding upon the parties as a result of the contract: not only terms stipulated by the parties but also terms implied by statute, and in the latter case, both suppletive and mandatory law. The concept of reasonableness and fairness makes it possible to solve many problems in a balanced way, without the parties or the court having to resort to extreme solutions such as setting aside the entire contract because a rule binding the parties is unacceptable or holding the parties to such an unacceptable rule.

The problem of the derogating function of bona fides has proved particularly urgent in cases of frustrated contracts. Like other civil law systems, Dutch law provides for the discharge of debtors in cases of impossibility of performance. Apart from this, unforeseen circumstances may create major difficulties in the performance of the contract. In cases of unforeseen circumstances, Article 6:258 provides for a possibility of modification or setting aside of the contract when reasonableness and fairness so require, *see infra*, paragraphs 172 ff. The derogating function of reasonableness and fairness thus lies at the base of other statutory provisions, such as Article 6:258. Article 6:248, paragraph 2 and Article 6:258 may be applied next to each other. The fact that a party may ask for modification of the contract on the grounds of unforeseen circumstances does not preclude the application of Article 6:248.[13] However, it is possible that not all legal effects of applying the special provision of Article 6:258 may be attained by invoking Article 6:248, paragraph 2.

§3. The Scope of the Concept of Good Faith

33. Article 6:248 and 6:258 apply directly only to contracts (but through Article 6:216 *mutatis mutandis* also to other multilateral patrimonial juridical acts). Article 6:2 applies to all obligations. The Code lacks a provision of such a general character as Article 2 of the Swiss Civil Code, according to which the provision on

12. HR 19-5-1967, ECLI:NL:HR:1967:AC4745, NJ 1967/261.
13. HR 25-6-1999, ECLI:NL:HR:1999:AD3069, NJ 1999/602.

'good faith' would be applicable to all '*Zivilrechtliche Verhältnisse*'. However, in practice, the Dutch Code has the same result.

Chapter 9. Style of Drafting

§1. Style of Drafting of the Code

34. The style of drafting of the Civil Code is in general somewhat more elaborate than the style of the French Code, but, compared to acts of Anglo-American origin, it is rather short. Perhaps it may be best compared to the style of drafting of the German Bürgerliches Gesetzbuch (BGB). Although Dutch law is distinctly less 'dogmatic' or 'conceptual' than German law, the Code does not provide easy reading, even to expert lawyers. For a correct interpretation of its provisions, it is advisable to consult the Explanatory Commentaries together with the text of the Code.

§2. Style of Drafting of Contracts

35. Generally speaking, the Dutch style of drafting contracts more or less fits into the civil law tradition and is much less detailed and elaborate than the Anglo-American style of drafting. Where American contracts may fill complete books, Dutch contracts are often restricted to a few dozen (rather short) articles.

If a contract is put down in writing, no special restrictions apply. There is no rule to the effect that only the written document may be taken into account. The contract must be interpreted in accordance with the general guidelines developed by the courts and all instruments of interpretation may be used.[14] As will be discussed *infra*, paragraphs 120 ff., the intention of the parties is considered more important than the literal meaning of the words used in the written contract.

Furthermore, the contract is not an isolated phenomenon; as was said before, its contents are supplemented by the rules of law, usage and the requirements of reasonableness and fairness (Article 6:248, paragraph 1 of the Civil Code) and, in extreme situations, the criteria of reasonableness and fairness may lead to derogation from the contract (Article 6:248, paragraph 2). The written contract therefore does not necessarily have to deal with all possible eventualities but may concentrate on the main points. This, of course, does not alter the fact that in cases of individual contracts dealing with specific subjects and large interests, contractual provisions may well be elaborated in full detail. In fact, under the influence of commercial relationships where the common law plays a role, this is often seen nowadays in Dutch legal practice.

---

14. This is true even when the contract contains an entire agreement clause: HR 5-4-2013, ECLI:NL:HR:2013:BY8101, NJ 2013/214.

Chapter 10. Sources of the Law of Contract

§1. Sources of the Law of Contract

36. The law of contract is codified in the Civil Code. The important titles for general contract law are Titles 2 of Book 3 (Title 3.2), 1 of Book 6 (Title 6.1) and 5 of Book 6 (Title 6.5).

As mentioned before, contracts are nowadays considered to be a species of the genus called juridical acts. The Code contains Title 3.2 on juridical acts (in patrimonial law), which deals with their formation, discrepancies between real and declared intention, nullity for lack of legal form or illegality, severability of null juridical acts and their transformation by operation of law into valid substitutes, annullability for threat (duress), fraud, abuse of circumstances (undue influence) and *fraus creditorum*, the technique and effects of annulment, *confirmatio* and *ratihabitio*. On error, however, the Code does not formulate provisions applying to all juridical acts but only to contracts. (But *see infra* on application by way of analogy to other juridical acts.)

When we discuss the law of contract, we have to take into account the relevant provisions relating to juridical acts in general.

The Code draws a distinction between unilateral juridical acts on the one hand and multilateral (including bilateral) juridical acts on the other. (Within the first group a further distinction is drawn between acts addressed to another person and acts which are not addressed to another person. The importance of this distinction appears especially in the field of nullities; a unilateral juridical act without address will sometimes be considered null in cases where a unilateral juridical act addressed to another person may only be annulled.)

Contracts constitute the most important class of multilateral juridical acts. The provisions on contracts in the Civil Code (in Title 6.5) only envisage obligatory contracts. By way of analogy, however, most of them are to be applied to other multilateral juridical acts in the field of patrimonial law (contracts that are not obligatory, like contracts on evidence or contracts in the field of public law, *see* paragraph 23 *supra*) to the extent that this is not incompatible with the necessary implication of the relevant provisions, taking into consideration the nature of the juridical act (Article 6:216).

They must not, but may, be likewise applied to yet other juridical acts where the courts deem fit to do so in the circumstances.

Title 5 of Book 6 – titled ‘Contracts in General’– contains general provisions, provisions on the formation of contracts, on general conditions, on the juridical effects of contracts and on synallagmatic contracts.

An obligatory contract is a source of obligations. Title 1 of Book 6 deals with obligations in general. The provisions of this title – which include provisions on performance of obligations, on the effects of non-performance and on legal obligations to repair damages – are also applicable to the obligations resulting from contracts.

Apart from the general provisions on contracts and obligations, the Code (especially in Book 7) and some other acts contain numerous provisions on special contracts.

Part I. General Principles of the Law of Contract

Chapter 1. Formation

§1. Offer and Acceptance

I. Offer and Acceptance

A. *Introduction*

37. Normally, a contract comes into being by mutual consent of the parties (but *see also* Article 3:35, mentioned *supra* in paragraph 15). Generally speaking, mutual consent is brought about when one party accepts an offer made by the other. The Dutch law on offer and acceptance is largely based on the 1964 Uniform Law on the Formation of Contracts for the International Sale of Goods and its successor, the 1980 Vienna Sales Convention. The Dutch Code contains provisions on the formation of contracts in Articles 6:217 ff.

Offer and acceptance are juridical acts, which means that they are not only governed by Articles 6:217 ff. but also by the general provisions on juridical acts in Book 3, Title 2. Title 3.2 deals with, among other things, matters such as declaration of will and reliance. An offer is a unilateral juridical act, but the question of whether an offer is valid, null or subject to annulment must be judged by the provisions on multilateral juridical acts (Article 6:218, *see infra*, paragraphs 98 ff.).

B. *Definitions*

38. An *offer* can be defined as a proposal to enter into a contract addressed to the other party, where the proposal is defined in such a manner that by acceptance thereof, a contract is immediately formed. An offer has to be distinguished from an invitation to negotiate. This distinction is important because, once an offer is made, the other party has it in his power to complete the contract by accepting the offer. In case of a mere invitation to negotiate, however, the other party does not have this power. The distinction played a role in a leading case on the sale of a house: an advertisement in which a price was mentioned was considered to be not an offer but only an invitation to negotiate.[15]

An *acceptance* is an expression of consent to the terms of an offer. An acceptance which varies the terms of the offer is considered to be a counteroffer and a rejection of the original offer. Unless the offeror objects to the differences without delay, where a reply intended to accept the offer only deviates from the offer on points of minor importance, the reply is considered to be an acceptance and the contract is formed according to the latter (Article 6:225, paragraphs 1 and 2).

An offer – like an acceptance – is the expression of an intention. The intention can be expressed by spoken or written words, gestures, signs, conduct and even by not acting if this inspires reliance in the other party that the intention is directed at the completion of a contract.

An offer can be addressed to one or more specific persons but can also be addressed to a group of persons or to the public in general ('public offer').

An offer takes effect when the proposal to contract has reached the person or persons to whom it is addressed. The offer can be withdrawn before it has reached the addressed person(s). In that case, no offer has been made.

C. *Duration of an Offer*

39. Article 6:219–222 sets out how long an offer continues to stand. An offer may lapse through time (Article 6:221, paragraph 1), through revocation (Article 6:219 and 6:220), or by being rejected (Article 6:221, paragraph 2). An offer does not lapse upon the death of one of the parties or his loss of legal capacity to act unless the offer, another juridical act or usage requires otherwise (Article 6:222 *jo* 6:217, paragraph 2).

An offer only stands for a limited time. If the offer is not made for a specific period, it depends on the circumstances for how long the offer remains open. A general rule is that the offer stands for the period the other party reasonably needs to consider the offer and communicate his decision. Article 6:221, paragraph 1 provides a rule for verbal offers and for offers in writing. Unless another inference is to be drawn from the offer itself, another juridical act or usage, the acceptance of a verbal offer must take place at once and the acceptance of a written offer within a reasonable period. In some exceptional cases, a late acceptance may still complete a contract, for example:

- if the fact that the acceptance is too late results from an act of the offeror, from an act of persons for whom he is responsible or from other circumstances which are personal to him and justify that he suffer the consequences (Article 6:224);
- if the offeror understands or ought to understand that the lateness was not apparent to the other party and the offeror omits to inform the other party forthwith that he considers the offer to have lapsed (Article 6:223, paragraph 2);

15. HR 10-4-1981, ECLI:NL:HR:1981:AG4177, NJ 1981/532.

– if the offeror is willing to consider the late acceptance as made in time and communicates this decision to the other party without delay (Article 6:223, paragraph 1).

D. Revocability

40. In the system of the Dutch Code, an offer is, in general, revocable. Unless it includes a term for acceptance or unless the offer itself, another juridical act or usage requires otherwise, an offer may be revoked as long as it has not been accepted and no communication containing an acceptance of the offer has been sent (Article 6:219, paragraphs 1 and 2).

From this provision, it also follows that an offeror may make his offer irrevocable, for example by expressly stating so or by fixing a time for acceptance. (However, the fact that the offer contains a time does not always mean that the offer is irrevocable during that time. The meaning *may* be that the offer lapses after the expiration of that time unless the offer is revoked beforehand). Revocation of an irrevocable offer is without effect. This means that acceptance of the offer in due time constitutes a contract.

An offer which states that it is without engagement can still be revoked immediately after acceptance (Article 6:219, paragraph 2). Sometimes, an offer 'without engagement' must not be considered a 'real' offer but as an invitation to negotiate. This depends on the circumstances.

An offer of a reward for a specific period may be revoked or modified for serious reasons. If an offer is revoked or modified, the court may grant fair compensation to a person who, on the basis of the offer, has begun to prepare the required prestation (Article 6:220). This is an example of precontractual liability based on a legal provision. About precontractual liability in general, *see infra*, paragraphs 65 ff.

E. Time and Place of the Contract

41. As mentioned before, mutual consent exists at the moment when a party accepts an offer made by another. According to Dutch doctrine and case law (in conjunction with Article 3:37, paragraph 3), the acceptance has no effect until the offeror learns that the offeree accepts the offer or until the offeror – as the offeree has good reasons to suppose – could have learned that the offeree accepts the offer.

Article 6:224 states that if a communication containing acceptance of the offer does not reach the offeror or does not reach him in time as a result of an act by the offeror himself or a person for whom he is responsible or as a result of other circumstances which are personal to him and justify that he suffer the consequences, the contract is deemed to have come into being at the moment when the communication would have been received without the intervening fact.

In general, the declaration of acceptance must be addressed to the offeror. There are exceptions to this rule. Usage, contract or the offer itself may imply that the communication of acceptance may or must be addressed to a third party or that, for example, acceptance may be expressed by the actual performance of the contract.

Sometimes – often as a result of practices established between the parties – the absence of a reaction may be regarded as an acceptance. The contract then comes into being at the moment when the other party should have made clear that he did not want the contract.

The contract is considered to have come into existence at the place where the offeror learned that his offer had been accepted.

F. Negotiations

42. Sometimes, the formation of a contract is preceded by lengthy negotiations. This may render it difficult in some cases to draw clear distinctions between offer and acceptance or, indeed, to assume altogether that there has been an offer and an acceptance. In these cases, it must be decided, on the basis of the conduct and declarations of the parties, whether they have agreed on the same terms. It may sometimes be difficult to ascertain whether the parties to a negotiation have reached an agreement or whether they haven't yet. The fact that parties have agreed on the essential elements of the deal (the price, the object of the transaction) does not always mean that they have reached an agreement, as the Supreme Court decided in a *Netherlands Antilles* case on the sale of a veterinarian's practice.[16] In cases of complex deals, where several different obligations have to be negotiated, the question of whether the deal is concluded even if not all different obligations have been agreed upon is dependent on the intention of the parties, as it appears on the basis of what was agreed upon and what was not and on whether they intended to further negotiate and the other circumstances of the case.[17] *See* further *infra*, paragraphs 65 ff., on the subject of broken negotiations and precontractual liability.

G. Battle of Forms

43. A final remark on the so-called battle of forms. The growing use of general conditions has raised some specific problems. Article 6:225, paragraph 3 contains a provision for the case that a contract has come into being by written declarations of offer and acceptance, in which both parties refer to their own general conditions. The article prescribes that the second reference is without effect unless it explicitly rejects the applicability of the general conditions as indicated in the first reference. In the latter case, the 'acceptance' will often have to be considered a counteroffer, but it can also be regarded as an acceptance that deviates from the offer on points of minor importance if the offeror has not, without delay, objected to the applicability of another set of general conditions.

---

16. HR 2-2-2001, ECLI:NL:HR:2001:AA9771, NJ 2001/179.
17. Cf. HR 16-9-2011, ECLI:NL:HR:2011:BQ2213, NJ 2011/572; HR 2-11-2018, ECLI:NL:HR:2018:2043; HR 17-12-2021, ECLI:NL:HR:2021:1889.

This rule applies equally when an invitation to negotiate (that refers to certain general terms and conditions) is followed by an offer that refers to different terms: the former is applicable.[18]

II. Contractual Obligation to Create Legal Relations

A. The *'Pactum de Contrahendo'*

44. A special kind of 'auxiliary contract' (*see* paragraph 24 *supra*) is the '*pactum de contrahendo*' (contract to contract), whereby one party binds himself – or both parties bind themselves – to enter into another contract, the contents of which are – at least on the main points – sufficiently determined or determinable.

A few different types of '*pacta de contrahendo*' can be discerned, for example:

(a) One party binds himself to enter into a certain contract as soon as the other party expresses his will to enter into this contract.
(b) Both parties bind themselves definitively towards each other to enter into a certain contract (possibly after the fulfilment of a certain condition).
(c) One party binds himself to give the other party before all others the opportunity to enter into a certain contract with him if he decides to conclude such a contract in the future.

Article 6:226 contains a special rule on the form of the '*pactum de contrahendo*', thus deciding a question that has stirred controversy in the past: where the law requires a formality for the formation of a contract, this rule applies *mutatis mutandis* to a contract whereby a party in whose interest the formality has been given binds himself to enter into such a contract.

B. Contracts to Negotiate

45. Apart from the '*pacta de contrahendo*', there are contracts intended to create an obligation for the parties to start or continue negotiations. On the basis of such contracts, the parties are obliged to negotiate in good faith. These kinds of contracts are, in particular, concluded when the parties are engaged in precontractual dealings, have not yet reached a full agreement, but already want to create a certain commitment. Contracts of this kind exist in various forms and under various names, of which 'letter of intent' is among the most common. *See* on precontractual relationships further *infra*, paragraphs 65 ff.

18. HR 13-7-2001, ECLI:NL:HR:2001:ZC3632, NJ 2001/497.

III. Consideration (Gratuitous Promises, Natural Obligations)

A. *Consideration*

46. The doctrine of consideration has always been unknown to Dutch law. A trace of it, however, could be found in the old law of donations, which used to prescribe writing (even a notarial deed) for a valid promise to be made. However, this provision has met with considerable resistance in legal practice and was abolished by the relevant title (Title 7.3) of the new Civil Code (Article 7:175–188, in force by 1 January 2003).

Moreover, the ideas behind consideration play a part in the law on the formation of contract in the case that a party is bound beyond his intent. A party may be bound beyond his will if it is due to him that another person believes, on good grounds, that he has agreed to consent (Article 3:35, *see supra* paragraph 15 and *infra*, paragraph 77). In this case, there is a valid contract.

Under the old Civil Code, which was silent on the subject, the courts were inclined to protect reliance only if the party relying on a promise which did not correspond with the actual intent of the promisor had either made a promise himself to the promisor or had acted on the promise in such a way that he would suffer a detriment if the promise were to be declared null and void. This position was changed under the new Civil Code, which did not adopt this nuance: Article 3:35 does not distinguish between gratuitous promises and promises made for value. However, it requires a reliance which is justifiable in the circumstances, and this poses a duty of investigation on the promisee, which may well be more extensive in the case of a gratuitous promise than in the case of a normal contract bestowing benefit on both parties.

And apart from this, even if, according to Article 3:35, a valid promise has come into existence, the promisee who has not given any benefit nor suffered detrimental reliance, may, through the operation of the provisions on good faith (*supra*, paragraphs 31 ff.) be stopped from asserting his rights against the promisor. All this not only applies to promises, but also to other unilateral juridical acts which do not correspond to the real intent of the party making the declaration.

B. *Natural Obligations*

47. Dutch law, like other systems originating from Roman law, accepts a category of non-enforceable obligations, labelled natural obligations. A restrictive theory admits the existence of a natural obligation only in the case of an '*obligation civile manquée ou dégénérée*', that is, where normally an action would lie, but for a statutory provision which deprives the obligation of its enforceability, either *ab initio* (as in the case of gaming and wagering contracts, *see infra*, paragraphs 243 ff.) or subsequently (e.g., as a result of the operation of the period of limitation).

Since 1926, however, the Supreme Court has adopted the extensive interpretation,[19] which, at the time, was already predominant in France. According to this approach, moral obligations of a certain intensity may also constitute natural obligations. The question as to which moral obligation may constitute a natural obligation was not always answered by the Court in the same way. At first, the Court would require that the duty reveals an urgent character; in later decisions, it was stressed that the duty of the debtor should correspond with an identifiable right of the creditor.

C. Provisions on Natural Obligations in the Civil Code

48. The Civil Code states in Article 6:3, paragraph 2 that a natural obligation exists: *a.* where the law or a juridical act deprives an obligation of its enforceability; *b.* where a person has a compelling moral duty towards another person of such a nature that its performance, although unenforceable at law, must in common opinion be considered as the performance of a prestation owed to that other person.

Examples of cases falling under *a* were mentioned above. Examples of cases *sub b* may be found in moral duties to grant a pension to a former employee, to pay alimony to a relative, to reward a wife for services rendered in the husband's business, etc. A particularly impressive example was a Supreme Court decision of 1945,[20] which ruled that a testamentary provision providing for reasonable maintenance of the surviving spouse is to be considered as the performance of a natural obligation and, for this reason, is not subject to the provisions on gifts and on the legitimate portion. At the same time, this decision is one of the finest examples to show that the Courts, by creative use of unwritten law, even in a system of codified law, may adapt statute law to meet the needs of a developing society (*see* for other examples, *supra*, paragraphs 4 ff.). The law of succession, which entered into force in 2003 (Book 4 of the Civil Code), has built on this judgment.

A natural obligation lacks enforceability (Article 6:3, paragraph 1), but not the other legal effects of obligations. According to Article 6:4, the provisions of the law with respect to obligations apply *mutatis mutandis* to natural obligations unless the law or its necessary implications entail that such a provision may not apply to an unenforceable obligation.

The old Civil Code contained a provision which excluded a claim for restitution in the case of a natural obligation voluntarily acquitted. Article 6:4 is more generally drafted and leads to the same result.

In principle, the debtor may transform a natural obligation into an enforceable obligation by means of a (express or implied) declaration that he wishes to do so. This declaration requires acceptance by the creditor so as to constitute a contract; acceptance is implied in the case where the creditor does not reject the offer immediately (Article 6:5, paragraphs 1 and 2). Neither the fulfilment of the natural obligation nor its transformation into an enforceable one is considered to be a gift (Article 6:5, paragraph 3).

19. HR 12-3-1926, ECLI:NL:HR:1926:AG1802, NJ 1926, p. 777.
20. HR 30-11-1945, ECLI:NL:HR:1945:14, NJ 1946/62.

IV. Modification of the Contract

A. *Modification by the Parties*

49. In the absence of the requirement of consideration in Dutch law, modification of the contract by the parties does not cause special difficulties. Like the formation of a contract, the modification of a contract is brought about by mutual consent. In fact, the parties conclude a new contract in order to modify the former one. If the parties agree on the fact that their contract should be modified and on the terms of the modification, the general rules of contract law apply.

B. *Modification by the Court: Unforeseen Circumstances*

50. A more controversial question in Dutch law has for a long time been the question of whether a contract may, without consent of the parties, be modified by the court. The Civil Code has introduced a few provisions which allow for the court to modify contracts in special cases. Probably the most interesting of these is Article 6:258 on *imprévision.*

The question of whether a contract should be modified arises, especially when the circumstances under which a contract is concluded have changed considerably after the conclusion but before the performance of the contract. Unforeseen circumstances may interfere with the intended equilibrium of the corresponding obligations or defeat the purpose the parties had in mind. The classic situation is that in which goods sold can be delivered and paid for only years afterwards because of a war which temporarily prevented performance but at the same time caused irreversible inflation. In cases decided after World War I, the Supreme Court has taken the view that even such events cannot alter the parties' contractual obligations. Later, however, the Court changed this position in anticipation of Article 6:258.

Article 6:258, paragraph 1 provides that the court, upon the demand of one of the parties, may modify the effects of a contract or set it aside in whole or in part on the basis of unforeseen circumstances, which are of such a nature that the co-contracting party, according to the criteria of reasonableness and fairness, may not expect that the contract be maintained in an unmodified form. The modification or the setting aside of the contract may be given retroactive effect. Paragraph 2 states that the modification or the setting aside of the contract is not pronounced to the extent that the person invoking the circumstances should be accountable for them according to the nature of the contract or common opinion.

It must be noted that the expression 'unforeseen circumstances' should not be taken in its literal sense. The test does not relate to what parties have foreseen or could foresee but asks whether the contract makes sufficient provision for the supervening event. *See* further *infra*, paragraphs 172 ff.

C. Modification by the Court: Obligations with Regard to Registered Property

51. Article 6:259 gives the court the possibility to modify a contract intended to oblige a person in the capacity of titleholder or user of registered property to a prestation which does not consist of or is not coupled with the suffering of continuing adverse possession (like a lease). Conditions for modification are that at least ten years have lapsed and continuation of the obligation is contrary to the general interest or the creditor no longer has a reasonable interest in performance. This article refers in particular to qualitative obligations and conditions-in-chain (*see supra*, paragraph 30 and *infra*, paragraphs 135 ff.). The article provides, among other things, a solution in cases in which obligations obstruct the exploitation of registered property in a way contrary to the general interest: for example, in case of a contractual prohibition to build contrary to the interest of public housing.

D. Modification by the Court: Error and Undue Influence

52. Finally, Article 3:54 and Article 6:230 should be mentioned. These articles state that in cases of error and undue influence between the parties, the court may, instead of pronouncing the annulment, modify the effects of the contract to remove the prejudice which the person entitled to the annulment suffers by the continuance of the contract. *See also infra*, paragraph 104.

E. Modification Through Conversion

53. Last but not least: Article 3:42 Civil Code provides for the possibility of *conversion*, the replacement of a juridical act which is null and void by a valid one, provided that both acts are sufficiently similar. *See* about conversion paragraph 101, *infra.*

§2. Requirements

I. Formal Requirements: Contracts under Seal

A. Formal Requirements

54. In Dutch law, contracts usually are binding *solo consensu* or by mere agreement (Article 3:37, paragraph 1).

As a rule, the formation of contracts and other juridical acts are not subject to requirements as to form so that they may be concluded or accomplished orally or even tacitly by conduct of the parties from which the relevant intention can be inferred. There are exceptions to this rule, however. Statutory requirements of form exist for certain types of contracts or for certain types of provisions in contracts. These formal requirements are often used to protect the weaker party. Examples may be found in labour law; for example, non-competition clauses will be valid only if they are in writing. The Supreme Court has also ruled that Article 3:37 does not imply that an oral statement is always enough; under certain circumstances (for instance, in very important matters), for a specific communication, a written form may be indicated.[21]

It is expected that the amount of formal requirements will be reduced under the influence of Union law, especially Article 9 of Directive 2000/31/EC on electronic commerce, because certain formal requirements cannot be met when contracts are completed electronically, for example, on the internet.

The most important varieties of form prescribed by statute are the following: writing, an instrument (which must be signed by the acting party or parties) and a notarial instrument. For example certain terms which occur in contracts of employment must be in writing. An instrument is required, among other things, for the assignment of a claim, for a contract of hire-purchase, collective labour contracts, and contracts concluded away from business premises. Instances where the law prescribes the use of a notarial instrument are a marriage contract, the conveyance of immovables, the formation of companies, cooperative associations and foundations.

The Code contains two general provisions on the juridical effects of formal requirements prescribed by law. One of these provisions, Article 6:226, concerning the form of the '*pactum de contrahendo*', was already mentioned in paragraph 44 *supra*. The other, Article 3:39, states that save as otherwise provided by the law, juridical acts which have not been performed in the prescribed form are null. The exception may apply, for example, when the requirement exclusively intends to protect the interest of one party to a contract, in which case only that party is entitled to rely on the provision (meaning in Dutch legal terminology that the contract is not null but annullable).

B. *Contracts under Seal*

55. The Anglo-American concept of contracts under seal is, as such, unknown to Dutch law.

II. Evidential Requirements: Proof, the Parol Evidence Rule, Function of the Notary

A. *Evidential Requirements*

56. Paragraph 54 *supra* dealt with formal requirements which are conditional for the existence of a contract and the absence of which leads, in principle, to nullity.

In addition to this kind of requirement, there are provisions which require writing or an instrument for the purpose of evidence only. The absence of the prescribed form does not influence the validity of the contract; it only places the contracting

21. HR 15-9-1995, ECLI:NL:HR:1995:ZC1805, NJ 1996/36.

parties in a disadvantageous position as regards the evidence. For example, the law prescribes the use of an instrument as an evidential requirement for an insurance policy.

Apart from these and similar exceptional provisions, the Dutch law of evidence does not impose many restrictions concerning the admissibility of proof, a fact which is easily explained by the tradition of the administration of justice by professional judges.

The law of evidence was thoroughly revised in 1988. Antiquated articles were deleted, and modernizations were introduced. A main principle of the law of evidence is that the court and the parties may, in general, use all conceivable evidence. New means of evidence, such as electronic data, (smartphone) camera images, etc., are admissible without restraint. However, the court is completely free in its assessment of this evidence.

The Code of Civil Procedure contains special provisions on some means of evidence, among other things, on authentic and private instruments and on witnesses.

B. *Restrictions to the Judicial Freedom of Assessment: No Parol Evidence Rule in Dutch Law*

57. A restriction to the general rule of freedom of assessment of the evidence by the court is that in case of compulsory evidence, the court is – if no counterevidence is produced – obliged to accept the contents of that evidence as true or is obliged to recognize the evidential value the law attaches to that evidence. The most important example of compulsory evidence is the authentic instrument, which is a signed instrument with an evidential purpose drawn up by an official (like a notary or a bailiff) who is especially charged by the law to do so. Authentic instruments provide compulsory evidence towards every one of the observations and actions of the official as laid down in the instrument. Also, private instruments – all instruments other than authentic instruments – have, to a certain extent, compulsory evidential value. Both authentic and private instruments provide compulsory evidence between the parties to the instrument as regards the truth of the declarations of the parties (with the restriction that the declaration in question must have been intended to provide evidence for the benefit of the other party).

These rules must be distinguished from the 'parol evidence rule' of the common law, which – in its original strict sense – prohibits the use of evidence by witnesses or other extrinsic evidence in case of a contract expressed in writing and provides that the intention of the parties may only be deducted from the writing. In Dutch law, counterevidence is always admitted, also in cases of compulsory evidence, and for that purpose all means of evidence may be used.

C. *Witnesses*

58. With regard to evidence by witnesses, there is, again, great freedom for the court. There are few restrictive rules. The old adagium 'one witness is no witness' no longer applies. Spouses and relatives of the parties are no longer incompetent to testify. It is left to the court to assess the value of the testimony.

In 1988, the possibility of the party witness was introduced. With regard to the testimony of a party witness, there are, however, some restrictions. The declarations of such a witness about the facts he has to prove have no full evidential value to the benefit of this party. His declarations may only serve to supplement incomplete evidence.

According to Dutch law, the court is, in general, obliged to enable a party to provide proof of his statements by means of witnesses when he offers to do so, even in appellate proceedings. This is not the case in arbitration procedures because in arbitration the rules of the Code of Civil Procedure relating to evidence do not apply.

D. Function of the Notary and Notarial Instruments

59. In the above, some references have already been made to notarial instruments. In some (rare) cases, the use of a notarial instrument is conditional to the existence of a contract (*see* paragraph 54 *supra*), but in general, a notarial instrument in the field of contract law is used for evidential purposes (*see* paragraph 57 *supra*).

The position of the notary is regulated in the Act on the Office of Notary, which originally dates from 1842 and was thoroughly revised in 1999. This Act defines the notary as a public servant who has the exclusive power to draw up authentic instruments with regard to all acts, contracts and decisions for which an authentic instrument is required by law or desired by the interested parties (always assuming that the law has not explicitly charged another civil servant with this task). The notary – who must have a university degree in law – is appointed by the Crown and is granted an honourable discharge at the age of 67. At his appointment, the notary is assigned a seat (or place of business) where he must have his office. Other than under the old law however, he is allowed to draw up notarial instruments throughout all of the Netherlands.

The Act contains – among other things – extensive provisions on the form of notarial authentic instruments and other requirements which must be met (e.g., the instrument must contain place and date and the names of the notary and the parties, the parties must be known to the notary, the instrument must be – fully or partially – read aloud and must be signed and sometimes the presence of witnesses is required). If the formal requirements for authentic notarial instruments are not met, the instrument is not authentic, which may have quite serious effects in cases where an authentic instrument is required (e.g., last wills). The evidential value of the authentic act has already been discussed (paragraph 57 *supra*). Another aspect worth mentioning is that the notary has the power to issue a special authenticated copy of an act (bearing the words 'In the name of the king'), which may serve as a writ of execution. In this way, for example, payment of a sum of money may be enforced. Execution through a notarial instrument is, however, no common practice.

Because of the fact that the tasks of the notary lie especially in the field of the law of matrimonial property and succession (he is appointed by law to draw up marriage contracts and wills), company law and the law of legal persons (he is appointed to establish and transfer associations, foundations and corporations) and the law of immovable things, the notary is pre-eminently expert on the aforementioned fields and the tax laws connected with these fields. The task of the notary exceeds the drawing up of instruments. Advisory services are a very important part of his task as well.

The notary must comply with high professional standards and must exercise due care in the execution of his activities, both as regards his client as – depending on the circumstances – vis-à-vis third parties. Several decisions of the Supreme Court have accentuated this duty to care; in general, a high degree of diligence is demanded of the notary. Moreover, notaries are subject to disciplinary jurisdiction.

E. Contracts in the Field of Evidence

60. The freedom of the court with regard to evidence may be restricted by the parties themselves. It frequently happens that parties to a contract insert special conditions into their contract with regard to their evidential position in the case of a trial; for example, they assign compulsory value to special means of evidence or exclude certain means of evidence. These conditions are, in general, valid but may not be applied by the court if they concern evidence with regard to facts with juridical effects that are not at the free disposal of the parties or if it would be contrary to good faith (reasonableness and fairness) for one of the parties to invoke the conditions. Some stipulations with regard to evidence are deemed to be unreasonably onerous if they are part of general conditions applicable to a consumer contract (a contract between a user of general conditions and a natural person not acting in the course of a business or profession, *see infra*, paragraph 112). Article 6:236, sub k, mentions in this respect stipulations excluding or limiting the right of the consumer to provide evidence or modifying the apportionment of the burden of proof under the law to the detriment of the consumer, either because it contains a declaration of the consumer regarding the adequacy of the prestation which is to be performed, or because it charges him with the proof that a failure of the user of the general conditions can be attributed to him.

III. Burden of Proof, 'Obligation of Means' and 'Obligation of Result'

A. Burden of Proof

61. A general rule of the Dutch law of evidence is that the party who invokes the juridical effects of certain facts has the burden of proof of these facts. The Code of Civil Procedure explicitly states this rule in Article 150 but allows an exception in case reasonableness and fairness or a rule of unwritten law requires another apportionment of the burden of proof.

In some cases in which the burden of proof lies with one party, the other party may have a duty of information in order to facilitate the onerous position of the party who has to produce the evidence. This will especially be the case when the facts to be proved have taken place within the sphere of the other party. For example, if an employee claims that he has been dismissed for a false reason, the employer will have a duty to provide information on the reason for the dismissal; in medical malpractice cases, the hospital or doctor will have a duty to provide information on the medical treatment the patient has undergone.[22] This duty to inform may make it easier for the other party to prove his position but does not change the apportionment of the burden of proof itself.

Sometimes, the substantive law – especially the Civil Code – takes the burden of proof into account. Many provisions of the Code indicate in their wording on which party the burden of proof should be placed. Cf. Article 6:74 states that every failure in the performance of an obligation obliges the debtor to repair the damage which the creditor suffers therefrom *unless* the failure cannot be attributed to the debtor. Such a formulation indicates that the party in whose interest the exception is inserted has to prove that this exception presents itself in his case. Another formulation with the same purpose is found, for example, in Article 6:237, which states that certain stipulations contained in general conditions *are presumed* to be unreasonably onerous (the 'grey list'). It follows that the party who is relying on the stipulation has to prove that, in the circumstances, it is not unreasonably onerous.

B. 'Obligation of Means' and 'Obligation of Result'

62. In Dutch law, a distinction is made between 'obligation of means' and 'obligation of result', but this distinction is a rather vague one. It is much discussed but does not play an important role in practice.

The distinction seems easy: the debtor of an obligation of result fails in the performance of his obligation if he does not reach the result agreed on (an obligation to give a thing is an example of an obligation of result); the debtor of an obligation of means fails in the performance if he did not make sufficient efforts to perform (an example of an obligation of means is the obligation of a lawyer defending a case in court: he does not have to stand in for a good result, that is winning the case). The distinction turned out to be not so easy in practice. One of the reasons for this is that, in general, more than one obligation results from one contract and these obligations may have a very different nature; for example, a lawyer (debtor of an obligation of means) must also take care that an appeal is lodged in time (obligation of result).

The distinction plays a role, however, as regards the weight of the burden of proof. In the case of an 'obligation of result', a failure in the performance is, in general, easier to prove than in the case of an 'obligation of means'. For the creditor of an obligation of result it suffices in general to prove that the result is not achieved, whereas the creditor of an obligation of means will have to prove that the debtor did not make the efforts required. (The efforts required will, in general, be the efforts that could have been reasonably and objectively expected from the debtor in the given circumstances.) Moreover, in the first case, if a failure has been proved, in order to escape liability, it lies with the debtor to prove that the failure may not be

22. E.g., HR 18-2-1994, ECLI:NL:HR:1994:ZC1269, NJ 1994/368; HR 7-9-2001, ECLI:NL:HR:2001:ZC3657, NJ 2001/615.

attributed to him, whereas in the second case, the proof of the failure (which implies a lack of care in the circumstances) normally amounts to proof of the debtor's liability.

As mentioned in paragraph 61 *supra*, according to Article 150 of the Code of Civil Procedure, the burden of proof may be apportioned in a different way if reasonableness and fairness or a rule of unwritten law so required.

C. *Obligation of Guarantee*

63. Sometimes a third type of obligation is distinguished, apart from the obligation of means and the obligation of result: the obligation of guarantee. An obligation of guarantee differs from an obligation of result in this respect that the debtor expressly guarantees a certain result (in general, the existence of a state of affairs or the occurrence of a fact) and therefore is not entitled to invoke 'force majeure'.

§3. Precontractual Liability and Negotiations

I. Precontractual Liability and Negotiations in Bad Faith

A. *Introduction*

64. If a contract comes into being after negotiations, the conduct and declarations of the parties in the precontractual phase can influence the juridical relationship of the parties created by the contract in several ways.

In the first place, the conduct and declarations are important with regard to questions such as what the contents of the contract are, whether a party may invoke error or fraud, whether, in the case of nullity of a contract, there is room for conversion (*see* on conversion paragraph 101 *infra*), whether the parties knew they were violating the law, etc.

In 1957, the Supreme Court decided that parties when negotiating a contract, enter into a juridical relationship dominated by the principles of reasonableness and fairness, which imposes on each of them the duty to take into account the others' reasonable interests.[23] The 1957 case concerned a case of error; the rule formulated by the Court led to the conclusion that it is contrary to reasonableness and fairness to annul the contract because of error if the party in error could and should have taken measures to prevent the error.

The rule that parties, when negotiating a contract, enter into a juridical relationship dominated by the principles of reasonableness and fairness, which imposes on each of them the duty to take into account the others' reasonable interests, also has its effect in cases where parties have been negotiating, but no contract has been concluded. The general duty of a negotiating party to take into account the reasonable interests of the other party may imply that a party lacks the freedom to break off

23. HR 15-11-1957, ECLI:NL:HR:1957:AG2023, NJ 1958/67.

negotiations (in which case the court may grant an injunction to continue or resume the negotiations) or that, when negotiations are broken off, he is under an obligation to pay damages; these may even amount to the '*positives Vertragsinteresse*' (expectation loss) including the loss of profits which the plaintiff would have made out of the envisaged contract, had it been concluded.

As we have seen *supra* paragraph 14, freedom of contract is one of the basic principles of Dutch contract law. The above-mentioned rule does not affect this principle to a considerable extent. A negotiating party is in general free to withdraw from the negotiations and to decide not to enter into a contract with the other participant(s) in the negotiations. The cases in which this freedom no longer exists are exceptional.

B. *Precontractual Liability*

65. The leading case on precontractual liability is a case from 1982,[24] in which a construction firm, whose proposal for the building of a municipal swimming pool had already been accepted by the major and aldermen, was passed over by the city council, which opted for a cheaper plan. The firm claimed damages: reparation costs and loss of profit.

The Supreme Court decided that it is not impossible that negotiations about a contract have reached a stage in which the breaking-off of the negotiations (itself) in the given circumstances may be considered contrary to reasonableness and fairness because the parties could mutually reasonably expect that in any case, a contract of some kind would result from the negotiations. In such a situation, there may also be room for compensation of lost profits. An obligation to compensate the other party for expenses made may even exist if the negotiations have not yet reached the stage mentioned above (in which the other party, according to reasonableness and fairness, is no longer allowed to break off the negotiations) but have reached a stage in which the party who breaks off is not free to do so without compensating the other party's expenses in part or in whole.

C. *Three Stages in the Negotiating Process*

66. From this decision authors conclude that the Court makes a distinction between three stages in the negotiating process:

(1) Parties are free to break off negotiations without any obligation to compensate the other party.
(2) According to the criteria of reasonableness and fairness, a party is still free to break off, however, under the condition that he compensates the other party for (all or some of) the expenses made.

---

24. HR 18-6-1982, ECLI:NL:HR:1982:AG4405, NJ 1983/723.

(3) According to the criteria of reasonableness and fairness, a party is no longer free to break off the negotiations. If that party nevertheless breaks off negotiations, he is obliged to compensate the other party for expenses and – in some cases – for the profits the other party would have made.

D. Further Developments

67. After this decision, the drafters of the new Code inserted an article in the Code in order to confirm this decision. The text of the new article read: 'Negotiating parties are obliged to have their conduct also determined by each other's reasonable interests. Each of them is free to break off negotiations unless this would be unacceptable on the ground of the justified reliance of the other party on the conclusion of a contract or on the ground of the other circumstances of the case.' This article was withdrawn because Parliament thought it better to allow case law to develop freely.

In a Supreme Court decision of 1987,[25] however (on negotiations about the participation of Shell in the capital of a certain company), the formula was almost literally quoted. The Court added that there can only be a duty to compensate for expectation losses due to the fact that a contract has not been concluded between the parties, 'if it is plausible that negotiations, had they been continued, would have led to a joint venture of any kind'. In the case at hand, this condition was not fulfilled.

In later case law, the above-mentioned rules were confirmed.

In a 1996 case,[26] the Supreme Court added that justified reliance on the conclusion of a contract will not under all circumstances render the breaking-off of the negotiations unacceptable. The extent to which and the way in which the party breaking-off the negotiations contributed to the reliance is relevant, as are the reasonable interests of this party. The fact whether or not unforeseen circumstances intervened during the negotiations may also be relevant.

In a 2005 case,[27] the Supreme Court has summarized its case law since 1982.

25. HR 23-10-1987, ECLI:NL:HR:1987:AD0018, NJ 1988/1017.
26. HR 14-6-1996, ECLI:NL:HR:1996:ZC2105, NJ 1997/481.
27. HR 12-8-2005, ECLI:NL:HR:2005:AT7337, NJ 2005/467.

Part II. Conditions of Substantive Validity

Chapter 1. Substantive Validity

§1. Capacity of the Parties

I. Capacity and Incapacity: Natural Persons

68. Article 3:32, paragraph 1 states that every natural person has the capacity to perform juridical acts to the extent that the law does not provide otherwise.

There are two exceptions to the rule. Minors (persons under 18 who are not married and have not been married) are capable of entering into contracts, provided they have the consent of their parents, either express or implied (Article 1:234). Persons under legal restraint are incapable of entering into contracts. To do so, they need the consent of their guardian (Article 1:381). The purpose of these provisions is the protection of minors and persons under legal restraint.

In the case of minors, the rule is that – with parental consent – they are capable of performing juridical acts. Without such consent, a contract concluded by a minor may be annulled (*see* the next paragraph). However, parental consent is supposed to have been given when the juridical act performed is a normal one for minors of this particular age (Article 1:234 sub 3). This means that in these cases, the contract is valid unless the parents prove that they have refused their consent before the contract was concluded and that this refusal was known to the other party. There are a few exceptions to the rule of legal incapacity: for example, a minor of the age of 16 may – without parental consent – enter into labour contracts (Article 7:612) and contracts concerning medical treatment (Article 7:447).

II. Effects of Juridical Acts of Incapable Persons

69. According to Article 3:32, paragraph 2, a juridical act of an incapable person is not null but may be annulled. Before the annulment the juridical act has full juridical effects. (Article 3:49–55 contains provisions on the annulment of juridical acts; *see infra*, paragraphs 102 ff.).

If the representative of the incapable person (or the former incapable person himself after the termination of his incapability) invokes the incapacity, the mere fact of the incapacity is enough to have the juridical act annulled, whether or not the incapable person has suffered a detriment is not relevant. Nor is it relevant whether the other party knew or should have known about the incapacity.

Article 3:32, paragraph 2, stating that a juridical act of an incapable person may be annulled, formulates an exception for a unilateral juridical act of an incapable person which is not addressed to one or more specifically determined other persons. Such an act is not subject to annulment but is null. An example of such a null act is the drawing up of a will by an incapable person.

III. Mentally Impaired Persons

70. A person whose mental faculties are impaired but who is not placed under legal restraint is not incapable of performing juridical acts. Impairment of mental faculties may occur in all kinds of forms and degrees. All situations in which the person who acts does not possess a normal will and is not able to understand what he does or what his actions lead to are situations of mental impairment. Causes may be hypnosis, drunkenness, great excitement, etc. For the acts of these persons, the Code contains a special provision in Article 3:34:

(1) Where a person whose mental faculties are permanently or temporarily impaired makes a declaration, the intention corresponding to that declaration is deemed to be absent if the impairment prevented a reasonable appraisal of the interests involved or if the declaration was made under the influence of that disturbance. Unless the prejudice was not reasonably foreseeable at the time of the juridical act, a declaration is presumed to have been made under the influence of the disturbance if the juridical act was prejudicial to the mentally disturbed person.
(2) A juridical act without such intention may be annulled. However, the absence of intention renders a unilateral juridical act null where it is not addressed to one or more specific persons.

Despite the absence of intention on the part of the mentally impaired person, the other party may claim that he has interpreted the declaration or conduct of that person in conformity with the sense which he could reasonably attribute to it in the circumstances as a declaration of a particular implication made to him by that person. In that case, the absence of intention in the declaration cannot be invoked by the person whose mental faculties were impaired. This follows from the general rule of Article 3:35, which deals with all cases of discrepancy between intention and declaration, *see infra*, paragraphs 73 ff.

IV. Legal Bodies

71. Not only natural persons are capable of performing juridical acts. From Article 2:5, it follows that legal bodies are capable too. In this field, there are no exceptions.

§2. 'MISTAKE' (DISTINCTION FROM MOTIVE)

I. Introduction

72. As mentioned above, in Dutch law a contract comes into being by mutual consent of the parties. Moreover, it is necessary that the intention of the parties to enter into a contract has manifested itself by a declaration addressed to each other (Article 3:33). Sometimes, however, a declaration is erroneously made which does not correspond to the actual will. (In Dutch law, this is called 'error improperly so-called'.)

Before discussing how the problems that arise from such a situation are to be solved, first, some attention will be paid to the different types of cases where there is a discrepancy between intention and declaration of the declaring party or between the intentions of both parties and to the possible causes thereof.

II. Discrepancy Between Declaration and Intention

73. The declaration of one of the parties was not intended by that party. In this case, a party's declaration does not correspond to its intention. There can be several causes for this type of discrepancy:

(a) '*Vis absoluta*'. (e.g., someone's hand is, against his will, led by someone else to sign a declaration. These cases must be discerned from cases of (psychological) threat, discussed later on).
(b) Impairment of mental faculties. This comprises all situations in which the person in question does not dispose of a normal will and is not aware of his actions. For example, drunkenness, narcosis, absent-mindedness and great excitement can lead to mental disturbance. The Code contains a special provision on the juridical acts of mentally disturbed persons, *see supra*, paragraph 70.
(c) Slip of the tongue or the pen.
(d) Wrongly delivered declaration by telegram or messenger.
(e) The signing of an instrument which is not in accordance with the intention of the signer.

III. The Declaring Party Does Not Want the Juridical Effects of the Declaration

74. The declaration and the way the other party understood it corresponds to the intention of the party who made the declaration, but this party did not want the juridical effects of the declaration:

(a) '*Reservatio mentalis*', the internal decision not to want that the effects of the declaration are hidden from the other party.
(b) Non-recognizable joke.

(c) Simulation. Simulation is a special case. In all other mentioned cases, the parties are, in a way, each other's adversaries, but in cases of simulation, two or more persons create the appearance that they concluded a certain contract while they agree in secret that this contract will not take effect between them. There is therefore a contradiction between the intention of the parties and their manifested declaration perceptible for third persons. As a general rule, the parties are not bound by the simulated contract, but third persons can – under the circumstances – refer to either the simulated contract or, if this exists, to the real contract or legal relationship between the parties.

IV. Declaration Corresponds to Intention, but the Other Party Understands the Declaration in a Different Way

75. The declaration of a party was intended by that party, but not in the way the other party understood it. In other words, the declaration corresponds to the intention of the party who made it, but this party did not want the other party to understand the declaration in the way the other party understood it. Here, the problem is not a discrepancy between the declaration and the intention of the declaring party but the fact that the declaration, by its ambiguity, covers both the intention of the declaring party and the different intention of the other party:

(a) The declaration is not clear enough or is misunderstood.
(b) There is uncertainty about the question to whom the declaration was addressed and therefore another person than the person for whom the declaration was intended has acted as the other party to the contract. (E.g., if a declaration is addressed to someone who transacts business in private as well as under a firm.).
(c) The declaration reaches another person than the person for whom it was intended.

V. Formation of a Contract on the Basis of the Declaration?

76. In the above-mentioned cases of discrepancy between intention and declaration (except in the case of simulation) or between the intentions of the two parties, the question of whether a contract comes into being on the basis of the declaration can be answered by applying Article 3:35 which states: 'The absence of intention in a declaration cannot be invoked against a person who interpreted another's declaration or conduct in conformity with the sense which he could reasonably attribute to it in the circumstances as a declaration of a particular implication made to him by that other person.' This provision has to be considered in connection with Article 3:11 on good faith (*see supra*, paragraph 32).

According to Dutch law, detriment is not an autonomous factor with regard to the coming into being of a valid juridical act. However, according to Article 3:35, in conjunction with Article 3:11, a party may be under a duty to investigate whether the other party's declaration is in accordance with his real intention. Of course, this depends on the circumstances of the case; among the relevant circumstances will be the gratuitous character of the declaration and the grave consequences which it might have for the declaring party (e.g., a resignation by an employee has serious consequences for the employee and the employer to whom the declaration is addressed will therefore in general have to make an effort to make sure that the resignation is really wanted).

In this sense detriment is one of the factors which come into play in determining whether a party could reasonably rely on the declaration of the other party being in conformity with his intention. Moreover, as was pointed out *supra*, in paragraph 46, it is also possible that even though the requirements of Article 3:35 and 3:11 are met, and a valid act (e.g., a promise or a contract) has come into existence, the party who has not given any benefit nor suffered detrimental reliance, may, through the provisions on good faith be stopped from asserting his rights against the other party.

If the requirements of Article 3:35 are met, the juridical act is valid, and unlike German law (Articles 119 ff. BGB), it cannot be annulled by the party whose intention did not correspond to his declaration, even if he would be prepared to pay compensation to the other party.

If the requirements of Article 3:35 are not met (or if the other party chooses not to invoke the article), the absence of intention to a declaration or the ambiguity of the declaration covering two differing intentions leads, in principle, to the nullity of the juridical act. An exception is made in Article 3:34 for declarations made by a person whose mental faculties are impaired. As we saw, in that case, a juridical act without intention (except a unilateral non-addressed act) is not null but annullable.

VI. Protection of Third Persons

77. The Code contains in Article 3:36 a special provision for the protection of third persons, based on the same principle as Article 3:35:

> A third person who, on the basis of another's declaration or conduct, assumes the creation, existence or extinction of a certain juridical relationship, which is reasonable in the circumstances and who acts reasonably in reliance on the accuracy of that assumption, cannot have the inaccuracy of that assumption invoked against him by the other person.

For example, A assigns a claim against B to C, who relies on an instrument signed by the parties A and B. The instrument does not mention a stipulation between A and B that the claim would be non-assignable. Under Article 3:36 B may not invoke the stipulation against C.

VII. Distinction Between 'Error Improperly So-Called' and Defects of Consent

78. The problems of 'error improperly so-called' we have just discussed must be distinguished from the actual defects of consent, where the consent of one of the parties was formed defectively. In these cases, there is no discrepancy between intention and declaration, but the intention was formed under the influence of error ('error properly so-called'), duress, fraud or undue influence. These defects of consent will be discussed in the next paragraphs.

§3. Misrepresentation, Improper Pressure, Gross Disparity

I. Defects of Consent: Terminology

79. The defects of consent known by Dutch law (error, duress, fraud and abuse of circumstances (or undue influence)) can roughly be compared to 'misrepresentation, improper pressure and gross disparity' in Anglo-American law. There are differences, however, and the borderline between these legal concepts is not drawn in the same way, so – to prevent confusion – we will use the terms 'error, duress, fraud and undue influence' instead of the Anglo-American terms and discuss each of these concepts in the next paragraphs.

A preliminary remark. The rules on duress, fraud and undue influence are formulated in Article 3:44, which means that they apply to all juridical acts in the field of patrimonial law. The provisions on error, however, are to be found in the titles on contract (Article 6:228) and partition (Article 3:196) and may be applied by way of analogy to other juridical acts.

II. Error: Three Types

80. Error is the most important and the most problematic defect of consent. It has given rise to a considerable amount of case law.

Article 6:228, paragraph 1 recognizes three types of relevant error: error caused by a misrepresentation (regardless of whether it was fraudulent, negligent or innocent); error caused by or reinforced by the breach of a duty to disclose information; and error existing on both sides. The first case is inspired by the common law, the third by the German doctrine of '*subjektive Geschäftsgrundlage*'.

Article 6:228, paragraph 1 states:

> A contract which has been entered into under the influence of error and which would not have been entered into had there been a correct assessment of the facts may be nullified:
>
> (a) if the error is due to information given by the other party, unless the other party could assume that the contract would have been entered into irrespective of such information;
> (b) if the other party, in view of what he knew or ought to have known regarding the error, should have informed the party in error;
> (c) if the other party in entering into the contract made the same incorrect assumption as the party in error, unless the other party, even if there had

been a correct assessment of the facts, need not have understood that the party in error would therefore be prevented from entering into the contract.

III. Further Requirements for Annulment, Based on Error

81. Article 6:228 requires, in the first place, a causal connection between the error and the conclusion of the contract. This means that the error must concern facts or circumstances (which may be extrinsic to the object of the contract) essential for the party in error – in the sense that without the error, he would not (or not on the same terms) have entered into the contract. The party in error does not have to state in court what other conditions he would have concluded the contract if he had known the facts that caused the error, but he must state and make plausible which specific parts of the contract he would not have entered into.[28]

Furthermore, at the time of the conclusion of the contract, it must have been known to the other party that the facts or circumstances concerned were essential for the erring party in the sense just explained. (This requirement is formulated a little differently for the three different types of error but comes down to the same thing.)

It is not required that the other party understands that his co-contracting party is in error, though this might influence a possible claim for damages based on unlawful act (Article 6:162). Nor is it required that the erring party has suffered detriment due to the conclusion of the contract, as was decided in the case of the sale of a stolen car: the buyer could invoke error (he did not know the car had been stolen) even though this fact would not be detrimental to him.[29]

IV. Error as to Future Circumstances and Error for Which the Party in Error Should Remain Accountable

82. Article 6:228, paragraph 2 reads:

> The annulment cannot be based on an error regarding a strictly future circumstance or an error which should remain for the account of the party in error, given the nature of the contract, common opinion or the facts of the case.

Error as to future circumstances is inoperative in itself but may nevertheless be relevant if it is the consequence of some error in past or present circumstances.

Under paragraph 2, which gives much discretion to the courts, important decisions of the Supreme Court under the old Code will retain their relevance. For example, the Court has decided that a party may not rely on his error if he could have taken reasonable measures to prevent it, but this rule may, in principle, not be

28. HR 17-1-1997, ECLI:NL:HR:1997:ZC2250, NJ 1997/222.
29. HR 19-1-2001, ECLI:NL:HR:2001:AA9559, NJ 2001/159.

invoked by the other party who has caused the error by the information he has given (paragraph 1, sub a) or ought to have given (paragraph 1, sub b) before the conclusion of the contract in order to prevent the first party's forming of wrong ideas on the relevant point.[30] In two more cases,[31] the Supreme Court again made it clear that a party who should have provided certain information before the conclusion of the contract but did not do so may not, when the other party wants to annul the contract because of error, put forward that the other party did not duly investigate the issue.

It is conceivable however, that the information which was given was so vague that the erring party should have made further inquiries before entering into the contract. In that case, the erring party will remain accountable; it all depends on the circumstances of the case.[32]

V. Error '*Iuris*'

83. If all requirements for error are fulfilled, error with regard to the law (*error iuris*) can also be a cause for annulment. In most cases of *error iuris* however, the erring party will remain accountable according to Article 6:228, paragraph 2.

VI. Error with Regard to the Person of the Other Party

84. Finally, an error with regard to the identity of the other party – or his qualities – can give rise to annulment when the contract is concluded with the intention to bind the person of the other party.

VII. Non-exclusivity of the Provisions on Error

85. The possibility to invoke error does not exclude the possibility to invoke failure in the performance of an obligation (*see* paragraphs 177 ff. *infra*) or to invoke another ground for annulment if the conditions therefore have been fulfilled (e.g., fraud). As briefly indicated above, the party in error may claim damages on the basis of Article 6:162 (unlawful act) if the error is caused by negligent behaviour of the other party. *See also infra*, paragraph 106.

VIII. Duress

86. Article 3:44, paragraph 2 states that:

30. HR 15-11-1957, ECLI:NL:HR:1957:AG2023, NJ 1958/67; HR 21-1-1966, ECLI:NL:HR:1966:AC4621, NJ 1966/183; HR 30-11-1973, ECLI:NL:HR:1973:AC5383, NJ 1974/97.
31. HR 10-4-1998, ECLI:NL:HR:1998:ZC2629, NJ 1998/666; HR 16-6-2000, ECLI:NL:HR:2000:AA6237, NJ 2001/559; HR 16-12-2016, ECLI:NL:HR:2016:2885, NJ 2018/223.
32. *See* for an example on how a duty of care of a professional party can influence the information that this party must give HR 28-6-2019, ECLI:NL:HR:2019:1046, NJ 2020/257; HR 4-10-2019, ECLI:NL:HR:2019:1499, NJ 2020/258; HR 4-10-2019, ECLI:NL:HR:2019:1500, NJ 2020/259.

> Duress occurs where a person induces another to perform a specific juridical act by unlawfully threatening him or a third party with harm to his person or property. The duress must be such that a reasonable person would be influenced by it.

Duress in Dutch law has a wider sense than duress in English law. It comprises not only threats to the person but also to property. The threat may be of an economic nature, e.g., a threat to commit a breach of contract or to go on strike.[33] A threat of committing an unlawful act against any person may be sufficient, provided that it is such as to influence a reasonable person.

IX. Fraud

87. Article 3:44, paragraph 3 contains a provision on fraud:

> Fraud occurs where a person induces another to perform a specific juridical act by intentionally providing him with inaccurate information, by intentionally concealing any fact he was obliged to communicate, or by any other artifice. Representation in general terms, even if they are untrue, do not, as such, constitute fraud.

It has been a much-disputed question if and under what circumstances fraud can be committed by silence. The Code has followed Meijers' opinion, according to which this is possible where the person concealing some information was under a duty to give that information.

Fraud causes error. On the one hand, the law contains sterner requirements for fraud than for error; fraud requires conduct which is intentionally misleading. On the other hand, fraud does not require that the error caused by it complies with the requirements of Article 6:228.

X. Undue Influence

88. Finally, Article 3:44 states in paragraph 4 on undue influence:

> Undue influence occurs where a person knows or ought to understand that another is being induced to perform a juridical act as a result of special circumstances – such as a state of necessity, dependency, wantonness, abnormal mental condition or inexperience – and promotes the realisation of that juridical act, although what he knows or ought to understand should cause him to refrain from so doing.

33. *See* e.g., HR 27-3-1992, ECLI:NL:HR:1992:ZC0555, NJ 1992/377.

This so-called fourth defect of consent springs from the English doctrine of undue influence, which had already been adopted in other countries like Germany, Switzerland and Italy.

XI. Consequences of Duress, Fraud or Undue Influence

89. When a juridical act has been entered into as a result of duress, fraud or undue influence, this act may be annulled (Article 3:44, paragraph 1). As in the case of error, these defects of consent may only be invoked if there is a causal connection between the duress, fraud or undue influence and the conclusion of the contract.

Like in cases of error, the fact that certain conduct can be classified as duress, fraud or undue influence does not derogate from the possibility to invoke failure in the performance of an obligation or another ground for annulment, nor from the possibility to institute an action for damages based on unlawful act (Article 6:162).

Paragraph 5 of Article 3:44 contains a special provision in case a declaration has been made as a result of duress, fraud or undue influence on the part of a person who is not party to the juridical act. In that case this defect cannot be invoked against a party to the juridical act who had no reason to assume its existence.

XII. *'Iustum Pretium'*

90. The doctrine of '*iustum pretium*'– the rule that the prestations resulting from a synallagmatic contract must have a more or less equivalent value – is not as such a part of Dutch law. The parties are, in principle, free to stipulate and bind themselves to the prestations they want. Someone may well conclude a disadvantageous contract out of motives of generosity or business motives as in the case of suretyship. Mere disparity will never be a sufficient cause of action. If the lack of equivalency is, however, a result of one of the defects of consent, the other party may, of course, have the contract annulled or institute the other actions mentioned above. Furthermore, Articles 3:33 ff. on intention and declaration (*see supra*, paragraph 15) and Article 6:233 on unreasonably onerous stipulations in general conditions – not concerning stipulations going to the essence of the prestations, like the price – (*see* paragraphs 113 ff.) provide possibilities to act against unreasonable detriment on the part of one of the contracting parties. Finally, Article 6:2 and 6:248 (*see supra*, paragraphs 31 ff.) may sometimes prevent the party who has benefitted from the contract to invoke the contract if this would be contrary to reasonableness and fairness (*see supra*, paragraphs 5 and 31 ff.). As mentioned, mere disparity will not be enough in this respect, but additional circumstances may lead to unreasonableness and unfairness. If the disparity is a result of circumstances that have occurred since the conclusion of the contract, Article 6:258 on unforeseen circumstances (*see supra*, paragraphs 32 and 50, *infra*, paragraphs 172 ff.) may be of avail.

§4. OTHER CONDITIONS OF VALIDITY

I. Determinability of the Obligations

91. The Code requires for a contract to be valid that the obligations which the parties assume must be determinable (Article 6:227). This does not mean that their object has to be specified in detail at the time of the conclusion of the contract. It is sufficient that the rights and obligations of the parties can be ascertained afterwards. Certain circumstances, like the market price or the customary practice between the parties or in the branch of trade concerned, may be a relevant factor, but the parties can also leave the determination to a third person or even to one of the parties themselves. Such powers must, of course, be used in accordance with reasonableness and fairness, which may be reviewed by a court or arbitrator.

In light of this provision, Article 7:4 (*see infra*, paragraph 246) must be seen, which stipulates that where a sale has been entered into without a determination of the price (the contract is not null), the buyer owes a reasonable price. *See also* Article 7:405, paragraph 2 (mandate) and 7:601, paragraph 2 (deposit, *see infra*, paragraph 239). This means that a contract of sale can come into being without the price being determined; in this sense, the price is not an *essentiale* of the contract.

II. Future Things or Rights

92. Contracts can relate to future things or patrimonial rights. The old Code contained a provision that explicitly stated this rule, but in the new Code, such a provision has been omitted as superfluous. Two important exceptions to this rule are the prohibition to donate future property and the prohibition to dispose of a future inheritance.

III. 'Cause'

93. The old Code stated that a contract without a 'cause' is invalid. 'Cause' was in general understood to mean the implication of the contract, that which the parties intended by the contract.

The requirement of a cause has created great uncertainty but has only proven useful in a few specific cases; therefore, the provision was not maintained in the new Code. Its function has been taken over by other, partly new provisions. The practical meaning of the rule that a contract needed a cause was especially felt in cases of contracts in furtherance of an already existing juridical relationship between the parties, which afterwards proved not to exist. For these cases, the Code contains a special provision in Article 6:229, according to which such contracts can be annulled. In other cases, the solution must be found by applying general provisions such as Articles 3:33 ff. (intention and reliance) and 6:74 ff. (rules on non-performance) (*See supra*, paragraph 15 and *infra*, paragraphs 164 ff.).

The old Code stated moreover that a contract with an 'unlawful cause' was invalid. Unlawful cause was defined as a cause contrary to law, good morals or public order. The concept of the unlawful cause did not return in the new Code, but Article 3:40 contains a provision for all juridical acts that has the same effects as the old article on unlawful cause. *See* further *infra*, paragraphs 95 ff.

§5. Initial Impossibility

I. Initial Impossibility

94. Sometimes the performance of obligations resulting from a contract is impossible *ab initio.* For example, a contract of sale concerning a thing that does not exist or that already belongs to the buyer. Under the old Code, such a contract was invalid because of lack of 'cause'. In the present Code, the provisions on non-performance are applicable in such cases. This means that the party who was entitled to the impossible performance can set aside the contract (Articles 6:265 ff.) and, if the failure in the performance can be attributed to the debtor, claim damages (Articles 6:74 ff.). *See* further *infra*, paragraphs 164 ff.

§6. Illegality and Public Policy: Unenforceable Contracts

I. Contracts Contrary to Good Morals, Public Order or Statutory Provisions

95. Article 3:40 states that a juridical act which, by its content or necessary implication, is contrary to good morals or public order is null (paragraph 1). Juridical acts which are as such contrary to statutory law are dealt with in paragraphs 2 and 3 of Article 3:40, *see infra*, paragraph 97.

II. Contradiction with Good Morals or Public Order

96. In order to determine whether a juridical act is – not by its content but – by its necessary implication contrary to good morals or public order, the foreseeable effects of the act and the motives of the parties with regard to these effects should be examined. For example, a contract of sale which would lead to the frustration of the lawful exercise of a right by a third party and which was concluded with the intention to frustrate that exercise, has been judged contrary to good morals.

If only one of the parties had a motive contrary to good morals or public order, the contract is in general only null if this motive was or should have been known to the other party. If not, the contract is valid. The internal motive renders the act morally condemnable but has only juridical effects if this motive is recognizable from the outside.

The contract must be judged on the basis of the situation at the moment of the conclusion of the contract. Later developments are irrelevant.

The opinion of what is contrary to good morals or public order, of course, varies with place and time.

Some examples of contracts that were judged to be contrary to good morals are contracts concerning indefeasible rights (such as the right of a guardian to decide in accordance with his own views about the education of a child; for example, the Supreme Court judged a contract, whereby a man undertook to pay alimony to his wife after their divorce and the wife assumed an obligation to send their child to a catholic school, to be null);[34] contracts concluded with abuse of the function or the profession of one of the parties; contracts which have the purpose of causing harm to third parties;[35] and contracts which, when executed, will lead directly or indirectly to the violation of a statutory rule.

An example of changing morals is found in a Supreme Court decision of 1990 concerning a case of the last-mentioned category.[36] A contract of sale with regard to the goodwill and inventory of a brothel (which would lead to a violation of the prohibition to gain profit from prostitution) was not deemed *eo ipso* contrary to good morals.

'Public order' is a concept that is even more vague than 'good morals'. Most contracts that were judged contrary to public order were also held to be contrary to good morals. An example of a contract contrary to public order is a contract whereby a person assumes an obligation to vote for a certain person on the occasion of the parliamentary elections. Another example is a contract between a private person and a government body (such as a municipality) which abuses its powers by requiring, without a legal basis, remuneration or other counter-performance for carrying out a public task.[37]

A contract which can only be performed by violating a statutory rule, for example, because acts indispensable for the preparation of the performance are forbidden, may be contrary to good morals or public order if both parties were (or could have been) aware of the fact that performance of the contract would imply the violation of a statutory rule.

Under the old Code, the Supreme Court ruled that a contract which creates an obligation to a performance forbidden by law is always null. Article 3:40, paragraph 1 will, as a rule, lead to the same result.[38]

III. Contradiction with Imperative Statutory Provisions

97. As mentioned, Article 3:40, paragraphs 2 and 3 are concerned with juridical acts, the conclusion of which is, as such, forbidden by a statutory provision. Unless the necessary implication of the provision implies otherwise, violation of an imperative statutory provision entails nullity of the juridical act concerned (paragraph 2). This is different from the rule discussed in the last paragraph because here (under

34. HR 20-5-1938, ECLI:NL:HR:1938:82, NJ 1939/94.
35. HR 19-12-2014, ECLI:NL:HR:2014:3650, RvdW 2014/137.
36. HR 2-2-1990, NJ 1991/265.
37. HR 13-4-2001, ECLI:NL:HR:2001:AB1055, NJ 2001/581; HR 5-12-2014, ECLI:NL:HR:2014:3532, RvdW 2015/36.
38. HR 1-6-2012, ECLI:NL:HR:2012:BU5609, NJ 2013/172.

paragraph 2), the nullity follows from the fact that *performing* the juridical act is contrary to an imperative statutory provision, whereas (under paragraph 1) a contract may be null as being contrary to good morals or public order if its *performance* implicates the violation of a statutory rule.

If, however, the provision is intended solely for the protection of one of the parties to a multilateral juridical act, the act is not null but may only be annulled unless, again, the necessary implication of the provision implies otherwise (paragraph 2). In a case where employer and employees had agreed that employees would have a right to share in the profits on the condition that there would not be a strike and employees invoked the annulment of this provision because the condition was in violation of the European Social Charter, the Supreme Court ruled that the annulment may only be invoked by the party to be protected and in such a way that the interests of that party are not, again, impaired by the annulment (in this case only the condition had to be annulled and not the entire provision, so that the employees would have a right to a share in the profit whether or not there had been a strike).[39]

Statutory provisions which do not purport to invalidate juridical acts contrary to them, are not affected by paragraph 2 (paragraph 3). This will generally mean that a juridical act in violation of such a statutory provision will not be contrary to good morals or public order either, as the Supreme Court decided in a case on a building contract which was concluded in defiance of Union law on public tenders. Since the Dutch provisions implementing the relevant Directive do not purport to invalidate juridical acts that are in conflict with them, the contract at hand was not null because of the conflict with the statutory provisions, and neither could it, because of that conflict, be deemed contrary to good morals or public order.[40]

The provisions of paragraphs 2 and 3 only concern imperative statutory provisions proclaimed by the national legislature (Crown and Parliament). Legislation of lower public bodies or foreign legislation may play a part in an indirect way, by applying the principles of Article 3:40, paragraph 1 to a juridical act contrary to such legislation.

39. HR 24-9-1999, ECLI:NL:HR:1999:ZE0527, NJ 1999/737.
40. HR 22-1-1999, ECLI:NL:HR:1999:ZC2826, NJ 2000/305; HR 4-11-2005, ECLI:NL:HR:2005:AU2806, NJ 2006/2014.

Chapter 2. Annulment, Nullity

§1. Introduction

98. Above, when discussing the various defects with which a contract (or a juridical act in general) may be affected, we mentioned whether the defect in question could lead to nullity or annulment of the contract or juridical act.

In order to summarize and complete the enumeration above, here follows a list of the most important grounds for nullity or annulment of a contract.

§2. Nullities

99. (Mentioned in Book 3, Title 2):

- Unilateral, non-addressed juridical acts of an incapable person (Article 3:32, paragraph 2).
- Unilateral, non-addressed juridical acts of a person whose mental faculties are impaired (Article 3:34, paragraph 2).
- Juridical acts which have not been performed in the form prescribed by law (Article 3:39).
- Juridical acts which, by their content or necessary implication, are contrary to good morals or public order (Article 3:40, paragraph 1).
- Juridical acts contrary to an imperative statutory provision which purports to invalidate juridical acts concluded in violation of that provision, unless the statutory provision is intended solely for the protection of one of the parties to a multilateral juridical act or the necessary implication of the provision produces a different result (Article 3:40, paragraphs 2 and 3).
- Juridical acts intended as a means of acquiring property, which are forbidden by Article 3:43 (e.g., the acquisition by a judge of property in respect of which procedures are pending before his court).

These nullities of Book 3, Title 2, are the most important nullities for our subject. There are, however, provisions elsewhere in the Code and in numerous specific Statutes which declare certain juridical acts null.

§3. Juridical Acts Which May Be Annulled

100. (Mentioned in Book 3, Title 2):

- Multilateral and unilateral addressed juridical acts of an incapable person (Article 3:32, paragraph 2).
- Multilateral and unilateral addressed juridical acts of a person whose mental faculties are impaired (Article 34, paragraph 2).
- Juridical acts which have been entered into as a result of (a) duress, (b) fraud, (c) undue influence (Article 3:44, paragraph 1).

- Juridical acts, to which a debtor is not obligated and which, as he knew or ought to have known, adversely affect the recourses of one or several of his creditors against his patrimony; multilateral and unilateral addressed juridical acts (acts by gratuitous title excepted) may only be annulled if the other party to the act knew or ought to have known that prejudice to one or more creditors would result from it (Article 3:45, paragraphs 1 and 2). This so-called *actio Pauliana* will be discussed *infra*, paragraphs 144 ff.

There are many cases of annullable juridical acts outside title 2 of Book 3 also. I only list those mentioned in Book 6:

- contracts which have been entered into under the influence of error (Article 6:228, paragraph 1);
- contracts in furtherance of an already existing juridical relationship which proves afterwards to be non-existent (Article 6:229);
- a stipulation in general terms and conditions if this stipulation is unreasonably onerous to the other party or if the user has not afforded the other party a reasonable opportunity to take cognizance of the general terms and conditions (Article 6:233);
- a stipulation in general terms and conditions which a person against whom a prohibition to use such a stipulation has been issued, included in a contract in violation of the prohibition (Article 6:243).

§4. Nullity and Its Effects

101. A juridical act is null when, as a result of a defect by which the act is affected, the intended juridical effects do not come into being. Just as the expression suggests, nullity operates automatically. In this respect, there is a major difference between, e.g., French (Article 1178 Code Civil) and Belgian (Article 5.59 *BW*) law, which require a judicial declaration of nullity. In Dutch law such a declaration is considered to be superfluous as far as substantive law is concerned. This does not alter the fact that parties who disagree on the validity of a juridical act will need a decision of the court. The function of the judicial decision is purely declaratory. A party has, of course, also to resort to a court decision when the other party is not willing to return what he has received in the performance of a null juridical act or to pay damages if he is obliged to do so on account of the nullity (*see infra*, paragraphs 105–106).

Nullity does not always affect the juridical act as a whole. If a ground for nullity only concerns a part of the act, the rest of the act is not affected to the extent that it is not inextricably related to the null part (Article 3:41). For example, a null stipulation in a contract does not necessarily invalidate the contract as a whole.[41]

41. *See* for an example in a case where a clause in a contract was null and void due to an infringement of competition law, which however did not prevent the remainder of the contract to remain in force: HR 20-12-2013, ECLI:NL:HR:2013:2123, NJ 2014/347.

Partial nullity may also be applied to a clause in a contract. However, this may be prevented by the purport of the rule, the infringement of which causes the nullity. If such rule purports to protect a party to the contract (e.g., an employee or a consumer), it may well be in his interest that the clause will not be held upright partially.[42]

Article 3:42 deals with the legal concept of '*conversion*', that is, the *ipso iure* replacement of a null juridical act by another juridical act. When the necessary implication of a null juridical act corresponds to such a degree to that of another juridical act, considered as valid, so as to imply that the latter juridical act would have been performed had the former been abandoned because of its invalidity, then the former shall be given the effect of the latter juridical act, unless this would be unreasonable to an interested person, not party to the act. Especially in cases of unilateral acts addressed to a person, conversion might lead to unreasonable results, for example, in case of a null dismissal addressed to an employee. Conversion may also be excluded for reasons comparable to those mentioned for partial nullity.

Where the nullity of an act results from the non-fulfilment of a legal condition for its validity, the act may be *validated* (or regularized) when this legal condition is fulfilled afterwards. Article 3:58, paragraph 1 states that where a legal condition for the validity of a juridical act is fulfilled only after its performance, but all directly interested parties who could have invoked this defect have regarded the act as valid during the period between the act and the fulfilment of the legal condition, the juridical act is thereby ratified. Such ratification has a retrospective effect: the act is considered to have been valid from the start. An exception to the rule of ratification is made for juridical acts of incapable persons who become capable afterwards (paragraph 2). It is possible that, in the meantime, third persons have acquired rights which are incompatible with the juridical act. These rights need not be a bar to ratification, provided that they are respected (paragraph 3). For example, if someone transfers a thing invalidly to a person and subsequently establishes a servitude for the benefit of another person, validation of the transfer is possible with maintenance of the servitude.

If a null juridical act, which is not replaced or regularized, has been carried out, the performance has been 'unduly paid'. On this ground, the undoing of the performance can be claimed. (*See also* paragraph 333 *infra*).

The fact that a legal act is null and void does not imply that a court will apply the nullity of its own motion. The duty of ex officio application has been formulated by the European Court of Justice in consumer law[43] and accepted by the Hoge Raad.[44] Apart from this, Dutch courts do not apply a nullity ex officio in case of violation of a statutory provision; they only do so if the nullity is based on an infringement of public order or good morals.

---

42. This solution has been chosen e.g., in Dutch labour law and in European consumer law. Applying partial nullity might lessen the deterrent effect of the statutory prohibition.
43. ECJ 26-10-2006, C-168/05, ECLI:EU:C:2006:675 (Mostaza Claro) and many subsequent judgments.
44. HR 13-9-2013, ECLI:NL:HR:2013:691, NJ 2014/274.

§5. Annulment and Its Effects

102. The most important difference between null and annullable juridical acts is that null juridical acts do not have juridical effects *ipso iure*, whereas, in the case of annullable juridical acts, it depends on the will of the party in whose interest the ground for annulment has been prescribed whether the juridical act will be valid or null. Until the act has been annulled, it is valid. If a juridical act is annulled, the annulment has retroactive effect on the time the act was performed (Article 3:53, paragraph 1). This means that the legal relationship of the parties is in principle restored to the state in which it was before the act was performed.

Once it is accomplished, the annulment, in most cases, has its effect against everyone; in some situations, however, the resulting nullity is only effective against certain persons. For example, in the case of the so-called *actio Pauliana* (Article 3:43, paragraph 4; *see infra*, paragraphs 144 ff.).

When a juridical act is subject to annulment, it can be annulled either by extra-judicial declaration (addressed by one of the parties to the contract to the other party or, as the case may be, by a third person to the party or parties to the juridical act) or by judgment (Article 3:49 and 3:50, paragraph 1). Only in cases where the juridical act concerned relates to the transfer of registered property is a judgment required unless all parties agree to the annulment (Article 3:50, paragraph 2).

With a view to annulment by judgment, a ground for annulment may be invoked by way of an explicit action but also as a defence against a claim or other legal measure based upon the juridical act (Article 3:51, paragraph 3). The latter is often done when the plaintiff bases a claim on his general terms and conditions: the defendant will then invoke the nullity of such provisions on the grounds of their being unreasonably onerous.[45] The annulment takes effect by means of the judgment by which a ground for annulment is accepted (Article 3:51, paragraph 1).

§6. Prescription of Actions to Annul

103. Actions to annul a juridical act are prescribed by three years (Article 3:52, paragraph 1, which also deals with the moment at which the prescription period of three years starts to run). Once prescription of the action has been completed, the act can no longer be annulled upon the same ground by an extrajudicial declaration (paragraph 2). However, invoking this ground as a defence remains possible.

§7. Lapse of the Power to Annul

104. The power to invoke a ground for annulment lapses:

(a) when the person who possesses the power to annul confirms the juridical act after the prescription period for the action to annul upon that ground has started to run (Article 3:55, paragraph 1);

45. An example may be found in HR 17-12-1999, ECLI:NL:HR:1999:AA3876, NJ 2000/140.

(b) when, after the commencement of the prescription period, a directly interested person has given notice to the person who possesses the right to annul, requiring him to choose between a confirmation and an annulment within a reasonable period, and this person has made no choice within that period (Article 3:55, paragraph 2);
(c) in cases of undue influence with regard to a multilateral juridical act, error or contracts in furtherance of a non-existing legal relationship, when the other party timely proposes a modification to the effects of the juridical act, which adequately removes the prejudice (Article 3:54, paragraph 1 and Article 6:230, paragraph 1). Moreover, if in a judicial procedure directed at annulment, one of the parties judicially demands modification, the judge may, instead of pronouncing the annulment, modify the effects of the juridical act to remove the prejudice (Article 3:54, paragraph 2 and Article 6:230, paragraph 2).

§8. Further Effects of Annulment

105. Annulment leads to nullity. This means that some provisions discussed above, with regard to nullity, are also applicable in cases of nullity after annulment. This goes for the provisions on partial nullity (Article 3:41) and conversion (Article 3:42). Ratification, however, only concerns juridical acts which are null *ipso iure.*

The further effects of annulment are the same as in cases of nullity: if performance has already taken place, the undoing of the performance can be claimed on the basis of undue payment (*see also* paragraph 328 *infra* on undue payment). If the juridical act has already produced effects which can only be undone with difficulty, the court may refuse to give effect to an annulment in whole or in part. He may order that a party who is prejudiced by his decision be compensated in money by a party who unjustly benefits from it (Article 3:53, paragraph 2).

§9. Damages

106. With regard to juridical acts which are null or subject to annulment, an obligation to repair damages may come into play on two grounds.

In the first place, as mentioned above, a performance effected as a consequence of a null juridical act must be undone. Sometimes, however, recovery is impossible. This may be the case because of its nature (e.g., the transportation of a person to a certain place), or later circumstances may have made it impossible to undo the performance (e.g., the delivered thing has perished). In the first case, the recipient of the performance will in general have to reimburse the value of the performance (Article 6:210, paragraph 2).[46] In the second case, Articles 6:203 ff. (on undue payment, *see also infra*, paragraphs 328 ff.) and 6:74 ff. (on the effects of the non-performance of an obligation, *see* paragraphs 164 ff. *infra*) are applicable. The

46. *See* HR 5-12-2014, ECLI:NL:HR:2014:3532, RvdW 2015/36; HR 28-06-2019, ECLI:NL:HR:2019:1046, NJ 2020/257; HR 4-10-2019, ECLI:NL:HR:2019:1500, NJ 2020/259.

recipient of the act will have to repair damages if the impossibility of restitution (the failure in the performance of the obligation to undo the performance) can be attributed to him.

Second, entering into a null contract or a contract which can be annulled may constitute an unlawful act by one of the parties towards the other, namely if the conclusion of such contract is contrary to proper social conduct (Article 6:162). In this case, the party who acted unlawfully must not only undo the performance received but must also repair the damage the other party suffered as a result of the fact that he entered into a null contract or a contract which can be annulled. The general provisions on legal obligations to repair damages (Articles 6:95 ff.) are applicable, *see infra*, paragraphs 202 ff.

Part III. The Contents of a Contract

Chapter 1. Express and Implied Terms

§1. Express Terms: Implied Terms

I. Terms of the Contract

107. As mentioned *supra* in paragraph 32, Article 6:248, paragraph 1 states that a contract has not only the juridical effects agreed to by the parties but also those which, according to the nature of the contract, result from law, usage or the requirements of reasonableness and fairness.

II. Agreement

108. The agreement – express or implied – of the parties is the most important source of contractual obligations. Which effects the parties (expressly) have agreed to is a matter of interpretation of the contract. It should be noted that in Dutch legal parlance, the expression 'implied terms' is to be distinguished from effects which result from law, usage or reasonableness and fairness (*see infra*): the expression refers to effects which, although not expressly stipulated, may – through interpretation of the contract – be assumed to be founded in the agreement of the parties.

Not all obligations resulting from a contract are based on the agreement of the parties. It is almost impossible for the parties to regulate their juridical relationship in full. If the agreement of the parties is not complete, the contents of the contract have to be supplemented by the rules of law, usage and equity.

III. Law

109. The most important supplementary source of contractual obligations is the law. The Civil Code contains many rules concerning contractual relationships, and many of these rules concern specific types of contracts. Most of these provisions are only applicable when the contracting parties do not deviate from them, but some of the legal provisions, especially in the field of such contracts as labour contracts, lease and consumer law, have a mandatory character.

IV. Usage

110. Usage is the second supplementary source of obligations mentioned in Article 6:248, paragraph 1. There is a usage, if in a certain class of persons, with regard to a certain kind of contract, a certain line of conduct is taken and is expected to be taken. All who belong to the circle where the usage is in force are submitted to the usage.

V. Reasonableness and Fairness

111. Reasonableness and fairness (traditionally called 'good faith') are a separate supplementary source of obligations, apart from law and usage. *See* on reasonableness and fairness *supra*, paragraphs 31 ff. In general, reasonableness and fairness only play a role as supplementary sources of obligations when a lacuna is not filled by law or usage. The derogatory function of reasonableness and fairness plays an important role in Dutch legal practice; it often happens that the Court judges a party's reliance on an express term of the contract contrary to the standard of reasonableness and fairness, for example, when a party invokes a stipulation in his general terms. About general terms (also called general terms and conditions or standard terms), *see* below, paragraphs 112 ff.

In order to determine which rights and obligations result from law, usage and reasonableness and fairness, the nature of the contract has to be taken into account. The nature of the contract is, in the first place, defined by the kind to which it belongs (e.g., a contract of sale has a nature different from a labour contract), but all kinds of other circumstances may play a part (e.g., whether a contract of sale concerns a moveable or an immoveable thing, whether one of the parties is a consumer, etc.).

§2. General Terms and Exemption Clauses: Penalty Clauses and Arbitration Clauses

I. General Terms and Conditions: Applicability

112. The Civil Code contains a section (section 3 of book 6, Article 6:231–247) on general terms and conditions. It may be summarized as follows. Article 6:231, sub a, describes general terms and conditions as one or more written stipulations which have been drafted to be included into a number of contracts, with the exception of stipulations involving the essential prestations (provided they are drafted clearly and understandably).

The starting point is that, in the interest of legal certainty, the applicability of a set of general terms and conditions is easily attained. It is sufficient that a party has accepted, in writing or in any other way, the applicability of general terms and conditions. The question of whether a party has accepted the applicability of general terms and conditions has to be answered by applying the principles of Article 3:33 and 3:35 (*see supra*, paragraph 15) and Articles 6:217 ff. (*see supra*, paragraphs 37 ff.). In general, it will be sufficient that the conditions are printed (or a reference to the conditions is printed) on an offer or acceptance which is sent to the other party and which is not followed by a protest by the other party as regards the applicability of the conditions. As mentioned in paragraph 43 *supra*, Article 6:225, paragraph 3 states that, in case of a 'battle of forms', the second reference in general conditions is without effect unless it explicitly rejects the applicability of the general conditions as indicated in the first reference.

The reliance principle only applies to the assent to the terms as such, not to the knowledge and approval of the individual terms. Article 6:232 states that the other party is bound by general terms and conditions even if, at the time of entering the contract, the user of those conditions understood or ought to understand that the other party did not know the content of the conditions.

However, the party using the conditions must allow the other party a reasonable opportunity to take note of the general terms and conditions. If the user has failed to do so, the other party may annul one or more of the stipulations in the general terms and conditions on the grounds of Article 6:233, sub b. The way in which a reasonable opportunity can be afforded is elaborated in Article 6:234. Generally speaking, the user of the conditions has to supply a written or electronic copy of the general terms and conditions to the other party before or at the time of entering into the contract. If the contract is not completed electronically, the user of the conditions needs to have the explicit consent of the other party for supplying the conditions by electronic means. The Supreme Court has ruled that this provision has to be read in a reasonable way, conforming to practice. Even if the user has not given the other party a copy of his general terms and conditions at the conclusion of the contract, he is still deemed to have given the other party a reasonable opportunity in the sense of Article 6:234 if the other party was aware of the terms, for instance, because he had contracted with the user before, under the same standard terms.[47] Invoking the nullity of standard terms because no reasonable opportunity to take note of them was afforded may, moreover, under the circumstances, be contrary to reasonableness and fairness.

II. Unreasonably Onerous Stipulations

113. In the system of the Code, the undesirable results to which the use of general terms and conditions sometimes leads are combated by granting the courts the possibility to judge whether the contents of the conditions comply with the standards of reasonableness and fairness. The Code contains a general provision according to which unreasonably onerous stipulations in general terms and conditions which are part of a contract may be annulled. It also contains an elaboration of this general provision in two lists of stipulations that are deemed to be or presumed to be unreasonably onerous when used in consumer contracts. Finally, stipulations in general conditions may be declared to be unreasonably onerous upon the demand of consumers or professional/business organizations.

The general provision is laid down in Article 6:233, sub a and states that a stipulation in general terms and conditions may be annulled if it is unreasonably onerous

47. HR 1-10-1999, ECLI:NL:HR:1999:ZC2977, NJ 2000/207.

to the other party, taking into consideration the nature and the further content of the contract, the manner in which the terms and conditions were established, the mutually apparent interests of the parties and the other circumstances of the case. This provision protects both consumers and legal persons acting in the course of a business or profession, provided that legal persons do not exceed a certain size (Article 6:235, paragraph 1). However, consumers are (directly) protected by the lists of Article 6:236 and 6:237, in which over thirty (types of) clauses often found in general terms and conditions are deemed or presumed to meet the test of Article 6:233, sub a.

Article 6:236 contains the so-called black list, a list of stipulations which are deemed to be unreasonably onerous. This means that these stipulations are always unreasonably onerous, irrespective of the circumstances of the case, and therefore subject to annulment. The list in Article 6:237 is called the 'grey list'. The stipulations mentioned in this article are only presumed to be unreasonably onerous. This presumption may be rebutted. In this respect, the circumstances of the case play a part.

If a stipulation is not mentioned in Article 6:236 or 6:237, it does not mean, of course, that such a stipulation is never an unreasonably onerous one. Whether this is the case must be determined by applying the general rule of Article 6:233, sub a. The same is true if the party invoking the unreasonable character of the clause is not a consumer.

The lists of Article 6:236 and 6:237 are structured according to the same principle. They begin with some stipulations in which the rights of the other party or the obligations of the user of the terms and conditions are limited compared to the rights or obligations provided for by the law. Then, stipulations follow in which the obligations of the other party or the rights of the user are extended. Finally, some stipulations of another nature are inserted.

Some of the most important provisions of Article 6:236 are the provisions under b and c, according to which all stipulations that limit or exclude the right which, pursuant to the law, the other party has to set aside the contract or to suspend performance of the contract are deemed to be unreasonably onerous.

As was mentioned in paragraph 112, the party who wants to defend himself against unreasonable general conditions can also invoke Article 6:248, paragraph 2 (reasonableness and fairness). So, the protection provided by Articles 6:233 ff. is not exclusive in relation to the more general Article 6:248.[48]

III. Arbitration Clauses, Exemption Clauses and Penalty Clauses

114. Article 6:236, sub n, restricts the clauses providing for dispute resolution other than by the regular state courts. The other party must at least have the possibility to choose a regular court. In the original draft of the article, this provision also concerned arbitration clauses, but the reference to arbitration clauses was deleted due to opposition in the circle of arbitration experts. However, in the amendment of the Code that entered into force in 2015, the original provision was restored.

48. HR 14-6-2002, ECLI:NL:HR:2002:AE0659, NJ 2003/112.

Arbitration clauses may also be reviewed under the general provision of Article 6:233, sub a. In a well-known case, decided before the present Code came into force, the Supreme Court judged an arbitration clause, included in a contract between two parties who were both acting in the course of their professional activities, unreasonably onerous because of its contents.[49] The arbitration clause in that case had, among other things, the effect that the other party could not address the arbitrators himself and that he could not influence the choice of the arbitrators.

Probably, in practice, the most important provision of Article 6:237 is the provision under f, according to which stipulations which free the user or a third person in whole or in part from a legal obligation to repair damage (exemption clauses) are presumed to be unreasonably onerous.

Furthermore, we mention Article 6:237, sub b, which refers to stipulations that materially limit the scope of the obligations of the user with respect to what the other party could reasonably expect without such a stipulation, also taking into account the rules of law, which pertain to the contract.

On the basis of Article 6:237, sub h, stipulations providing for the forfeiture of rights of the other party or of his power to raise certain defences as a sanction for certain conduct of the other party, including omissions, are presumed to be unreasonably onerous, except to the extent that the conduct of the other party justifies the forfeiture of those rights or defences.

Article 6:237, sub i, concerns stipulations obliging the other party to pay a sum of money in the event that the contract is terminated for a reason other than the fact that he has failed in the performance of his obligation, except to the extent that they concern a reasonable compensation for loss suffered by the user or profit of which he has been deprived. Other kinds of penalty clauses can be put to the test of Article 6:233, sub a. Article 6:94 gives the court the power to reduce a stipulated penalty upon the demand of the debtor if it is evident that fairness so requires. Stipulations derogating from this provision are null.

IV. Non-consumer Contracts

115. As mentioned before, Article 6:236 and 6:237 only protect consumers. They can play a role, however, beyond their scope of application. For example, if a party who is not a consumer invokes the general provision of Article 6:233, sub a, the court may be inspired by the fact that the clause concerned is mentioned in Article 6:236 or Article 6:237.[50] The same applies if a party who is a 'large firm' in the sense of Article 6:235, to which Article 6:233, sub a does not apply, invokes Article 6:248, paragraph 2 (containing a provision on the derogating function of reasonableness and fairness, *see supra*, paragraph 32). In practice (both in the regular courts and in arbitration), this happens frequently.

49. HR 23-3-1990, ECLI:NL:HR:1990:AD1068, NJ 1991/214.
50. HR 8-9-2023, ECLI:NL:HR:2023:1197, NJ 2023/333.

V. The Final Provisions of Section 3, Title 5 of Book 6

116. Articles 6:240 ff. concern the abstract review of general conditions upon the demand of consumer or professional organizations. The Court of Appeal at The Hague has exclusive jurisdiction to judge an action as referred to in Article 6:240. A declaratory decision by that Court that a certain stipulation is unreasonably onerous may be accompanied by, among other things, a prohibition to use or to promote the stipulation. A stipulation used in violation of the prohibition may be annulled. This possibility has hitherto been used sparingly: only once did the Supreme Court have to judge such a case. It upheld the decision of the Court of Appeal at the Hague that an exemption clause used in the general conditions of a large energy firm was unreasonably onerous towards consumers.[51]

Article 6:244 affords some protection to a dealer (retailer) who uses general terms and conditions annulled or prohibited according to the previous articles but which are closely related to (general) conditions which he himself has been 'forced' to accept by his seller in the previous link of the distribution chain, for example, a wholesale dealer or a producer. The wholesale dealer or producer is not allowed to invoke his (general) conditions in so far as this would be unreasonable towards the retailer because of such a connection.

Section 3 of the Book applies to all contracts, with the exception of contracts of employment and collective labour contracts (Article 6:245). No derogations from Article 6:231–244 are allowed (Article 6:246).

In the remaining article of the section (Article 6:247) attention is paid to private international law aspects. Article 6:247, paragraph 1, stipulates that the section on general conditions applies to contracts between parties who act in the course of a profession or business and who are both residents of The Netherlands, irrespective of the law governing the contract. According to Article 6:247, paragraph 2 – which is inspired by the English Unfair Terms Act – the section does not apply to contracts between professional parties who are not both resident in the Netherlands, no matter which law governs the contract. Article 6:247, paragraph 4, states that the section applies to contracts between a user and a consumer if the consumer has his habitual place of residence in The Netherlands, irrespective of the law applicable to the contract.

51. HR 16-5-1997, ECLI:NL:HR:1997:ZC2372, NJ 2000/1.

Chapter 2. Interpretation

§1. No Statutory Rules

117. The old Code contained some provisions on the interpretation of contracts. These provisions did not return in the present Code because they were thought to be in part superfluous, and in part incorrect because of their generality. This means that it is left to the courts to develop rules and principles for the interpretation of contracts.

§2. Definition of Interpretation

118. Interpretation of a contract can be defined as the determination of the meaning that must be attached to the declarations made by the contracting parties and of the juridical effects created by these declarations. In interpreting a contract, reasonableness and fairness play a part.

§3. Criteria for Interpretation

119. In 1981, the Supreme Court stated in a landmark decision that in interpreting terms of a contract, the literal sense of the term is not decisive, but 'the sense the contracting parties could mutually reasonably attach to the stipulations in the present circumstances and that which they could reasonably expect from each other in this regard', to which was added that in this respect it could be important 'to which social circles the parties belong and which legal knowledge could be expected from such parties'.[52] According to this rule, all surrounding circumstances are to be taken into account in order to assess what meaning each party could reasonably attach to the terms of the contract, and what the parties could reasonably expect from each other at the moment they concluded the contract. This formula, which – after the name of the plaintiff – became known as the '*Haviltex*' formula, has been frequently repeated, and the Supreme Court subjects decisions of lower courts to this test. If the interpretation has been carried out along the lines of the formula, the outcome of the interpretation is, in procedural terms, a matter of 'fact' (as opposed to 'law'), which is not further examined by the Supreme Court. The outcome may only be subjected to the control which the Court in all cases exercises as to the consistency of the motivation.

The '*Haviltex*' criteria have not lost their importance under the present Code. They apply in case of complicated commercial contracts[53] and have been supplemented in cases where one or even both of the parties have not taken part in concluding the contract, the most important being the interpretation of collective labour

52. HR 13-3-1981, ECLI:NL:HR:1981:AG4158, NJ 1981/635.

53. *See*, for example, HR 19-1-2007, ECLI:NL:PHR:2007:AZ3178, NJ 2007/575. Even in this case – a complicated commercial contract in writing – the Haviltex criteria were upheld, but the lower court was entitled to take a specific clause at face value, subject to subsequent proof that the parties had

agreements. In such cases, in principle, the text of the document is decisive.[54] However, other elements may also be of relevance, provided that they are of an objective nature. The intentions of the parties that have concluded the collective agreement will not be taken into consideration unless they can be deducted from a written and published explanation.[55] Also, in cases where a contract affects third-party interests, such as a contract containing a stipulation in favour of a third party (*see* paragraph 131 below) or a contract containing an obligation to pledge claims against third parties, case law shows a tendency to attach more prima facie value to the written text of the contract.

§4. No Distinction Between Clear and Unclear Declarations

120. In the past, the opinion has been advocated that only unclear declarations need interpretation. This opinion disregards the preliminary question when a declaration can be called unclear. Linguistic clarity is not enough; also when the words of a contract seem clear, the intentions of the parties or other circumstances can be of importance to determine whether the words are really clear and what they mean. The prevailing opinion nowadays is that a distinction between clear and unclear declarations cannot be drawn and that every declaration needs interpretation in order to determine its meaning.

§5. Some General Principles

121. Some general principles of interpretation adopted by Dutch Courts are the following:

(a) the intention of the parties must be examined rather than the literal sense of the words of a contract;
(b) a contractual stipulation must be understood in the sense in which it would have any effect rather than in a sense in which it would have no effect;
(c) the words of a contract must be taken in accordance with the nature of the contract;
(d) when interpreting a contract, regional, local, professional and trade customs must be taken into account;
(e) in case of uncertainties (general), conditions drawn up by a professional party are in principle construed in favour of the other party, especially when the other

---

intended a different meaning. The *Hoge Raad* held that courts when interpreting lengthy and detailed commercial contracts concluded by parties who have been assisted by professional advisers are allowed to rely on the literal meaning of the wording of the contract, unless such interpretation is proved to be wrong by the party who has an interest to show that the wording of the contract is at variance with the intention of the parties when they concluded the contract. In bringing this proof the Haviltex criteria apply.

54. HR 17-9-1993, ECLI:NL:HR:1993:ZC1059, NJ 1994/173; HR 24-9-1993, ECLI:NL:HR:1993:ZC1072, NJ 1994/174; HR 26-5-2000, ECLI:NL:HR:2000:AA5961, NJ 2000/473.
55. HR 20-2-2004, ECLI:NL:HR:2004:AO1427, NJ 2005/93.

party is a consumer. In 1999, Article 6:238 sub 2 was added to the Code, under the influence of the Directive on unfair terms in consumer contracts (1993/13/EEC). This Article stipulates that general terms and conditions should be clear and understandable. When doubt arises about the meaning of general terms and conditions, the interpretation which favours the consumer shall prevail;

(f) written or typed additions to printed general terms and conditions prevail (in case of difference) over the printed conditions. The same is true for other 'individual' conditions;

(g) *a contrario* arguments must be used with great caution.

The above-mentioned principles represent by no means a complete list of principles of interpretation. They only provide some general guidelines. Some of these principles are derived from the provisions on interpretation in the old Code.

Chapter 3. Conditional Contracts

§1. Introduction

122. Article 3:38, paragraph 1 states that unless the law or the nature of a juridical act provides otherwise,[56] a juridical act can be performed subject to a term or subject to a condition. The fulfilment of a condition does not have retroactive effect (paragraph 2).

Against the background of the general rule of Article 3:38, the Code contains in section 5 of Title 1 of Book 6 some special provisions on conditional obligations resulting from juridical acts. An obligation is conditional where, by virtue of a juridical act, its effect has been made dependent upon a future and uncertain event (Article 6:21). Conditions can be stipulated explicitly or tacitly.

§2. Suspensive and Resolutory Conditions: Positive and Negative Conditions

123. Conditions may be distinguished into suspensive conditions and resolutory conditions.

A suspensive condition causes the obligation to take effect upon the occurrence of the event; a resolutory condition extinguishes the obligation upon the occurrence of the event (Article 6:22). For example, the obligation to sell my house to you in case I find a job in Canada this year is suspensive and the obligation to sell my house to you under the condition that the sale will be annulled if you will find a job in Canada this year is resolutory. Whether a condition must be considered as a suspensive or a resolutory one is a matter of interpretation.

A condition is positive or negative as the effect depends on the occurrence or the non-occurrence of an event.

§3. Characteristics of a Conditional Obligation

124. A conditional obligation is an obligation. This is of interest for the obligation under suspensive condition: not the obligation, but its effect is suspended until the fulfilment of the condition. The provisions regarding unconditional obligations apply to conditional obligations to the extent that the conditional nature of the obligation in question so permits (Article 6:26).

The main characteristic of a conditional obligation is that it is for some time uncertain whether it will have effects or whether it will keep its effects. At the time of the stipulation of the condition, it must be objectively uncertain whether the event will take place or not.

56. HR 2-11-2012, ECLI:NL:HR:2012:BX0348, NJ 2012/700.

Conditions concerning an event that already has taken place or that will certainly take place (including those events that, in the contemplation of the parties, will certainly take place) or concerning an impossible event are no real conditions in the sense of Article 6:21.

§4. Further Requirements

125. A condition must not be contrary to good morals or public order or forbidden by the law. Depending on the circumstances, such a condition may lead to nullity of the contract, or the condition itself may be null. (*See supra*, paragraphs 96 ff.).

§5. Fulfilment of a Condition: Effects

126. If the fulfilment of a suspensive condition only depends on the will of the debtor, the obligation is null. Sometimes, the debtor has the power to influence the fulfilment of a condition. In this case, he may not, contrary to the intention of the parties, undo the element of coincidence that is part of the condition.

Article 6:23, therefore, states that if reasonableness and fairness so require, the condition is deemed fulfilled in the event that the party who had an interest in the non-fulfilment of the condition has prevented its fulfilment and the condition is deemed not to be fulfilled in the event that the party who had an interest in the fulfilment of the condition has caused its fulfilment.

As mentioned above, the fulfilment of a condition does not have retroactive effect. One of the consequences of this rule is that a prestation performed on the basis of an obligation which has been extinguished by the fulfilment of a resolutory condition has not been performed without legal ground. The provisions on undue payment can therefore not be invoked to bring about the undoing of the prestation. For that reason, Article 6:24, paragraph 1 contains a special provision, according to which, after the fulfilment of a resolutory condition, the creditor must undo the prestations which have already been performed, unless the content or the necessary implication of the juridical act otherwise require. If the obligation to undo the prestation cannot be performed, the general rules on non-performance apply, *see* paragraphs 178 ff. *infra.*

§6. Delivery on the Basis of a Conditional Obligation

127. In case the prestation consisted of the transfer of property, Article 3:84, paragraph 4, is of interest. This paragraph states that where delivery (required for transfer of property) is made in the performance of a conditional obligation, the right so acquired is subject to the same condition as the obligation. This means that in case of transfer of property under a suspensive condition, the transferee will acquire a right of property under suspensive condition; the right will automatically (*ipso iure*) become a full right of property upon the fulfilment of the suspensive condition. And it means that in case of transfer of property under a resolutory condition, upon the fulfilment of the condition in principle, the (ownership of the) property automatically returns to the person who transferred the property. This person will, therefore have both an obligatory action (based on Article 6:24) and a real action to the restitution of the property.

§7. Performance Before Fulfilment of a Suspensive Condition

128. Where a prestation owed pursuant to an obligation under a suspensive condition has been performed before the fulfilment of the condition, a demand may be made that the prestation be undone according to the principles on undue payment (Articles 6:203 ff., *see* paragraph 328 *infra*) as long as the condition has not been fulfilled (Article 6:25).

§8. Judicial and Statutory Conditions

129. The rules of Article 3:38 and Articles 6:21 ff. apply only to conditions agreed upon by the parties. These rules may, however, be applied *per analogiam* to conditions laid down by a judicial decision (e.g., on the basis of Article 6:260 *jo* 258 – *see also* paragraph 174 *infra* – the court may set aside a contract on the grounds of unforeseen circumstances, subject to conditions determined by him) and to certain requirements, prescribed by law, for the validity of a juridical act which usually is fulfilled after the conclusion of the act itself. Examples of such 'statutory conditions' are the entry in the public registers of the notarial deed of transfer, necessary for the transfer of registered property and the granting of a permit by official authorities, necessary for the validity of certain obligatory contracts (e.g., the approval of a bureau of price control, required for some sales). *See also infra*, paragraph 327.

Part IV. Contracts and Third Persons

Chapter 1. Privity of Contract: Contract for the Benefit of a Third Party

§1. The General Principle: Contracts Affect the Contracting Parties Only

130. As is usual in other legal systems, the general principle is that contracts only have effects between the contracting parties and those assimilated to them (e.g., heirs). This principle was reaffirmed in a Supreme Court case about a quarrel between owners of apartments in the same building.[57] In the contract between the builder/seller of the apartments and the buyers, the buyers obliged themselves to let the apartment only through a central organization. When one of the owners subsequently refused to do so, the others sued him. The Supreme Court judged that the other owners could not base their action solely on the contractual obligation since this was binding between the buyer and the seller only. The ground for this general rule is obviously based on the freedom of contract: the freedom to bind oneself entails the freedom from being bound by someone else without one's consent.

There are, however, several exceptions to the general principle that contracts only have effects between the contracting parties.[58]

I. Stipulation for the Benefit of a Third Party

131. It is clear that from a practical point of view, there is less reason to frown upon a contract conferring a right on a third person than upon terms imposing some obligation on a non-contracting person. For this reason, the Code admits the stipulation for the benefit of a third person without restriction (Article 6:253–256).

Article 6:253, paragraph 1 states that a contract creates the right for a third person to claim performance of a prestation from one of the parties or to otherwise invoke the contract against any of them (e.g., by relying on a clause which excludes his liability) if the contract contains a stipulation to that effect and if the third party accepts it. The third party acquires his right by accepting the stipulation. At the moment of acceptance, the obligation between the third party and the promissor

57. HR 26-5-2000, ECLI:NL:PHR:2000:AA5964, NJ 2000/640.
58. The doctrine of representation is not dealt with here since this doctrine in Dutch law is not a part of the law of contract. *See* para. 225 below.

comes into existence. Until its acceptance, the stipulation can be revoked by the stipulator (paragraph 3). Article 6:253, paragraph 4 provides that an irrevocable stipulation which, with respect to the third person, has been made by gratuitous title is deemed accepted if it has come to the attention of the third person and he has not rejected it without delay. Once the third person has accepted the stipulation, he is deemed to be a party to the contract (Article 6:254, paragraph 1).

If the promissor fails in the performance of his obligation towards the third party, both the stipulator and the third party may claim performance. Article 6:256 states expressly that the stipulator may claim performance towards the third person unless the latter objects. The third party and the stipulator together may set aside the contract; this follows from Article 6:279,[59] paragraph 3. The third party may not set aside the contract by himself because the contract only provides him with a right, not with an obligation; the stipulator may not set aside the contract by himself because this would mean that he would frustrate the right of the third party. The stipulator may, however, suspend performance of his obligation.

The right of the third party depends in principle on the validity of the contract between stipulator and promissor. If the stipulation for the benefit of the third party is itself null or subject to annulment, it depends on the circumstances if this affects the contract as a whole. Where a stipulation for the benefit of a third party is without effect with respect to that person, the stipulator can designate either himself or another third person as beneficiary (Article 6:255, paragraph 1). This article is in keeping with common practice in, for example, the life insurance branch.

The possibility of making a stipulation for the benefit of a third person has proven to be useful in many different situations. These stipulations abound in many different types of contracts, for example, in contracts of life insurance (the insured assigns a third person to whom the money is to be paid in the event the insured occasion arises), in transportation contracts (the addressee gets a right as a third party to delivery of the transported goods) and in banking law (the legal construction of payments by check or credit card is based on such stipulations).

II. Contracts Which Impose Obligations on Third Parties

132. In principle, a contract cannot impose obligations on third parties, but even here, exceptions may be noted. A collective labour contract may bind the employers and employees affiliated with the contracting organizations, and if the Minister of Social Affairs has declared the agreement 'generally binding', even non-affiliated persons will be bound.

III. Qualitative Rights and Obligations

133. Sometimes contractual rights or obligations are so closely related to some property – especially immovable property – belonging to one of the parties that on

59. Article 6:279 contains some general provisions on contracts resulting in obligations between more than two parties, in particular on setting aside such contracts in case of breach.

transfer of that property to a third person, they will be nugatory if not transmitted to the latter person as well. In such cases already under the old Code, contractual rights could, in fact, automatically be transmitted.

Article 6:251 of the present Code expressly states that a contractual right capable of transmission, which is so closely linked to certain property belonging to the creditor that the right is of interest to him only as long as he retains the property, shall automatically be transmitted to the person who acquires the property by particular title unless the transferee declares to the transferor that he does not accept the transmission of the right. Where in exchange for the right, a counter-prestation has been agreed to, the obligation to perform that counter-prestation also passes to the transferee to the extent that it relates to the period following the transfer.

Under the old Code, obligations with regard to property could not automatically be transmitted, but the present Code recognizes a contract stipulating that the obligation of one of the parties to suffer or refrain from doing something in respect of his registered property will be transmitted (i.e., will automatically pass) to persons who will acquire the property by particular title and that the stipulation may also bind those who will acquire a right to use the property from the titleholder (Article 6:252, paragraph 1). For such a stipulation to have effect, a notarial deed must be drawn up of the contract between the parties, followed by its entry in the public registers (paragraph 2). Where in exchange for the obligation a counter-prestation has been agreed, the right to that counter-prestation is also automatically transmitted to the extent that it relates to the period following the transmission and the stipulation with respect to the counter-prestation has also been entered in the registers (paragraph 4).

The article does not apply to obligations which limit a titleholder in his power to dispose of or encumber the property (paragraph 5).

The qualitative obligation is in its contents and main effect related to a servitude, but as a result of the different nature of these concepts (obligation versus real right), other effects are entirely different. The concept of the qualitative obligation is, as such, not found in the legal systems around the Netherlands.

IV. Stipulations-in-Chain

134. The obligation referred to in Article 6:252 may only consist of a 'duty' to tolerate or not to do something in respect of the property. Therefore, contracting parties who want to create duties going with the property obliging to active conduct (e.g., a duty to construct a building or to buy goods from a specific company) will continue, as they used to do under the old Code, to insert terms obliging the owner to stipulate on any transfer of the property from the transferee that he will assume the obligations concerned and that he will in his turn make the same stipulations if he transfers the property to another person, and so forth. These stipulations – made for the benefit of the original stipulator and secured by means of penalties – are known by the term stipulations-in-chain.

A stipulation-in-chain is weaker than a qualitative obligation because it does not pass automatically to the transferee of the property. If an owner fails to insert the stipulation upon transfer, the original stipulator can claim compensation from the transferor but cannot claim the performance from the transferee. Furthermore, the chain will be broken if the property is executed by a creditor or a receiver in case of bankruptcy.

V. Modification of Qualitative Obligations and Stipulations-in-Chain

135. Both the qualitative stipulations under Article 6:252 and stipulations-in-chain may be modified or set aside by the judge if at least ten years have elapsed since the contract was entered into and the unmodified existence of the obligation is contrary to the general interest or if the creditor no longer has a reasonable interest in the performance of the obligation and if it is unlikely that this interest will revive (Article 6:259). *See also* paragraph 51 *supra.*

VI. Transfer of Ownership Leaves Lease Intact

136. Another important exception to the rule that contractual obligations are not automatically transmitted to a subsequent owner of the property to which the obligations are related goes back to ancient Dutch law: where the property in a leased object passes from the lessor to a new owner, the latter henceforth takes the place of the lessor as contracting party and for the future automatically acquires his rights and duties; this rule applies among other things to lease of residential and commercial space and to agricultural holdings (Article 7:226 and 7:361 Civil Code, *see also infra*, paragraph 283).

VII. Other Ways in Which Contracts May Influence the Position of Third Parties

137. There are still other ways in which contracts may have an effect against or for third parties. Several provisions in the Code give a contracting party the power to invoke a contract as a defence against a third person who institutes an action against him. In such cases, the third person is, in a sense, bound by the contract. For example, a creditor who has a right of retention relating to goods may (under the conditions set out in Article 3:291) invoke this right against third persons claiming the goods from him, or a co-debtor may invoke the defences he had against the creditor also against the solidary debtor who calls upon him to contribute to a debt (Article 6:11).

Sometimes, however, a third party is allowed to derive defences from a contract to which he was not a party against a contracting party. If A hands over a thing to B for repair and the reparation is carried out by B's employee C, who causes damage to the thing, according to Dutch law, the fact that A may claim compensation from B in itself does not prevent him from bringing an action in tort based on negligence against C (Article 6:162). However, if B has exempted himself from liability (which may either be contractual liability on account of non-performance of his obligation, Article 6:76, or vicarious liability in tort, Article 6:170), the Code allows the employee to invoke the same exemption clause. Article 6:257 explicitly states that where a contracting party has a defence under the contract against his co-contracting party which shields him from liability for the conduct of his subordinate, the subordinate may also invoke this defence as if he were party to the contract if he is sued by the co-contracting party on the basis of his conduct. Rules of the same type exist in the law of deposit (Article 7:608) and in the law of transport (Articles 8:361 ff.), where they are not restricted to employees but also protect sub-transporters and sub-depositaries.

Under some circumstances, it may be possible that a party who has exempted himself from liability may invoke the clause not only against the other party to the contract but also against a third person (e.g., the owner of the thing). Such rules can be found in the articles of Books 7 and 8 just mentioned, but not in Book 6, the law of obligations in general. In the general law of obligations such an effect of exemption clauses may nevertheless be based on the principle of reasonableness and fairness, although the Supreme Court shows reluctance in doing this. The Court has decided in this sense in a case where the owner A had handed over goods to B, granting him full discretion to conclude a contract for work on the goods with a third party, C.[60] When the goods were damaged, A brought an action based on tort against C, but (although the doctrine on representation did not apply) C could successfully invoke the exemption clause he had contracted with B.

General rules about the question of when contracts have this kind of effect on third persons cannot be inferred from the case law. Courts must find justification for such an exception in the special circumstances of the case, for example, the fact that the stipulating party undertook his obligation while he had reasonable grounds to believe that he could invoke the stipulation against a third party, the nature of the contract, the nature of the stipulation, the relation between the third party and the stipulating party, and, if the contract in question is regulated by law, the system of the law.

60. HR 7-3-1969, ECLI:NL:HR:1969:AB7416, NJ 1969/249.

Chapter 2. Transmission of Contractual Rights

§1. Introduction

138. There are several ways in which contractual rights can be transmitted. I will briefly discuss three important ways of transfer: assignment, subrogation and the take-over of contracts. The second Title of Book 6 contains provisions on subrogation in section 2 and provisions on the take-over of debts and contracts in section 3. Assignment is not provided for in Book 6; a special provision concerning assignment is found in Article 3:94.

§2. Assignment

139. Assignment can be defined as the transfer of a claim. Assignment takes place on the basis of a contract to do so, followed by an act of delivery. Article 3:94, paragraph 1 states that rights to be exercised against one or more specific persons are delivered by means of an appropriate instrument and notice thereof given by the alienator or acquirer to those persons. As long as no notice has been given, the alienator remains the creditor.

§3. Subrogation

140. Normally, performance of the obligation leads to the disappearance (extinction) of the obligation. This is, however, not always the case. In cases where the obligation is not performed by the debtor himself but by a third person, the obligation may sometimes pass from the original creditor to the third person. This is called 'subrogation'. As a result of the subrogation the third person acquires the claim of the original creditor and the rights which are accessory to this claim.

Subrogation must always have a legal basis. One important case of subrogation is found in Article 6:12: a solidary debtor who pays the debt for more than his share is subrogated for the excess to the rights of the creditor against the co-debtors and third parties, in each case up to the share of each co-debtor or third party according to his relationship with that debtor. Another important example of subrogation is the provision of Article 7:962 Civil Code, which deals with the transfer by subrogation of the insured's claim against a third person to the insurer. For example, when a car is damaged by someone's (not the owner's) negligence, the insurer, who has reimbursed the owner, may exercise the owner's claim for damages by way of subrogation. Article 6:150 provides for four other cases of subrogation. The article states that a claim is transferred to a third person by way of subrogation:

(a) if property belonging to the third person is seized and foreclosed in satisfaction of the claim (e.g., a pledge or a hypothec provided by the third party);
(b) if the third person satisfies a claim because property belonging to him constitutes security for the claim;

(c) if the third person satisfies a claim in order to prevent the foreclosure of property not belonging to him, provided that, as a result of the foreclosure, he would lose a right which he has in the property or that the satisfaction of a claim to which he is entitled would be jeopardized;
(d) pursuant to a contract between the third person who satisfies the claim and the debtor, provided that the creditor was aware of this contract at the time of its satisfaction or had been notified of it.[61]

Article 6:151–154 contain some specific consequences of subrogation and deal, among other things, with the subrogated party acquiring rights of the creditor against sureties and persons other than the debtor and on the apportioning of the unpaid part among the subrogated party and these persons in case of impossibility of recourse.

§4. The Take-Over of Contracts

141. In Article 6:159 the Code deals with the take-over of contracts. According to this article, a contracting party can, with the cooperation of his counterparty, assign his juridical relationship with this counterparty to a third person by a deed drawn up between himself and the third person (paragraph 1).

As a result thereof, all rights and obligations shall be transferred to the third person save as otherwise provided with respect to rights and obligations which are secondary or have already become exigible (paragraph 2). Article 6:157, paragraphs 1–3 (concerning the take-over of debts but declared *mutatis mutandis* applicable to the take-over of contracts) contains some special provisions on rights which are accessories to the claim. The take-over of contracts is not the same as assignment and the take-over of debts combined. It is a separate figure that is often used when a company is being bought or sold.

§5. General Consequences of the Transmission of Claims

142. Section 1 of Title 2 deals with some general consequences of the transmission of claims. Some of its provisions are applicable to all modes of transmission, others only to a special mode of transmission. The most important ones are the following.

The new creditor to whom a claim is transmitted acquires the rights which are accessory to the claim, such as rights of pledge, hypothec, suretyship, priority rights and the right to enforce executory titles relating to the claim and the accessory rights. The ancillary rights also include the right of the predecessor creditor to contractual interest, to a penalty or to a forfeiture, except to the extent that the interest, the penalty or the forfeiture were already exigible at the time of the transmission of the claim (Article 6:142). On the transmission of a claim the predecessor creditor must hand over to the successor creditor the documentary evidence pertaining to the

61. HR 29-2-2008, ECLI:NL:HR:2008:BC2199, NJ 2008/144.

claim and the ancillary rights, the executory judgments, orders and deeds and any pledged property. On transmission of a claim secured by hypothec the predecessor creditor must, upon demand, give his cooperation so that the public registers will reflect such transmission (Article 6:143). The predecessor creditor must, after the transmission, warrant the performance of the obligations flowing from the creditorship or the ancillary rights (Article 6:144). The transmission of a claim does not affect the debtor's defences (Article 6:145). This follows from the long-accepted principle that the predecessor creditor may not assign more rights than he has himself.[62]

62. HR 2-11-1933, ECLI:NL:HR:1933:248, NJ 1934/302.

Chapter 3. The Special Case of a 'Subcontract': For Example, the Contract with a Subcontractor

§1. 'Action Directe'

143. In general, a contracting party may make use of the services of other persons in order to fulfil his contractual obligations. According to Article 6:76 of the Code, the debtor who uses the services of other persons is responsible for their acts as if they were his own (*see* further *infra*, paragraph 167 and paragraph 273 on subcontractors.) If a contractor makes use of a subcontractor, the fact that there is a contract between employer and main contractor on the one hand and a contract between main contractor and subcontractor on the other hand does not create direct contractual relations between employer and subcontractor. The '*action directe*' of French law is, as such, unknown in Dutch law. However, there are exceptions in insurance law. In cases of car accidents, the injured party has a direct action (based on statutory law) against the insurer of the motor vehicle which inflicted the damage. Third-party insurance is mandatory for possessors of motor vehicles. A more general rule is provided by Article 7:954: an injured party has a claim for payment against the insurer of the party who inflicted the damage. There are dogmatic differences between the two rules, which cannot be dealt with here.

In some cases, a creditor may have an action based on unlawful act against a sub-debtor. With regard to subordinates, sub-transporters and sub-depositaries, the creditor can, however, not successfully use this roundabout way to escape contractual exemption clauses or legal limitations of liability which apply in his relation with the main debtor. As has been discussed *supra*, paragraph 137, the sub-debtors just mentioned may invoke the defences of the main debtor as if they were party to the contract. This power is based on specific legal provisions and may not be seen as a general rule of Dutch contract law. When the draft Article 6:257 – considering subordinates – was discussed in Parliament, the question was raised whether the power to invoke the defences of the main debtor should not be extended to all persons whose services were used by the main debtor in the performance of his obligation. This option was expressly rejected. The principal argument was that – apart from sub-transporters and sub-depositaries – the provision should be limited to those who, on the one hand, are as subordinates less equipped to take liability and who, on the other hand, in general, do not have to bear the damage themselves but may shift the damage to their employer. This argument does not apply to independent sub-debtors.

A rule as laid down in Article 6:257 does not exist with regard to subcontractors. In special cases, depending on the circumstances, a subcontractor may invoke an exemption clause in his contract with the main contractor against the employer who brings an action based on unlawful act against him. *See* on this subject also *supra*, paragraph 137.

Chapter 4. *Actio Pauliana*

§1. Introduction

144. In principle, third persons must respect contracts by which they are in fact prejudiced. However, there are exceptions to this rule. One of them was mentioned in paragraph 96 above: contracts which have the purpose of causing harm to third parties may be null and void because they infringe good morals. Another one is the '*actio Pauliana*'. This regulation, laid down in Article 3:45–48, protects a group of creditors by granting them, in certain circumstances, the right to stand up against juridical acts entered into by their debtor with other persons.

§2. Requirements for the '*Actio Pauliana*'

145. Article 3:45, paragraph 1 states that if a debtor, in the performance of a juridical act to which he is not obligated, knew or ought to have known that this act would adversely affect the possibility of recourse of one or more of his creditors, the act may be annulled; any creditor whose possibility of recourse has been adversely affected by the juridical act may invoke this ground for annulment, irrespective of whether his claim arose before or after the act. It is not only required that the debtor knew or ought to have known that prejudice would result from the act but also that the persons with whom or in respect of whom the debtor performed the juridical act must have had this knowledge (paragraph 2).

Only if the act concerned is an act by gratuitous title knowledge of the debtor suffices. However, in this case, annulment has no effect against a beneficiary who neither knew nor ought to have known about the prejudice to the extent that he shows that, at the time of the declaration of annulment or the institution of the annulment action, he did not derive benefit from the juridical act (paragraph 3). This is, for example, the case if the acquired property is no longer in his patrimony because it perished or was used.

§3. Relative Effects of Annulment

146. Annulment on the basis of Article 3:45 has only a relative effect. A creditor attacking a juridical act as being prejudicial to him only annuls the act on his own behalf and no further than is necessary to remove the prejudice which he has experienced (paragraph 4).

With regard to all other persons, the juridical act is valid and has, in principle, normal effects. Contrary to this rule, rights which third parties in good faith have acquired, other than by gratuitous title, in property which was the subject of the annulled juridical act are respected. With respect to a third party who has acquired property in good faith by gratuitous title, the annulment has no effect to the extent that he shows that at the time the property is claimed from him, he does not derive profit from the juridical act (paragraph 5).

§4. Burden of Proof: Presumptions

147. In principle, the creditor who invokes the *Pauliana* must prove the elements of Article 3:45. Especially the knowledge of the debtor and (in case of multilateral or unilateral addressed juridical acts not by gratuitous title) of the persons with whom or in respect of whom the debtor performed the juridical act will in many cases be difficult to prove.

Article 3:46 and 3:47 therefore contain some (rebuttable) presumptions.

In case of some juridical acts (like contracts whereby the value of the obligation on the debtor's side considerably exceeds the value of the counter-obligations or juridical acts to satisfy or furnish security for a debt which was not exigible) or juridical acts performed with or with respect to some persons (like members of the debtor's family or, in case of a legal person, the debtor's officers, directors or shareholders and their relatives), there is a presumption that, if such an act has been performed within one year prior to the invocation of the ground for annulment, on both sides one knew or ought to have known that prejudice to a creditor or creditors would be the result of the juridical act.

In the event of prejudice caused by a juridical act by gratuitous title which the debtor has performed within one year prior to the invocation of the ground for annulment, there is a presumption that he knew or ought to have known that prejudice to one or several creditors would be the result of the juridical act.

Some important additional legal provisions facilitating the use of the *Actio Pauliana* may be found in the Bankruptcy Act, enabling the trustee in bankruptcy to invoke the Pauliana where the person who is bankrupt tried, prior to his bankruptcy, to remove his assets in order to prevent recourse by the trustee in bankruptcy. These provisions contain, apart from some rebuttable presumptions like the ones just mentioned, a rebuttable presumption that in case of prejudice caused by a juridical act by gratuitous title performed by a debtor within one year before the bankruptcy order, it will be presumed that he knew or ought to have known that the creditors would be prejudiced thereby.

Part V. The End of the Contract

Chapter 1. Performance and Breach

§1. Performance

148. Performance of an obligation (whether contractual or not) means the fulfilment of its contents, as a result of which the obligation reaches its goal and, in principle, ceases to exist.[63] In general, the term 'payment' is used as synonymous with 'performance', which means that the term 'payment' is not restricted to performance of an obligation to pay a sum of money.

The Code contains a special section (section 6 of Title 1 of Book 6; Articles 27–51) on the performance of obligations. The provisions in this section deal with, among other things, the persons who can perform an obligation, the person to whom payment must be made, the object of payment and the time and place of payment.

Generally speaking there is no such thing as an independent obligation to make the necessary preparations for the performance. Only after the breach of contract (e.g., when the performance itself has proven to be late or inadequate) does the creditor have a remedy, a legal ground on which to sue the debtor. In some cases, however, such an independent obligation to make the necessary preparations is created by the law or by contract. It may also follow from the nature of the obligation. *See* paragraph 153 *infra* about the duty to care for a certain thing until delivery.

§2. Person Who Can Perform an Obligation

149. An obligation can in general be performed not only by the debtor but by every other person unless this is contrary to its terms or necessary implication (Article 6:30, paragraph 1). Especially in cases of obligations to do something, personal performance will often be required. In case of obligations to give something (especially money), the person of the debtor will hardly ever play a part.

An obligation will in general only be brought to an end by payment by a third person if this person acted with the intention to discharge the debtor. Payment made by a third person who erroneously believes that he is bound himself gives rise to an action based on undue payment.

63. Sometimes however, for example in the case of subrogation, the obligation does not cease to exist. *See* para. 140 *supra*.

The third person may pay because this is in his own interest (for instance, when his house is mortgaged against the debt), but also when it is not (for instance, to help the debtor). He may also pay in his own name (Article 6:30 is then applicable) or in the name of the debtor. This last difference is quite important because when a payment is made in the name of the debtor, it is regarded as made by the debtor. In such cases, the third person may not become the creditor of the obligation by subrogation, to name but one consequence.

§3. The Person to Whom Payment Must Be Made

150. The Code contains provisions on the question to whom payment must or may be made, which are mostly relevant with regard to obligations that require someone to *receive* payment. Sometimes, of course, the payment does not have to be made 'to' someone. In the case when the debtor is obliged not to do something, his performance is not made 'to' someone in particular. Payment must be made to the creditor or to someone who is entitled to receive payment together with or on behalf of the creditor.

In some cases, however, the debtor is not released when he pays to the creditor himself.

First of all, in case of an incapable creditor, payment must be made to his legal representative. Payment to an incapable creditor releases the debtor only to the extent that what has been paid has actually benefited the incapable person or has come under the control of his legal representative (Article 6:31).

Secondly, in some cases, performance towards the creditor releases the debtor in relation to the creditor but does not release him in relation to other persons. An example of this is payment to the creditor, made despite a seizure or during a period in which the creditor was unable to receive payment because of a dismembered right (e.g., the claim is the object of a right of pledge or usufruct), a regime of administration or a similar impediment. If, as a consequence of this, the debtor is made to pay again, he has recourse against his creditor (Article 6:33).

Payment to someone who is entitled to receive payment together with the creditor may take place when the creditor has granted a procuration to this other person to receive payment for him.

The power to receive payment on behalf of the creditor follows in general from a judgment or from the law (e.g., the parents or guardian of a minor are entitled to receive payment on behalf of the minor, Article 1:247 and 1:337).

§4. Effects of Payment to the Wrong Person

151. If payment has not been made to the creditor or a person who was entitled to receive payment, the payment does not release the debtor, and he has to pay again, this time to the right person. In such a case, of course, the debtor may reclaim the sum paid from the 'wrong' person on the ground of undue payment, but the risk of this person not being able to pay is his.

In some cases, however, the law makes an exception to this rule. The payment releases the debtor to the extent that the person to whom the payment had to be made has ratified it or has benefited from it (Article 6:32). Furthermore, the debtor can invoke the payment as a discharge against the person to whom the payment should have been made if he had reasonable grounds to believe that the recipient of the payment was entitled to the prestation as creditor or that payment was to be made to him for another reason (Article 6:34, paragraph 1). The formula that there must have been 'reasonable grounds' is a good faith criterion, which is elucidated in Article 3:11, *see supra*, paragraph 32. Dutch law has chosen to protect the debtor if he is, in good faith, mistaken about the person of the creditor. This may happen because, for instance, the creditor has changed without the knowledge of the debtor, for example, in cases of subrogation. This protection of the debtor is deemed just and practically important because otherwise, people could not pay their obligations without fear of having to pay twice.

The provision of Article 6:34, paragraph 1, only applies if the debtor believed that the person to whom he paid was someone to whom he had to pay. The provision therefore does not apply if the debtor believed the person to whom he paid to be the procurator of his creditor. In that case, Article 3:61, paragraph 2 (part of the general rules on procuration) is applicable: the debtor is released if, on the basis of a declaration or conduct of the creditor, he has assumed and, in the given circumstances, could reasonably assume the existence of a sufficient procuration. This difference with Article 6:34 may be explained by the fact that when the debtor wrongly believes the person to whom he paid to be the procurator of the creditor, he could have protected himself against mistakes by paying to the creditor himself. Because of this reason, the balance in the choice of protecting the debtor or protecting the creditor in cases of payment to the wrong person is laid somewhere else.

Article 6:34, paragraph 1, may be applied in several cases, for example, in case of payment to the original creditor after the claim has been transferred to another person or in case of payment to a creditor whose right is subject to annulment. This last case is specifically provided for in Article 6:34, paragraph 2: if a person loses his right to claim payment in such a way that the right belongs retroactively to another person, the debtor can invoke against that other person a payment made in the meantime unless he should have refrained from payment on account of what he could have foreseen with regard to such loss.

When payment is made by a third person, Article 6:34 also applies. When the requirements of this article are fulfilled, the third person can invoke the releasing effect of the payment in his favour (Article 6:35, paragraph 1). The debtor can also invoke the releasing effect of that payment in his own favour, but only if through that payment, he would also, with respect to himself, have complied with the requirements of Article 6:34 (Article 6:35, paragraph 2). If the debtor invokes Article 34 (and he is free to do so or not) and he is successful, the real creditor has recourse against a person who has received payment without entitlement (Article 6:36).

The debtor is entitled to suspend the performance of his obligation if he has reasonable doubts as to the person to whom the payment must be made (Article 6:37).

§5. The Object of Payment

152. Payment must consist of what is due. From this rule, it follows that the creditor is not obliged to accept another prestation than the one that the debtor owes him. Only with the consent of the creditor can a debtor discharge his obligation by performing a prestation other than that due, albeit equal or even greater in value (Article 6:45).

The debtor is not entitled to make partial payments of his debt without the permission of the creditor (Article 6:29).

The Code contains supplementary provisions on the performance of obligations to deliver a thing and on the performance of obligations to pay a sum of money.

§6. The Object of Payment with Regard to Obligations to Deliver a Thing

153. Article 6:27 states that a person who is obliged to deliver a certain and determinate thing must care for it until delivery in the manner in which a prudent debtor would do so in the circumstances. This article creates, apart from the obligation to deliver, a separate obligation for the debtor to care for the thing. Non-performance of this obligation may give rise to a separate claim, which can be instituted even before delivery. This rule is an example of a statutory deviation from the principle that there is no such thing as a separate obligation to make preparations for the performance (*see* paragraph 148 *supra*).

According to Article 6:28, if the thing or the things due are only determined as to kind, and if there exists a difference of quality within the specified kind, the debtor may not deliver a thing of less than average good quality.

A special provision concerning the delivery of a thing the debtor had no right to dispose of is found in Article 6:42, which states that in such a case, the debtor can require that the delivered thing be given to the person to whom it belongs, provided that, at the same time, he offers to deliver another thing corresponding to the obligation, and that the interest of the creditor is not contrary to the thing being returned.

§7. The Object of Payment with Regard to Obligations to Pay a Sum of Money

154. The provisions on obligations to pay a sum of money are incorporated in section 11 of Title 1 of Book 6 (Articles 111–126). An obligation to pay a sum of money must be performed at its nominal value unless otherwise required by law, usage or a juridical act (Article 6:111). Payment must be made in money or by having credited a postal account of the creditor. If money is paid to perform the obligation, it must, at the time of payment, be current money in the country in whose currency the payment is made (Article 6:112). Where the creditor has a postal account in a country where the payment must or may be made, the debtor can perform the obligation by having that account credited with the amount due unless the creditor has validly excluded payment into that account (Article 6:114, paragraph

1). If payment is nonetheless made into the excluded account, the creditor may refuse it and demand payment into a permitted account; however, if he was enriched by the first payment, he must refund the amount of his enrichment.[64] Payment is made at the time when the account of the creditor is credited (Article 6:114, paragraph 2). This article puts an end to a controversy among legal writers about the question of whether payment into an account is a valid payment.

The creditor may refuse payment other than in money or by payment into an account.

Where the creditor takes delivery of a cheque, postal order, transfer order, or another document tendered to him by way of payment, his acceptance presumes a condition that it will be honoured (Article 6:46, paragraph 1, which is not found in section 11, but in section 6, the general section on performance of obligations). If it is not honoured, the creditor can still claim payment from the debtor.

Where pursuant to an obligation, payment must be made in a currency other than that of the country where payment must be made; the debtor is entitled to pay in the currency of the place of payment unless he is obliged to make effective payment in the currency which is the object of the obligation (Article 6:121). Where the obligation is performed by payment in a currency other than that which is the subject of the obligation, conversion shall be calculated on the basis of the exchange rate on the day of payment (Article 6:124). If the debtor is in default, the creditor may also claim damages caused by a fluctuation of the exchange rate during the period the debtor was in default (Article 6:125).[65]

§8. TIME OF PERFORMANCE

155. As mentioned the Code contains in the general section 6 of Title 1 some provisions on time and place of performance of obligations.

If no term has been set for the performance of an obligation, it may be performed as well as demanded immediately (Article 6:38). However, from the standards of reasonableness and fairness as laid down in Article 6:2 (*see supra*, paragraph 31) it follows that the debtor must be given the time he reasonably needs for performance.

An obligation can be subject to suspensive or resolutory terms. A stipulation is called a term when it is certain that the indicated event will take place, even if it is uncertain when that will be. A term may be set explicitly or tacitly. Not all juridical acts may be subject to a term, however. From the Code or the nature of the juridical act, it may follow that it may not be subject to a term. For instance, it is not possible to transfer property subject to a term. A clause like that will be interpreted as creating a right of usufruct.

The Code only contains some provisions on the suspensive term. Article 6:39, paragraph 1, states that where a term for performance has been set, it is presumed only to prevent the obligation from being demanded earlier. This article supposes

64. HR 28-2-1997, ECLI:NL:HR:1997:AG7207, NJ 1998/218.
65. *See also* HR 17-2-1995, ECLI:NL:HR:1995:ZC1636, NJ 1995/423.

that the term has been set only on behalf of the debtor. The debtor is allowed to perform before the due date but cannot be compelled to do so. Sometimes, from the juridical act, the nature of the obligation or other circumstances, it may be concluded that a term is set not only on behalf of the debtor but also on behalf of the creditor. An example is the case of a loan against interest: in such a case, a term may be set on behalf of the creditor as well to prevent the debtor from paying back the loan prematurely and thus making the creditor forfeit the interest. In such cases the debtor is not allowed to perform before the due date. If the term is set only on behalf of the creditor (a rare case, but possible), the creditor may claim performance before the due date.

Article 6:39, paragraph 2 states that payment before the due date is not considered undue. From this provision it also follows that the Code considers the obligation under suspensive term an obligation which is not suspended itself, but the performance of which is suspended by the term.

Other consequences of the suspensive term are dealt with in scattered provisions, for example, Article 6:127, paragraph 2 (a non-exigible claim cannot be compensated by the creditor), Article 6:52, paragraph 1 (the creditor of a non-exigible claim is not entitled to suspend the performance of his own debt) and Article 3:307, paragraph 1 (no prescription term runs with regard to a non-exigible claim).

According to Article 6:40, a debtor loses the benefit of the term:

(a) when he has been declared bankrupt or when he is subject to a debt rescheduling scheme;
(b) when he is in default in providing security promised by him;
(c) where security which has been provided for the debt has been diminished by a cause which can be attributed to him, unless the remaining security still constitutes a sufficient guarantee for the performance of the obligation.

A resolutory term extinguishes the obligation when the indicated period expires. Resolutory terms especially play a part in cases of continuous obligations, like a labour contract or a contract of rent for a certain period.

§9. Place of Performance

156. The place of performance is important for several reasons. The debtor who does not perform at the right place does not fulfil the obligation. An offer to pay, necessary to bring about creditor's default (Article 6:58, *see infra*, paragraphs 158 ff.), must be made at the place where performance should take place. The costs of payment (e.g., transportation costs to the place of payment) shall be for the account of the person who performs the obligation (Article 47, paragraph 1).

Payment must be made at the place which is determined by the contract. Whether a place of performance is agreed upon is a matter of interpretation of the contract.

Article 6:41 states that if no place of payment has been determined for the performance of the obligation, delivery of a thing due must take place (a) in the event of a thing certain and determinate at the place where it was at the time when the obligation has arisen; (b) in the event of a thing determined as in kind, at the place where the debtor conducts his profession or business, or, in the absence thereof, at his address.

Article 6:116–118 contains provisions on the place of payment of a sum of money, which apply when law, usage or a juridical act does not point at another place of payment (Article 6:115). According to Article 6:116, payment must be made at the creditor's address at the time of payment. The creditor is entitled to designate another place of payment in the country where he has his address at the time of payment or at the time when the obligation arises. In this respect, we may think of the designation of a transfer bank.

At the time of the conclusion of the contract, the debtor will assume that payment must take place at the creditor's address at that time. The application of Article 6:116 may, however, sometimes result in another place of payment, for example, if the creditor has moved or if the claim has been assigned. Article 6:117 states that if this would make performance considerably more onerous, the debtor is entitled to suspend payment until the creditor has designated another place of payment in one of the countries referred to in Article 6:116, paragraph 2 to which such an inconvenience does not apply.

If the obligation has arisen in carrying out the creditor's business or professional activities, the place of business where those activities are carried out is considered to be the address of the creditor for the purpose of Article 6:116 and 6:117 (Article 6:118).

§10. The Remaining Articles of Book 6, Title 1, Section 6

157. The remaining articles of section 6 (which is, as I mentioned in paragraph 148, the section on the performance of obligations) deal with:

- rules which prescribe to which obligation a payment must be attributed if the debtor has more than one obligation of the same kind towards the creditor (Article 6:43 and 6:44);
- proof of performance (Article 6:48–50; Article 6:48, paragraph 1 states that the creditor must issue a receipt for each payment unless contract, usage or fairness otherwise required and Article 6:50 states that where prestations of the same kind must be performed in succession, the receipts for two successive instalments create the presumption that the previous ones have also been performed);
- the provision of security (Article 6:51).

§11. Creditor's Default

158. In some cases, the debtor may perform his obligation without any cooperation from the creditor, for example, in case of an obligation not to do something or an obligation to give something to a third person. In many cases, however, the debtor needs the cooperation of the creditor, for example, in case of an obligation to deliver a thing. For the fulfilment of the obligation an act of the creditor is required, namely acceptance of the prestation. Sometimes, the creditor has to contribute to the preparation of the performance and then his cooperation is already required in an earlier stage.

Articles 6:58 ff. deal with creditor's default and some of its consequences.

According to Dutch law, a creditor, as a rule, is not under an obligation to accept the prestation which is owed to him. A buyer is, as a rule, not obliged to accept the goods he bought; a creditor of a sum of money is not obliged to accept payment. If the creditor, according to the contract, is obliged to cooperate in accepting performance, he is, in that respect, debtor and the regular provisions on failure in the performance of an obligation will apply. For those cases, the provisions on creditor's default are not written, which does not mean, however, that their application is excluded.

§12. Definition of Creditor's Default: Requirements

159. Article 6:58 and 6:59 define when a creditor is in default. Unless the cause of non-performance cannot be attributed to him, the creditor shall be in default when the performance of the obligation is prevented because he does not cooperate where necessary or because another impediment arises on his part (Article 6:58). The creditor shall also be in default where, for reasons attributable to him, he does not comply with a duty which he owes to the debtor, who, for that reason rightfully suspends the performance of his obligation towards the creditor (Article 6:59).

Creditor's default arises when the following conditions are fulfilled: performance is not possible without cooperation of the creditor, or another impediment attributable to the creditor obstructs performance; for example, the creditor has destroyed the thing to be delivered to him or the creditor refuses to name the third party with regard to whom the debtor must perform or the creditor's creditor serves a garnishee order on the debtor.[66] The debtor must be capable and ready to perform and in general, the debtor must have informed the creditor that his cooperation is required. The creditor must have failed to give the necessary cooperation.

From Article 6:58, it follows that there is no creditor's default if the non-cooperation cannot be attributed to the creditor. In that case, the creditor can invoke force majeure on his part.

§13. Effects of Creditor's Default

160. If the creditor's default has a permanent character, performance will never be possible, and the debtor may be regarded as released from his obligation. If the default is temporary, the debtor is, in principle, still bound. He will, however, be able to reject all claims based on failure in the performance.

It may be in the interest of the debtor to be freed from his obligation if the creditor obstructs performance. Article 6:60 states that where the creditor is in default,

66. HR 3-5-1991, ECLI:NL:HR:1991:ZC0254, NJ 1992/261; HR 13-4-2012, ECLI:NL:HR:2012:BV2629, NJ 2012/445.

the court may discharge the debtor, upon his demand, from his obligation, with or without conditions to be determined by the court.

The creditor's default terminates the debtor's default. The debtor cannot come into default as long as the creditor is in default (Article 6:61). The creditor is not entitled to initiate execution while he himself is in default (Article 6:62). This provision is linked to the provision of Article 6:61. The creditor, who is not entitled to claim performance, damages or to set aside the contract (*see* further in this paragraph on Article 6:266, paragraph 1), should neither be capable of forcing the debtor to perform by initiating execution.

The debtor is, within the bounds of reasonableness, entitled to compensation for costs attributable to the default (Article 6:63). The debtor can only claim compensation for costs and not damages.

An event occurring during the default of the creditor, making proper performance wholly or partially impossible, is not attributed to the debtor unless, by his fault or that of his subordinate, he has failed to exercise the care which could have been expected from him in the circumstances (Article 6:64).

This article restricts the liability of the debtor in several ways and increases the risk of the creditor. In the first place, the obligation to exert reasonable care for the thing to be delivered (*see supra*, paragraph 153 on Article 6:27) is reduced. Secondly, the debtor is only liable for faults of his subordinates, not for the faults of other persons whose services he uses in the performance of his obligation (*see* paragraph 167 on Article 6:76). Finally, Article 6:64 shifts the burden of proof with regard to the attributability of the failure in the performance from the debtor to the creditor.

Where in an obligation to deliver things determined as to kind, the debtor has designated for delivery certain things corresponding to the obligation and has informed the creditor thereof, he is only obliged to deliver these things if the creditor is in default (Article 6:65). This means that contrary to the general rule, the debtor has in case, of default of his creditor, the power to individualize unilaterally the things to be delivered. The debtor remains entitled, however, to deliver other things corresponding to the obligation (Article 6:65).

If the obligation results from a synallagmatic contract, the creditor in default remains obliged to perform on his part. The setting aside of a contract cannot be based upon a failure of an obligation in respect of which the creditor is himself in default (Article 6:266, paragraph 1).[67] This is, in principle, also true when the act of the debtor becomes wholly or partially impossible. In that case, the risk with regard to the counter-prestation lies with the creditor. The contract may be set aside, however, if the debtor or his subordinate have, through their fault, failed to exercise the care which, in the given circumstances, could have been expected from them (Article 6:266, paragraph 2).

67. *See also* HR 7-12-2018, ECLI:NL:HR:2018:2255, NJ 2020/196.

§14. Deposit and Sale

161. Where the debtor is under an obligation to pay a sum of money or to deliver a thing, and the creditor is in default, the debtor is entitled to deposit for the benefit of the creditor what is owed (Article 6:67). During the custody, the debtor does not incur interest charges on a deposited sum of money (Article 6:68). During the custody, the creditor can only remedy his default by accepting what has been deposited (Article 6:69, paragraph 1). As long as the creditor has not accepted what has been deposited, the depositor is entitled to remove it from custody (Article 6:69, paragraph 2).

In certain circumstances the debtor is entitled or sometimes even obliged to sell the things that were not accepted by the creditor and then to keep the proceeds at the disposal of the creditor instead of the things. This rule may apply, for example, in the case of things subject to decay or depreciation.

§15. Plurality of Creditors and/or Debtors

162. Sometimes, there are more creditors and/or debtors, and this may complicate the situation in cases of creditor's default. Article 6:72 and 6:73 contain some special provisions in this respect.

In the event of solidarity, the legal effects of the default of the creditor apply to each of the debtors (Article 6:72). This is an exception to the general rule that claims against debtors who are solidarily liable are independent and do not influence each other.

Where the creditor rejects tender by a third party, Article 6:60, 6:62 and 6:66–70 (most of them discussed above) apply *mutatis mutandis* to the benefit of the third party, provided that this tender corresponds to the obligation and that the third party has a legitimate interest in its performance (Article 6:73).

§16. Breach

163. Failure in the performance of a contractual obligation may give rise to several remedies. The effects of failure in the performance are laid down in section 9 of Title 1 of Book 6 and – where it concerns synallagmatic contracts – in section 5 of Title 5 of Book 6. The already mentioned term 'failure in the performance' is a key term. When a debtor does not fulfil his obligation on time, in a proper way or when he does not fulfil his obligation at all, he fails in the performance of his obligation. The term failure in the performance has a broad and neutral meaning. It contains all cases in which the debtor, in one way or another, falls short of what the obligation requires. Moreover, it comprises both the case that the failure can be attributed to the debtor and the case that it cannot be attributed to him.

When a failure in the performance cannot be attributed to the debtor or when performance is permanently impossible, there is a failure in the performance right away. In all other cases, there is in principle only a failure in the performance when the debtor is in default. (*See* default, when it commences and what are its effects, *infra*, paragraphs 180 ff.).

Section 9 of Title 1 sets out when a failure in the performance can be attributed to the debtor and under which conditions the creditor may claim damages. The content of the legal obligation to repair damage is laid down in section 10 of Title 1. The failure in the performance of an obligation resulting from a synallagmatic contract may furthermore give rise to the setting aside of the contract; this is provided for in section 5 of Title 5.

Of these subjects, the concept of force majeure and its effects will be dealt with in the next chapter (paragraphs 164 ff.) and the others in the next part on Remedies (Part VI, paragraphs 177 ff.).

Chapter 2. Impossibility, Hardship and Frustration

§1. Impossibility

I. Force Majeure: Introduction

164. Article 6:74, paragraph 1, states that every failure in the performance of a contractual obligation obliges the debtor to repair the damage which the creditor suffers therefrom unless a failure is not attributable to the debtor. Article 6:75 specifies when a failure is not attributable to the debtor, namely if the failure 'is neither due to his fault nor for his account pursuant to the law, a juridical act or generally accepted principles'. This article lays down the principle of force majeure.

In Dutch legal doctrine, as in other continental systems, there have been several theories on the concept of force majeure. The objective theory demanded absolute impossibility of performance, which would apply to everyone (e.g., the thing to be delivered had perished), not resulting from a fault of the debtor, while in the 'subjective theory', it sufficed that performance had become impossible *for the debtor concerned*, i.e., practically too problematic for him (e.g., the debtor had fallen ill or had lost all his money), provided that this was not to be blamed on the debtor. Both theories have been elaborated and extended and despite their different starting points, came to resemble each other more and more. The subjective theory accepted the concept of risk, meaning that the debtor must be held responsible for certain causes of impediment not attributable to his fault. The objective theory enlarged the concept of impossibility in the direction of situations in which performance would be excessively burdensome and mitigated impossibility 'for everyone' by accepting, in some cases, depending on the nature of the obligation, impossibility based on personal circumstances.

The present Code is based on the subjective theory, supplemented with the concept of risk. In short, a debtor can invoke force majeure in case of a failure in the performance which does not result from his fault and is not at his risk.

II. Impediment to Performance

165. Failure in the performance, which constitutes force majeure, will almost always be a result of an impediment to performance. In exceptional cases, this may be different; an example is the case in which a debtor does not know about the existence of the obligation due to a cause that cannot be attributed to him, for example, a successor who does not perform in time because he does not know about the death of the testator.

The impediment must concern the prestation itself.

There is no force majeure if the equilibrium between the prestations of the parties is disturbed by unforeseen circumstances, for example, as a consequence of a price rise. For such cases *see* paragraph 50 *supra* and paragraphs 173 ff. *infra*.

There is no impediment which results in force majeure either if an obligation may be performed in several ways or by several persons and the impediment only concerns one way of performance or one person.

As mentioned above, there may be an impediment to performance resulting in force majeure not only when performance is absolutely impossible for everyone but also when performance is impossible or practically too problematic for the debtor concerned. The prevailing question is, therefore, to which degree the prestation must be impeded to result in force majeure. The answer to this question depends on the circumstances of the case. A general rule cannot be given; societal views will be the deciding factor.

III. No Force Majeure If the Impediment Results from a Fault or Is at the Risk of the Debtor

166. The impediment may not result from the fault of the debtor. The non-performance must be the consequence of an event the debtor could not reasonably have prevented and the effects of which he could not have averted; the cause of the non-performance must not be attributable to him. For example theft of a thing to be delivered is in itself not enough for force majeure; if the debtor had left the thing in an unclosed car, the impediment is a result of his fault.

Furthermore, the impediment must not be the result of a cause for which – according to the law, a juridical act (especially the contract) or common opinion – the debtor is responsible.

IV. Statutory Provisions on Risk: Responsibility for Persons or Things

167. There are several statutory provisions which lay the risk of a certain impediment to perform on one of the parties. Section 9 of Title 1 of Book 6 contains two such provisions.

Article 6:76 states that where, in the performance of an obligation, the debtor uses the services of other persons, he is responsible for their conduct as if it were his own. For the application of this article, it is not relevant whether the other person is a subordinate or not; neither is it relevant whether the debtor has called in the other person on his own initiative or on request of the creditor. In the latter case, however, the nature of the contract, together with the criteria of reasonableness and fairness, may bring about a deviation of the responsibility rule of Article 6:76.[68] The question whether a person is someone whose services have been used in the performance of the obligation in the sense of Article 6:76, should be answered in a restricted way however, namely restricted to only those persons who assist in the performance of the obligation on which the claim is based, as the Supreme Court ruled in the following case. A transporter of money and valuables was robbed of the money he had in deposit for his client. One of the robbers worked for the transporter but was not assisting in the transport of this particular amount of money. He

68. HR 21-5-1999, ECLI:NL:HR:1999:ZC2903, NJ 1999/733.

was therefore not considered to be a person whose services were used by the transporter for the performance of this particular obligation. The transporter's liability could not be based on Article 6:76.[69]

If it is contrary to the obligation to employ the help of others, the debtor may also be held responsible for acts that would not have been attributable to him if he had performed himself. The same is true if the debtor is to blame for the choice of the other persons (*culpa in eligendo*).

Article 6:77 concerns the responsibility for things. Where in the performance of an obligation, a thing is used which is unfit for the purpose, the resulting failure is attributed to the debtor unless this would be unreasonable in view of the contract and necessary implication of the juridical act from which the obligation arises, common opinion and other circumstances of the case. In this respect, we may think of circumstances such as the value of the counter-prestation, the level of professionalism of the debtor, the question of who provided the thing, insurance taken out by the debtor or by the creditor, etc.[70] The provision on responsibility for things is less strict than the provision on the responsibility for persons due to the exception which is formulated in the last part of Article 6:77. In the Explanatory Note, the motives given for this exception are that on the one hand, modern social and technical developments result more often in defective products and on the other hand, the producer of a defective product will be liable in tort. The use of defective equipment or medicine by a hospital or a doctor is mentioned as an example of a case in which the responsibility of Article 6:77 must not be accepted too soon. In this regard, the Supreme Court ruled in recent case law that Article 6:77 is not applicable when a hospital or doctor has used a thing in the performance of an obligation arising from a medical treatment contract that at the time of use was considered 'state-of-the-art' but due to medical research deemed in retrospective unfit for the treatment; in this situation the hospital or doctor has not failed in the performance of the contract.[71]

V. Contractual Stipulations

168. Apart from the law, a juridical act, especially a contract, may determine liability in a certain way. Parties are in general free to derogate from the legal provisions on liability for failure in the performance. They are therefore also free to restrict or extend the facts, which must be regarded as facts of force majeure in their relationship. They may, for example, agree that the debtor guarantees a certain result or undertakes responsibility for the occurrence of a particular cause of impediment. In these cases, events which would otherwise be looked upon as facts of force majeure will now not be considered as such. The other way around, the parties may define facts as facts of force majeure, which would otherwise not fall under the term.

69. HR 14-6-2002, ECLI:NL:HR:2002:AE0657, NJ 2002/495.
70. HR 19-6-2020, ECLI:NL:HR:2020:1090, NJ 2021/16.
71. HR 19-6-2020, ECLI:NL:HR:2020:1082, NJ 2021/15.

A contractual exemption of liability does not always have the desired effect. A stipulation of non-liability made by one party to the contract which is clearly contrary to the interests of the other party, may be null as violating conflict with good morals or may be annulled due to undue influence. If the clause is a part of general conditions, it may be subject to annulment as unreasonably onerous to the other party. Moreover, a debtor is not free to invoke an exemption clause if this would be unacceptable according to the standards of reasonableness and fairness (*see* on this function of good faith paragraph 32 above). *See* further on exemption clauses, paragraph 114 *supra* and paragraph 221 *infra.*

VI. Common Opinion

169. Article 6:75 mentions, apart from the law and a juridical act, common opinion as a possible determining factor with regard to the question if a failure in the performance, not resulting from the fault of the debtor, may or may not be attributed to the debtor.

The answer to the question if a failure in the performance is, according to public opinion, at the risk of the debtor, depends largely on the circumstances of the case.

With regard to some impediments, however, the general opinion is that these in principle do not justify the debtor to invoke force majeure:

(1) Impediments which were foreseeable at the time of the conclusion of the contract. An impediment is in general considered to be foreseeable if the occurrence of such an impediment was probable to such a degree that a prudent debtor would have taken it into account.
(2) Insolvency of the debtor.
(3) Inexperience of the debtor.

Some impediments which will in general justify the debtor to invoke force majeure are:

(1) Illness of the debtor, in case the obligation must be performed personally by the debtor (provided of course that the illness was not foreseeable and not due to a fault of the debtor). The relevant criterion is whether the illness would impede a normal debtor from performing; personal circumstances which can be considered abnormal (e.g., extreme sensitivity) must remain at the risk of the debtor.
(2) Danger for life, health, freedom, etc. In this respect, the same principles apply.
(3) Legal regulations and government measures, which impede all ways of performance. Also, foreign legal regulations or government measures may cause force majeure. Cases of this kind have to be seen in the same way as other cases of force majeure. Two questions have to be asked: (a) Is the foreign law or regulation an 'impediment' to the debtor? (b) Should the cause of this impediment be attributed to the debtor? If a regulation or measure is connected with the person of the debtor and must be considered as an abnormal personal circumstance which would not have affected all debtors equally, the

risk is to remain on the side of the debtor. For example, if a foreign government prohibits its nationals from paying a sum of money to another country, the citizenship of the prohibiting state may be a personal circumstance, and the impediment may, therefore, be attributed to the debtor.

Under the Code, an interesting case law has emerged on the question of whether a certain impediment to performance should, according to common opinion, be attributed to the debtor or not. In 1997,[72] the Supreme Court ruled that the impossibility of returning a rented car because it was stolen (by no fault of the person who rented it) is a circumstance which is, according to common opinion, the risk of the car rental company.

Another example is a case of 1998,[73] in which the Supreme Court ruled that the mere fact that a sold thing does not correspond to the contract (in that case, a pure-bred dog which, after delivery, appeared to have a hitherto unknown physical defect), does not make the seller liable. Whether or not such a defect should be attributed to the seller depends on the circumstances of the case.

Last but not least, the Supreme Court ruled that, according to common opinion, the dealer selling an industrially produced good, which proves to be defective in a way the dealer did not cause and did not know about (because it was already defective when he bought it from the producer), is liable for the damage caused by the defective good. Such a dealer may not invoke force majeure as a defence to a buyer's claim for damages because the failure in the performance should, according to common opinion, be attributed to him. In that case a grower bought a fertilizer which was polluted and damaged the grower's plants. The dealer was held liable for this damage and could not invoke force majeure, even though the pollution was caused by the producer from which the dealer had bought the fertilizer and even though the dealer did not know about the pollution because this defective performance should, according to common opinion, be attributed to the dealer.[74] The practical impact of this judgment is smaller than it may appear, however, because dealers like this generally use exemption clauses.

VII. Burden of Proof

170. A creditor who claims damages must first of all state that there is an obligation in the performance of which the debtor has failed. As a rule, he will eventually also have to prove these statements, although the apportionment of the burden of proof with regard to the failure to some extent will also depend on the circumstances of the case. *See also supra*, paragraph 61 on the burden of proof with regard to obligations of means, respectively, obligations of result. If the obligation concerns the payment of a sum of money, the creditor must state that the debtor has failed in his obligation, but the burden of proof does not lie on him; if the debtor

72. HR 24-10-1997, ECLI:NL:HR:1997:ZC2469, NJ 1998/69.
73. HR 9-1-1998, ECLI:NL:HR:1998:ZC2541, NJ 1998/272.
74. HR 27-4-2001, ECLI:NL:HR:2001:AB1338, NJ 2002/213.

denies the failure, he must prove that he has paid. Furthermore the creditor must state and prove that as a consequence of the failure, he has suffered damage.

In order to escape liability, the debtor has to state and prove that the failure in the performance was the result of a cause which cannot be attributed to him.

VIII. Consequences of Force Majeure

171. The Code contains in Articles 6:78 ff. some provisions on the consequences of force majeure.

Force majeure can consist of a permanent or temporary, full or partial impediment to perform. Force majeure will bar a claim for performance to the extent that the debtor is impeded to perform. This means that if the force majeure is permanent, the obligation has lost its force. Temporary force majeure may also bring about this effect, for example, when the prestation should have been performed within a certain time limit. In other cases, temporary force majeure will only suspend the obligation.

If the impediment only obstructs a part of the prestation, the creditor is entitled to the remaining part unless it was the intention of the parties that the prestation should be performed as a whole or not at all.

Force majeure bars a claim for performance but does not obstruct the obligation as such. This is of practical interest if a debtor performs despite the impediment (e.g., the debtor delivers the thing despite a legal prohibition); in that case, the payment has not been undue.

The debtor who is impeded to perform as a consequence of force majeure will in principle not be obliged to pay damages. This means that, in case of a unilateral contract, the creditor will suffer the damage. After all, he has no right to claim performance or damages. But if the debtor derives benefits in connection with the non-performance which he would not have had in the case of proper performance, the creditor is entitled to compensation for his damage by application of the rules relating to unjustified enrichment, up to the maximum of the amount of the said benefit (Article 6:78, paragraph 1). Where the debtor is prevented from performing by a cause which cannot be attributed to him but the creditor is nevertheless in the position to obtain, by execution or by compensation, that what is owed to him, the creditor may do so (Article 6:79).

If force majeure permanently impedes the performance of an obligation resulting from a synallagmatic contract, the creditor of that performance is not obliged to perform either. As a consequence, both parties are equally prejudiced: the creditor has no right to claim performance or damages, and the debtor has no right to claim the counter-prestation. If the creditor has performed already, he may claim restitution.

The fact that the creditor is not obliged to perform does not mean that his obligation lapses automatically. As in other cases of failure in the performance, the obligation of the creditor only lapses after he has set aside the contract by a written declaration. In case of partial force majeure, the creditor also has the right to set aside the contract if the failure in the performance is such as to justify setting aside. A partial setting aside is also possible. *See infra*, paragraphs 190 ff. on Article 6:265.

If the force majeure is temporary, the obligations are mutually suspended. When the impediment has been removed, the obligations regain their force.

§2. Hardship: 'The Unforeseen'

I. Unforeseen Circumstances: Introduction and Definition

172. Article 6:258 (mentioned already *supra*, in paragraph 50) states in paragraph 1 that, upon the demand of one of the parties, the court may modify the effects of a contract, or it may set it aside in whole or in part on the basis of unforeseen circumstances which are of such a nature that the co-contracting party, according to the criteria of reasonableness and fairness, may not expect that the contract be maintained in an unmodified form. The modification or the setting aside of the contract is not pronounced to the extent that the person invoking the circumstances should be held accountable for them according to the nature of the contract or common opinion (paragraph 2).

As mentioned, the expression 'unforeseen circumstances' must not be taken literally. The decisive factor is whether the parties have made allowance for the occurrence of these circumstances in their contract and whether the contract has made sufficient provisions for *those* circumstances. This must be determined by the interpretation of the contract.

The unforeseen circumstances may be of a general nature – such as war or a natural disaster – or may concern one or more specific contracts.

It is not necessary that the unforeseen circumstances concern the basic assumption on which the contract was made; also, stipulations of secondary character may be modified, for example, the place or the time of delivery.

II. Application in Cases of Force Majeure

173. As we have just seen, Article 6:258 may be applied in cases in which there is no force majeure but in which performance has become very onerous for the debtor. However, application of the article in cases of force majeure is also possible.[75] The article may serve, in certain circumstances, as a means to overcome the impediment to perform. For example, if a port where a ship must be discharged has become inaccessible as a consequence of hostilities, the court may, upon the demand of one of the parties, change the place of performance and – depending on the circumstances – adapt the counter-prestation.

75. The distinction between cases of force majeure and cases of unforeseen circumstances is not always clear, *see infra.*

III. Judicial Decision Required for Modification or Setting Aside

174. The modification or setting aside must take place by judicial decision. The court may pronounce a modification of the contract or set it aside, subject to conditions to be determined by it (Article 6:260, paragraph 1). In this respect, we may think of conditions such as the restitution of a prestation or payment of a certain amount of money.

If the court modifies, or partially sets aside the contract, it may determine that one or more of the contracting parties may set aside the contract in its entirety by a written declaration within a period specified in the decision (Article 6:260, paragraph 2).

Article 6:258 may not be derogated by the parties (Article 6:250).

The provision of Article 6:258 has links with other concepts in the field of the law of obligations, such as the concepts of force majeure and error.

Sometimes, the situation in which the other party, as a result of unforeseen circumstances, may not expect the contract to be maintained in an unmodified form is difficult to distinguish from a situation in which performance has become practically too onerous for the debtor due to a cause which may not be attributed to him (one of the cases of force majeure).

Article 6:258 concerns circumstances changed *after* the formation of the contract, whereas in case of error circumstances existing *at the time of* the formation of the contract are involved. Also here, the distinction is not always easy to make. This may be illustrated by two cases on the sale of immovable property with polluted soil. In the first case,[76] buyer and seller were aware of the pollution and agreed that the seller would pay for the decontamination according to a certain plan. When later it became clear that decontamination according to this plan would last eternally, the appellate court decided that the seller's obligation to clean the pollution should be limited in time or money. The Supreme Court upheld this decision, deciding that in case of error, there are several ways of avoiding nullification of the contract by changing its contents instead, one of which is the application of Article 6:258, provided of course that the error concerns 'unforeseen circumstances' within the meaning of Article 6:258. In the second case[77] buyer and seller had not been aware of the pollution at the time of the sale. The Supreme Court upheld the appellate court's decision that the contract of sale had to be modified in such a way that the disadvantageous consequences of this error would be divided among the parties. The price of the sold property was halved.

From a theoretical point of view it is still important to sharply demarcate legal concepts like force majeure and error. From a practical point of view, a sharp distinction has become less important due to the provision of Article 6:258, which makes modification or setting aside of the contract possible in all cases of unforeseen circumstances.

76. HR 28-11-1997, ECLI:NL:HR:1997:ZC2509, NJ 1998/659.
77. HR 18-1-2002, ECLI:NL:HR:2002:AD7321, NJ 2002/106.

§3. FRUSTRATION

I. Frustration

175. With regard to the subject of frustration, I refer to what already has been said in paragraphs 164 ff. on force majeure and unforeseen circumstances.

Chapter 3. Discharge by Agreement

§1. Discharge by Agreement

176. As mentioned in paragraph 49 on modification of the contract by the parties, the absence of the requirement of consideration enables the parties to modify their contract by mutual consent. Modification does not present special difficulties; the general rules of contract law apply. The same remarks can be made about discharge by agreement. If the parties have reached a mutual consent about the discharge of one or both of them, there are no specific problems. In this respect, Article 6:160 may be mentioned. Paragraph 1 states that an obligation is extinguished by a contract between creditor and debtor whereby the creditor renounces his claim. According to paragraph 2, an offer to renunciate by gratuitous title, addressed by the creditor to the debtor, is deemed accepted when it has come to the attention of the debtor and he has not rejected it without delay.

Part VI. Remedies

Chapter 1. Remedies

§1. General Provisions

I. Remedies

177. If the debtor does not fulfil the obligation of his own free will, the creditor normally has a choice of different remedies. In general, the creditor may claim:

(a) performance;
(b) performance and compensation for late performance;
(c) damages instead of performance, and in the case of synallagmatic contracts, also;
(d) setting aside of the contract;
(e) setting aside and damages.

According to Dutch law, the creditor of an obligation in principle has a right to claim specific performance (Article 3:296). It should be stressed that as long as performance remains possible, the creditor is not obliged to content himself with a substitute. He may bring an action for specific performance, even in the case of an obligation to do or not to do. *See*, on specific performance and on the '*astreinte*' as an instrument to effect specific performance, further *infra*, paragraphs 184 ff.

Instead of performance, the creditor may choose one of the above-mentioned remedies for non-performance, the most important of which are damages and, in the case of synallagmatic contracts, the setting aside of the contract (invoking the consequences of discharge by breach). In this respect, different modes of non-performance should be distinguished.

II. Attributable and Non-attributable Non-performance

178. First, non-performance may be attributable to the debtor or may not be attributable to him; in the first case, he is responsible for the non-performance; in the second, he is not (Article 6:74, *see* further *supra*, paragraphs 164 ff.). This distinction is vital because, in the latter case, no action lies for damages. A failure in the performance attributable to the debtor gives the creditor a right to damages. This means that in the case of a failure in the performance, which is *not* attributable to the debtor, the only remedies available are the ones mentioned above under (a) (only if performance is still possible of course) and (d). In rare cases, the creditor may also claim the sum of the benefits the debtor may have had by non-performing. *See supra* paragraph 168 and Article 6:78, paragraph 1.

III. Permanent or Temporary Impossibility to Perform

179. To the extent that the performance is already permanently impossible, the right to damages comes into existence immediately and *ipso iure*. As we have seen (*supra*, paragraph 165), the concept of impossibility refers to both absolute impossibility and relative impossibility. Some cases of permanent impossibility have been mentioned already; furthermore, one can think of cases:

(a) in which the prestation of the debtor was only possible within a certain time, and this time has passed;
(b) in which an obligation not to do was violated;
(c) in which the prestation of the debtor has a permanent defect, and the creditor has definitively rejected the prestation;
(d) in which the creditor, as a result of a defect of the prestations, has suffered damage (to that extent, correct performance is permanently impossible).

IV. Default

180. Except where performance is already impossible, the debtor is fully responsible only when he is 'in default'.

Article 6:81 states that except to the extent that the delay cannot be attributed to him or performance is already permanently impossible, the debtor is in default during the period that the prestation is not rendered once it has become exigible and the requirements of Article 6:82 and 6:83 have been met. This rule applies both to cases in which performance has not been made at all and to cases where a defective performance has been made, provided that it may be cured, for example, by repairing the defect or by replacing the defective goods.

V. The Requirement of a Default Notice

181. In general, default requires a default notice. Article 6:82, paragraph 1 states that default commences when the debtor is given written notice of default granting him a reasonable period for the performance, and there is no performance within this period.

The notice may be served on the debtor by a bailiff, but any writing will suffice, including a telegram. The meaning of the warning is not simply to establish that the debtor has failed to perform, but it serves to let the debtor know the creditor insists on performance within a fixed reasonable time. The function of a default notice is primarily to specify until when timely performance is still possible. After this moment the debtor will be in default.[78] Accordingly, the warning may be sent before performance is due, but the time fixed in the document may not expire before that moment. If the debtor is in a temporary impossibility to perform or if it is evident from his attitude that a warning would serve no purpose, he may be put into default by a written declaration to the effect that he is held liable for his non-performance (Article 6:82, paragraph 2).

In certain cases the debtor is in default without default notice.

According to Article 6:83, default commences without the formality of putting into default:

(a) where a term set for satisfaction lapses without the obligation having been performed unless it appears that the term has another purpose (*'dies interpellat pro homine'*);
(b) where the obligation arises from an unlawful act or relates to reparation of damages as referred to in Article 6:74 (*viz.* as a result of failure in the performance of an obligation) and the obligation to pay damages is not immediately performed;
(c) where the creditor must conclude from a communication by the debtor that the latter will fail in the performance of the obligation.

Moreover, default commences without default notice:

(d) where the parties have agreed on this in their contract or where the debtor has afterwards, expressly or tacitly, relieved the creditor of the sending of a default notice;
(e) where it would be contrary to reasonableness and fairness to invoke the lack of a default notice. This possibility is of particular practical importance since it may easily happen that it is totally clear between the parties that one of them demands a certain thing from the other and (therefore) does not give written notice of default, granting the other a specific period for performing. An example may be found in the case where the lessee of a shop suffered water damage because the roof was defective. After having the electric circuit repaired, he demanded compensation of these costs from the lessor. The Supreme Court ruled that even though the lessee did not give written notice of default before calling in the repairmen himself, it would, under the circumstances of the case (from the lessor's conduct, it was clear he would not perform), be unacceptable according to the standards of reasonableness and fairness for the lessor to invoke the lack of a default notice. The list of Article 6:83 is enunciative.[79] On the other hand, from this case, it should not be inferred that the requirement of a default notice is taken lightly: the Supreme Court has held that reasonableness and fairness may be invoked successfully only when

78. HR 20-9-1996, ECLI:NL:HR:1996:ZC2140, NJ 1996/748; HR 31-1-2020, ECLI:NL:HR:2020:141, NJ 2020/60.
79. HR 6-10-2000, ECLI:NL:HR:2000:AA7364, NJ 2000/691.

the debtor's invoking the lack of a default notice would be unacceptable according to standards of reasonableness and fairness;[80]

(f) where the law provides that no default notice is required (e.g., in Article 6:205: he who receives a payment 'in bad faith', that is, knowing that it is undue, is in default *ipso iure*);

(g) where, because of the nature of the obligation to be performed, timely performance is only possible at a fixed moment. An example is the obligation of the lessee of a rented property to return the property in good order at the end of the lease; this obligation can, by its nature, only be performed adequately at the moment the lease ends. If the lessee does not return the property in good order at this moment, he shall be in default even without a default notice.[81]

VI. Effects of Default

182. As stated before, the provisions on default apply irrespective of whether the debtor performed in a defective way or did not perform at all.

Every impossibility of performance arising during the default of the debtor and not attributable to the creditor is attributed to the debtor; the latter must repair the damage incurred thereby unless the creditor would equally have incurred the damage on proper and timely performance (Article 6:84).

The debtor in default is liable to compensate the creditor for the damage caused by his late performance. Here, the creditor has a choice: he may either combine a claim for performance with a claim for compensation for late performance or may – provided that the breach is serious – renounce his right to performance and claim damages instead of performance.

If the creditor chooses the first option, the debtor must repair the damage for delay only for the time that he has been in default (Article 6:85). The creditor may refuse performance offered after commencement of the default when the offer does not include payment of (future) damages which have, in the meantime, become due as well as (future) costs (Article 6:86).[82]

If the creditor chooses the second option, the obligation is converted into one to pay damages in substitution, where the creditor notifies the debtor in default in writing that he claims damages instead of performance (Article 6:87, paragraph 1). This notice may also be combined with the default notice discussed above.

The creditor is furthermore entitled to set aside the synallagmatic contract from which the obligation results. (*See*, on this remedy, *infra*, paragraphs 190 ff.).

As long as the creditor has not claimed damages instead of performance nor taken steps with a view to setting aside the contract, the debtor is entitled to purge his default, provided that he offers payment of (future) damages and costs. If the creditor accepts the debtor's offer of performance without it, including damages and costs, his acceptance cannot be seen as a waiver of his right to claim damages.[83] He

80. HR 4-10-2002, ECLI:NL:HR:2002:AE4358, NJ 2003/257.
81. HR 27-11-1998, ECLI:NL:HR:1998:ZC2790, NJ 1999/380.
82. HR 7-12-2018, ECLI:NL:HR:2018:2255, NJ 2020/196.
83. HR 7-12-2018, ECLI:NL:HR:2018:2255, NJ 2020/196.

is also entitled to summon the creditor to choose between his remedies (performance, damages, setting aside); if the creditor does not comply with the request within a reasonable time, he in principle merely retains his right to claim damages (Article 6:88).

183. The Code contains a special provision on the damages which may be claimed for delay in the payment of a sum of money. These damages are confined to the legal interest on that sum over the period in which the debtor has been in default of payment (Article 6:119). Legal interest rates are set by Regulation (governmental decree) (Article 6:120, paragraph 1). This system has an advantageous and disadvantageous side for the creditor. On the one hand, the creditor is entitled to the legal interest without having to prove that he actually suffered any damage; on the other hand, the creditor may not claim more than the legal interest.

Under the influence of Directive 2000/35/EC on combating late payment in commercial transactions, replaced by Directive 2011/7 EU, two new provisions came into effect on 1 December 2002 (Article 6:119a and 6:120, paragraph 2). A commercial contract is defined as a contract for remuneration which leads to the provision of goods or the delivery of services and which is concluded between legal persons or natural persons acting in the course of a business or profession (Article 6:119a, paragraph 1).[84] In the case of a commercial contract, the damage due on account of delay in the payment of a sum of money shall consist of legal interest from the day after the day set for payment (Article 6:119a, paragraph 1). If no such day is set, the interest will generally be due when thirty days have passed since the debtor received the invoice (Article 119a, paragraph 2a). The legal interest rate for commercial transactions shall be the most recent main refinancing interest rate of the European Central Bank, plus eight percentage points (Article 6:120, paragraph 2). This is substantially higher than the legal interest rate for non-commercial debts. These regulations are further tightened where the debtor is a public authority (Article 6:119b).

§2. Specific Performance and Injuctions: '*Astreinte*'

I. Specific Performance

184. The creditor may bring an action for specific performance, even in the case of an obligation to do or not to do. Article 3:296, paragraph 1 states that unless it otherwise follows from the law, the nature of the obligation or a juridical act, the person obliged to give, to do or not to do something as regards another may be ordered to do so by the court upon the demand of the person to whom the obligation is owed.[85]

---

84. *See also* HR 8-12-2017, ECLI:NL:HR:2017:3106; HR 30-10-2020, ECLI:NL:HR:2020:1710, NJ 2020/408.
85. *See* HR 20-12-2019, ECLI:NL:HR:2019:2006, NJ 2020/41 for a case in which the Dutch government was obligated to achieve the reduction of greenhouse gas emissions with at least 25% by 2020.

An order to perform may in general not be given in case of obligations with a personal character, such as the obligation to write a book. In such a case, the creditor will have to settle for damages and/or the setting aside of the contract. If performance has become impossible (e.g., if the thing to be delivered is perished), an order to perform may not be given.[86]

A judgment by which a person has been ordered to give, to do or not to do something may be executed in a direct or an indirect way.

II. Direct Execution

185. Execution in a direct way is possible if the creditor is able to enforce performance from the debtor by means of power (such as police action) or to obtain performance without the debtor (e.g., if the creditor acquires the money the debtor owes him through seizure and compulsory sale of things owned by the debtor).

III. Obligations to Give

186. In case of an obligation to give (i.e., to deliver property, to provide actual control or enjoyment of a thing or to pay a sum of money), only the last form of direct execution is suitable. Provisions on execution of an order to pay a sum of money may be found in the Code of Civil Procedure. In Articles 439 ff. and 700 ff., there are detailed rules on seizure, attachment, compulsory sale, etc. In Articles 491 ff., there are also rules on execution of an order to give moveable non-registered things. Execution takes place through a bailiff taking control of the things and giving them to the creditor. The handing over of immovable things (eviction) is provided for in Articles 502 ff. Article 3:300 of the Civil Code renders possible execution of an obligation to deliver registered property. Unless it is incompatible with the nature of the juridical act, where a person must perform a juridical act towards another, the court may, upon the demand of the creditor, determine that its decision shall have the same force as a deed drawn up, in legal form, by the person who must perform the juridical act; or he may determine that a representative to be appointed by him shall perform the act. Where the court appoints a representative, it may determine that the act to be performed by the latter needs its approval.

Where the defendant must draw up a deed together with the plaintiff, the court may determine that its judgment shall take the place of the deed or part thereof. Article 3:301, paragraph 1 states that a decision whereby the court has determined that it takes the place of a deed or part thereof intended to transfer registered property cannot be entered in the public registers unless notice of it has been served upon the person ordered to transfer, and unless the decision has become final or unless the decision is provisionally enforceable and a period of fourteen days or as much longer or shorter as determined in the decision has elapsed since notice of the decision was served.

86. HR 27-6-1997, ECLI:NL:HR:1997:ZC2401, NJ 1997/641.

If there are several attachments on property in order to obtain the transfer of that property, the question arises as to which creditor has priority. This will often follow from the nature of the rights of the respective creditors. In case two or more creditors pursue conflicting rights to transfer in respect of one and the same property, the oldest right to the transfer has preference in their mutual relationship unless it otherwise follows from the law, the nature of their rights or the requirements of reasonableness and fairness (Article 3:298). Article 3:298 only concerns the mutual relationship of the creditors; with respect to the debtor, all creditors have a right to delivery.

IV. Obligations to Do Something

187. In case of obligations to do, Article 3:299 states that where a person does not do what he is obliged to do, the court may, upon demand, authorize the creditor of the obligation to procure for himself that which would have resulted from the performance (paragraph 1). In the same way, a person to whom another owes an obligation not to do something may be authorized to undo what has been done in breach of such obligation (paragraph 2). The expenses necessary to carry out the authorization shall be borne by the person who failed to perform his obligation. The decision granting the authorization may also order the payment of such expenses upon presentation of the documents which it declares to be required for this purpose (paragraph 3).

Article 3:299, paragraph 1 does not prevent the creditor from doing what his debtor had to do without the court's authorization and for the debtor's account and to his risk and to claim the costs he made afterwards as damages caused by the failure in the performance of the debtor. If he has acted reasonably in the circumstances and if the other requirements are met (default of the debtor, causal link), his claim will be sustained.

Article 3:299, paragraph 1 gives a remedy only in case of obligations to do with a non-personal nature. In case of obligations of a personal nature, direct performance may not be obtained. As mentioned, pressure on the debtor to perform personally is not allowed. If the obligation to do so consists in the performance of a juridical act, the above-mentioned Article 3:300 is applicable.

V. Obligations Not to Do Something

188. With regard to obligations not to do, the creditor may make use of means of power to prevent the debtor from doing what he is not allowed to do. The obligation not to do obliges the debtor not to do something that he would otherwise be allowed to do or to tolerate something that he would be otherwise allowed to prevent. For example, a debtor may be contractually obliged to give his creditor access to his premises; if he refuses such access, the creditor may effect entrance by police force.

A debtor who has already done what he promised not to do may be forced to undo what he has done. Such a court order may – as we have already seen – be executed in a direct way (*see* Article 3:299, paragraph 2, mentioned above). Another way for the debtor to bring about the old situation is to claim damages other than money (*see infra*, paragraph 203).

VI. Indirect Execution: *Astreintes*

189. The execution of a judgment may also be effected in an indirect way. In Dutch law, there are two indirect means of power: civil imprisonment and *astreinte* of which the latter is by far the most important. An *astreinte* ('dwangsom') is a sum of money (penalty) fixed by the court in case the debtor does not comply with the judgment. The *astreinte* may be determined as a lump sum or as an amount for every day (or other time-unit) the debtor does not comply with the judgment or for every time he violates the judgment. An *astreinte* may not be imposed in case of a judicial order to pay an amount of money. The *astreinte* is a powerful instrument to defer the losing defendant from obstinacy, all the more so since it may also be imposed in summary proceedings ('*kort geding*'). In this case, the defendant who does not comply with the judgment is obliged to pay the *astreinte*, even if the plaintiff loses the case afterwards in the regular proceedings.

An a*streinte* must be paid to the winning plaintiff, not to the state (as in the German system). The court has no power to grant a respite to the debtor. An *astreinte* is not a special form of damage; *astreintes* and damages are independent of each other and do not influence each other. Damages are calculated irrespective of the fact that *astreintes* are paid. The order to pay an *astreinte* has an accessory and conditional nature; such an order is only possible in combination with a principal order and is given under the suspensive condition that the debtor does not comply with the principal order. However, once *astreintes* are forfeited they may be separately collected. Finally, it is worth noting that in Dutch law, *astreintes* are – unlike the so-called *astreintes-comminatoires* in France – not subject to review, except in case of impossibility to perform (and of course on appeal).

The Dutch law on *astreintes* (Articles 611a ff. of the Code of Civil Procedure) is based on a Benelux Treaty. The Court of the Benelux has jurisdiction in cases in which interpretation of the relevant provisions is required. In such cases, Dutch courts may or sometimes must ask the Benelux Court prejudicial questions.

§3. Termination

I. Setting Aside

190. The remedies for non-performance of an obligation in general were discussed *supra* in paragraph 177. One of these remedies is the setting aside of a synallagmatic contract.

The right to set aside a contract is regulated in some detail in Article 6:265–277; the provisions are directed at bilateral contracts but may be applied *per analogiam* to comparable bilateral relationships (Article 6:261, paragraph 2) and to multilateral contracts (Article 6:279). An example of a bilateral relationship that is not a synallagmatic contract was found in the case where the owner of a horse handed the animal over to someone else for the other to sell it. When the other did not succeed in selling the animal, the owner could set the order aside.[87]

Every failure of one party, the debtor, in the performance of one of its obligations gives the other party, the creditor, the right to set the contract aside in whole or in part unless the failure, given its special nature or minor importance, does not justify a setting aside of the contract and the consequences thereof (Article 6:265, paragraph 1). It is for the debtor to state and prove that the failure does not justify the setting aside of the contract. Dutch law therefore does not adhere to the rule that setting aside is only possible in cases of *fundamental breach*, where the creditor has to prove that the breach is so fundamental as to justify the setting aside of the contract.

Following the system of Articles 6:74 ff., paragraph 2 of Article 6:265 provides that to the extent that performance is not permanently or temporarily impossible, the right to set the contract aside does not arise until the debtor is in default. The remedy is available both where the non-performance may be attributed to the debtor and where the impossibility of performance is due to force majeure, but the right to claim damages remains conditional upon attributable breach (Article 6:277). Unlike under the old Code, the setting aside does not require a lawsuit: it will suffice that the disappointed creditor declares so in writing to the other party (Article 6:267). If the contract has been concluded electronically, the declaration can be made electronically as well.

Although a lawsuit is not required, the setting aside may also be pronounced by the court upon the demand of the creditor. In more complicated situations it will be advisable to demand a judgment. In that case, the creditor may suspend performance of his own obligation (*see infra*, paragraphs 192 ff.), while an offer to perform made after the demand has no effect if the setting aside is pronounced (Article 6:269).

The creditor may set aside the contract in whole or in part. Article 6:270 provides for partial setting aside, which is defined as a proportional reduction, in quantity or in quality, of punctual obligations. In this way, a party may obtain a reduction of his obligations (such as the price he has to pay); for example, where the other delivers only part of the goods promised, but also where the prestation of the other party is insufficient in quality. In this way partial setting aside also will constitute a generalized '*actio quanti minoris*'. The creditor may also set aside the contract merely for the future, for example, when the debtor stops performing prestations such as paying rent or supplying services which are due continuously or at fixed intervals. A number of legal authors have defended the position that the right to set aside the contract should be regarded as *ultimum remedium*; that is, the creditor should exercise his rights to other less drastic remedies first. In this view, the creditor may not set aside the contract if he has a reasonable alternative. The Supreme Court repeatedly refused to accept such a principle, for example, in a case where the seller of a company did not inform the buyer about pollution on the premises: the buyer could

87. HR 14-4-2000, ECLI:NL:HR:2000:AA5516, NJ 2000/438.

set aside the contract and did not have to exercise his right to damages first.[88] One should keep in mind, however, that the right to set aside a contract (as any other contractual remedy) is subject to the principles of reasonableness and fairness.

Where both parties are unable to perform, they both have the right to set aside the contract.[89]

II. Effects of Setting Aside

191. Setting aside does not have retroactive effect (Article 6:269), which means *inter alia* that the section on undue payment does not apply to the obligation of the parties to undo the prestations which they had already received before the contract was set aside; for this reason, Articles 6:271 ff. contains a set of comparable rules. The principle is laid down in Article 6:271: the setting aside of a contract releases the parties from the obligations affected by it; to the extent that these obligations have already been performed, the legal ground for this performance remains intact, but an obligation arises for the parties to reverse the performance of the obligations already performed (Article 6:271).

Where the prestations, by their nature, cannot be reversed, compensation up to their value at the time of performance is substituted (Article 6:272, paragraph 1).

Where the prestations cannot be undone due to other reasons than their nature (e.g., the buyer resold the goods received), this in itself does not exclude the right to set aside the contract, but the recipient is considered to have failed in the performance of his obligation to undo the prestations; on this ground, he is obliged to pay compensation for the loss caused to the other party instead, which normally implies that he has to account for the value of those prestations. But this rule does not apply if the impossibility to restitute the goods cannot be imputed to him, for example, when he resold them before he discovered or should have discovered the defect which entitled him to set aside the contract. In such a case, his obligation to pay compensation is governed by the rule on unjustified enrichment (Article 6:273 *jo* 6:78).

The contracting party, who has been disappointed by his co-contracting party, may have suffered damages as a result of the failure in the performance and the setting aside of the contract. In that case, the party who has set aside the contract may also claim these supplementary damages, provided of course that the non-performance could be imputed to the other party.

§4. *Exceptio Non Adimpleti* Contractus

I. Rights to Suspend Performance: Introduction

192. The Code contains in section 7 of Title 1 of Book 6 (Article 6:52–57) general provisions on the right to suspend performance. In Article 6:262–264, these general principles are elaborated for synallagmatic contracts.

88. HR 4-2-2000, ECLI:NL:HR:2000:AA4728, NJ 2000/562. *See also* HR 28-9-2018, ECLI:NL:HR:2018:1810, NJ 2019/446.
89. HR 11-1-2008, ECLI:NL:HR:2008:BB7195, NJ 2009/342.

A right of suspension is, according to the Code, a right of a debtor (who also has an exigible claim against his creditor) to suspend the performance of his obligation until his claim is satisfied. The right of suspension is especially important in case of synallagmatic contracts, but also outside the field of synallagmatic contracts, the right to suspend may be of interest.

Article 6:52, paragraph 1 states as a general rule that a debtor has a right to suspend if there is a sufficient connection between the claim and the obligation to justify such suspension.

Apart from this general rule, section 7 contains some provisions which further develop the right of suspension. These provisions also apply to suspension rights that are regulated elsewhere to the extent that they are not derogated from. A special kind of suspension right is the right of retention, regulated in Article 3:290. The right of retention is the power vested in a creditor, in the cases specified by law, to suspend the performance of an obligation to surrender a thing to his debtor until settlement of the claim. Section 7 is applicable to the right of retention unless the articles on retention derogate from Article 6:52–57.

II. Requirements

193. From Article 6:52, paragraph 1, it follows that a debtor only has a right to suspend if the claim against his creditor is exigible and if the creditor does not perform. In this respect, non-performance is not the same as failure in the performance of Articles 6:74 ff. Article 6:52 does not require default. It is sufficient that the other party does not perform or does not continue performance, although the right to claim performance is exigible.[90]

Furthermore, in order to justify suspension, there must be a sufficient relationship between claim and obligation. This criterion may be regarded as an application of the general standards of reasonableness and fairness. A sufficient relationship may be assumed, *inter alia*, in the event that the reciprocal obligations result from the same juridical relationship or from regular previous dealings between the parties (Article 6:52, paragraph 2).

If both obligations are 'correlative' obligations, that is, counter-obligations in the same synallagmatic contract, a sufficient relationship does exist (Article 6:262, *see* further *infra*, paragraph 195).[91] Synallagmatic contracts may also result in obligations that are not counter-obligations in the sense of Article 6:262, such as the obligation of the lessee to pay rent and the obligation of the lessor to carry out reparations. In this case, the test of Article 6:52 must be met.[92]

90. HR 8-3-2002, ECLI:NL:PHR:2002:AD7343, NJ 2002/199.
91. HR 17-4-2020, ECLI:NL:HR:2020:723, NJ 2020/168.
92. HR 30-6-1978, ECLI:NL:HR:1978:AC6324, NJ 1978/693; but *see also* HR 6-6-1997, ECLI:NL:HR:1997:ZC2389, NJ 1998/128, where Art. 6:262 was held applicable.

Other examples of a relationship, as referred to in Article 6:52, are the relationship between obligations to undo after the annulment or the setting aside of a contract and the relationship between the obligation to restitute property given without legal ground and the obligation to reimburse the costs incurred in accepting and returning the property (paragraph 2).

Sometimes, a debtor does not have the right to suspend, although the requirements of Article 6:52 are met. No right to suspend exists (Article 6:54):

(a) to the extent that the performance of the obligation of the other party is prevented by the creditor's default. Such a case could arise, for instance, when a buyer does not accept the goods he bought because he thinks they are defective. He suspends paying the price. Later, he is proven wrong: the goods are fine. In hindsight, the buyer was in default (creditor's default). He therefore did not have the right to suspend paying the price. The seller may claim performance and sometimes even damages (i.e., interest, namely when the buyer is also in debtor's default);
(b) to the extent that the performance of the obligation of the other party is permanently impossible. This rule does not apply in case of synallagmatic contracts: in those cases, a party may suspend his obligation when the other party does not perform his, even when performance by the other party is already impossible. This is because, in the case of synallagmatic contracts, suspension is used as a first step towards setting aside the contract. It would make no sense when a party would not be allowed to suspend his obligation, even when the other party could not perform and then, after the setting aside, the performance of the first party would have to be undone again. On the other hand, when, for instance, the parties have a continuing trade relationship, a party is not allowed to suspend his payment for one transaction because the other party will not be able to deliver in another transaction. In such cases, this rule applies;
(c) to the extent that the claim of the other party is exempt from seizure. Some claims are exempt from seizure in order to protect the creditor. In such cases, the creditor is protected in other ways as well, one of which is this: the debtor may not suspend his obligation to pay such claims.

The right to suspension may also be excluded by contract, or the exercise of this right may be prevented by reasonableness and fairness.

A right to suspend performance can be invoked against the creditors of the other party (Article 6:53).

The right to suspend performance ceases as soon as security has been provided for the satisfaction of the obligation of the other party unless such satisfaction would thereby be unreasonably delayed (Article 6:55).

A right to suspend performance continues to exist even after the prescription of the action against the other party (Article 6:56).

III. Effects of the Exercise of a Suspension Right

194. If a debtor exercises his right to suspend, he does not perform his obligation, but his non-performance is not a failure in the performance in the sense of Articles 6:74 ff. and 6:265. This means that the other party has no right to claim performance and damages or, in the case of a synallagmatic contract, to set aside the contract. Furthermore, the creditor will, in general, come into creditor's default, which means, among other things, that he will not have the right of suspension on his part (Article 6:54, sub a) and that the debtor may invoke the other consequences of creditor's default (*see supra*, paragraphs 158 ff.).

IV. Synallagmatic Contracts

195. As mentioned before, the Code contains some special provisions with regard to obligations resulting from synallagmatic contracts.

Article 6:262 states that where one of the parties does not perform his obligation, the other party is entitled to suspend performance of his corresponding obligations (paragraph 1). In the event of partial or improper performance, suspension is only allowed to the extent justified by the failure to perform (paragraph 2).

The Code contains in Article 6:263 a special rule in order to protect the party to a bilateral contract who would normally be bound to perform his obligation first. Such party is nevertheless entitled to suspend the performance of his obligation if circumstances have come to his attention after the contract was entered into, giving him good reason to fear that the other party will not perform his corresponding obligations (paragraph 1). In the event that there is good reason to fear that there will be partial or improper performance, suspension is only allowed to the extent justified by the failure to perform (paragraph 2).

In the event of suspension on the basis of Article 6:262 and 6:263, Article 6:54, sub b and c and 6:55 do not apply.

§5. Faultive Behaviour of the Debtor

I. Faultive Behaviour

196. As we have seen, *supra*, paragraph 178, a debtor is responsible for non-performance, which is attributable to him. As mentioned, according to Article 6:75, a failure cannot be attributed to the debtor if the failure 'does not result from his fault and if he cannot be held accountable for it by law, juridical act or common opinion either'. Article 6:75 has already been discussed at some length in paragraphs 164 ff. *supra.* In this paragraph I will confine ourselves to a few extra remarks.

First of all, it should be noted again that not only faulty behaviour of the debtor gives rise to the remedies pointed out in paragraph 177 but also behaviour or events for which the debtor can be held accountable. As we have seen, several legal provisions lay the risk of a certain impediment to perform on the debtor. Furthermore, a juridical act (e.g., the contract) or common opinion may hold the debtor responsible for non-culpable behaviour or for events not resulting from his fault.

Sometimes, it may make a difference, however, whether the debtor is liable on the basis of faulty behaviour or on the basis of the fact that he bears the risk for his non-performance. For example, in case of fault, a causal connection (*see* paragraph 210 *infra*) may be accepted more readily; if there is fault on the part of the creditor, the question of whether there is faulty behaviour on the part of the debtor may influence the apportionment of the damage (*see* paragraph 214 *infra*); the ground for the liability may influence recourse between debtors who are solidarily liable – for example, one debtor has made a fault, and the other has not – (*see* paragraph 215 *infra*); faulty behaviour may prevent the debtor from invoking an exemption clause if this would be contrary to reasonableness and fairness (*see* paragraph 32 *supra* and paragraph 221 *infra*); the ground for the liability may also play a role with regard to the judicial power to reduce damages (*see* paragraph 217 *infra*) and with regard to the determination of maximum liability amounts as referred to in Article 6:110 (*see* paragraph 220 *infra*).

Finally, a remark about the meaning of the term 'fault'. To determine whether a debtor has been acting in a faulty way, first of all, an objective criterion should be used to decide how a prudent debtor should have behaved in the present case. But, taking this into account, the term 'fault' in Article 6:75 has a subjective nature: the question to decide is whether this debtor is to be blamed that he has not behaved as a prudent debtor.

§6. Limitation of Actions

I. Prescription

197. The actions described in paragraph 177 may be limited in several ways. One cause of limitation is prescription, in the sense of the passing of a certain period of time, determined by the law, during which no facts occur on the basis of which it may be concluded that the creditor claims performance or that the debtor admits his debt. After this period of time the debtor may successfully wave aside a claim for performance. The subject of prescription did not play an important role at all under the old Civil Code. Under the new Civil Code, however, it has come to everybody's attention by a constant flow of case law. This change is explained by the fact that under the old law, the usual prescription period used to be thirty years, whereas now it is, for a number of important types of claims, confined to five years.

The Code contains in Article 3:306 a general provision on prescription: unless otherwise provided for by law, rights of action are prescribed on the expiry of twenty years. In a lot of cases, however, the Code provides for a different period of prescription or a different regulation altogether.

Some actions are never prescribed; for example, a partner in a community may at any time demand partition of common property (Article 3:178, paragraph 1). In the field of the law of obligations, however, all actions are subject to prescription.

Prescription does not extinguish the obligation itself, but only the right of action. After prescription, a natural obligation remains (*see* paragraphs 47 ff. *supra*).

The court may not ex officio apply the defence resulting from prescription (Article 3:322, paragraph 1). Prescription only has effect when it is invoked by the debtor.

II. Moment at Which the Prescription Period Begins

198. The general principle is that the prescription period begins to run when performance is exigible. Article 3:307, for example, states that the prescription period of a right of action for the performance of a contractual obligation to give or to do begins to run at the beginning of the day following the one on which immediate performance can be claimed. In general, the day on which immediate performance can be claimed will be the day on which performance is exigible. With regard to obligations not to do, the prescription period only starts to run after the debtor has acted contrary to the contract.

The first day of the prescription period is always the day following the one on which the event due to which the prescription period starts to run has taken place.

III. Special Periods of Prescription

199. As mentioned before, the general prescription period is twenty years. However, with regard to the most important obligations the prescription period is determined at five years. This applies to:

- rights of action to claim the performance of a contractual obligation to give or to do (Article 3:307);
- rights of action for the payment of interests on sums of money, of annuities, dividends, rents and all amounts payable annually or in shorter instalments (Article 3:308);
- a right of action for recovery of things not due (Article 3:309);
- a right of action to compensate for damage or to pay a stipulated penalty (Article 3:310);
- a right to set aside a contract for failure to perform it or a right of action to correct such failure (Article 3:311).

Article 3:307–310 contains specific provisions on the time at which the five-year prescription period starts to run, mostly the moment when the creditor becomes aware of the obligation. Under Article 3:310, for instance, a right of action to compensate for damage is prescribed on the expiry of five years from the day following the one on which the prejudiced person becomes aware of both the damage and the identity of the person responsible therefor. The Supreme Court has ruled that this is a subjective test, which means that the prescription period starts to run when the prejudiced person really, in fact, becomes aware of the damage and the identity of the person responsible and not also when he ought or could have become aware of this.[93] In some cases, however, notably cases where the plaintiff claims damages because of sexual abuse, the plaintiffs are not able to start legal proceedings against the defendant within these five years due to psychological problems. The Supreme Court ruled that in such cases if these mental impairments are to be attributed to the defendant, it will be unacceptable according to standards of reasonableness and fairness to invoke the five-year prescription period as running from the moment the plaintiff was aware of the damage and the person responsible. In such cases, the Supreme Court ruled the plaintiff may invoke the prescription period only when more than five years have passed since these impairments have stopped, preventing the plaintiff from taking action against the defendant.[94] Subsequently, the Supreme Court has brought together its various decisions into the criterion that the prescription period starts to run when the plaintiff is 'effectively capable' of bringing an action against the tortfeasor.[95] Although the plaintiff's incapability to judicially assess the facts and circumstances with regard to the damage and the person responsible does not bar the prescription period from running, the lack of specific (e.g., judicial or medical) knowledge and insight required to assess whether the performance is correct can influence whether or not the plaintiff is effectively capable of bringing a claim, i.e., sufficiently aware of the damage and the person responsible.[96]

Article 3:312 states that rights of action for failure in performance, for payment of legal or conventional interest or for the delivery of fruits are, save interruption or extension, prescribed no later than the rights of action for the performance of the principal obligation or, where the failure is susceptible to correction, no later than the right of action to claim correction of the failure.

Article 3:307 and 3:309–3:311 furthermore all contain a second prescription period of (mostly) twenty years and, in some types of cases, even thirty years, with the effect that in any event, the claim expires twenty/thirty years after the event giving rise to the claim (for instance the event that caused the damage), even when the creditor was not aware of the claim.[97]

This system has been the source of a vast body of case law, especially in asbestos cases, where employees claimed damages from their employers after they developed an asbestos-related disease long after working with asbestos. In such cases it may easily happen that the disease is discovered only after the long prescription term of twenty (or thirty) years has lapsed, which term is not contingent on the plaintiff's knowledge of the damage and the tortfeasor. The result is that the action is prescribed before the plaintiff has been able to defend his rights. This was considered to be so unsatisfactory that the Supreme Court ruled that, depending on the circumstances, it may be unacceptable according to standards of reasonableness and fairness for an employer to ground his defence on the expiry of the prescription

93. HR 6-4-2001, ECLI:NL:HR:2001:AB0900, NJ 2002/383; HR 20-4-2001, ECLI:NL:HR:2001:AB1208, NJ 2002/384.
94. HR 23-10-1998, ECLI:NL:HR:1998:ZC2748, NJ 2000/15; HR 11-10-2002, ECLI:NL:HR:2002:AE4430, NJ 2002/558.
95. HR 31-10-2003, ECLI:NL:PHR:2003:AL8168, NJ 2006/112; HR 4-4-2008, NJ 2008/203. Most cases deal with medical and legal malpractice (HR 9-7-2010, ECLI:NL:HR:2010:BM1688, NJ 2012/194).
96. HR 9-10-2020, ECLI:NL:HR:2020:1603, NJ 2021/187.
97. HR 27-11-2020, ECLI:NL:HR:2020:1887, NJ 2020/437.

period when the employee had fallen ill *after* the prescription period had expired.[98] In most contractual cases, however, the long prescription period of twenty or thirty years will be of minor significance next to the five-year prescription period. Nevertheless, the legislature intervened and added, in 2004, a fifth paragraph to Article 3:310, excluding the twenty-year prescription term in case of bodily injury and death caused by a tort or by breach of contract.

The parties may agree on a different prescription period than the legal one, provided that the contractual period is shorter than the legal period.

IV. Interruption of the Prescription Period: Extension of the Prescription Period

200. Prescription of a right of action shall be interrupted by the institution of action or by any other act of juridical recourse instituted in the required form by the person entitled to do so (Article 3:316, paragraph 1). Prescription of a right of action to claim performance of an obligation shall be interrupted by a written warning or by a written communication in which the creditor unequivocally reserves his right to performance (Article 3:317, paragraph 1). 'Unequivocally' means that the message should be clear enough for the creditor to understand that he should hold on to his evidence, etc., to be able to defend himself against a claim.[99] Prescription of other rights of action shall be interrupted by a written warning followed within six months by an act of interruption as described in Article 3:316 (Article 3:317, paragraph 2). Acknowledgement of the right which a right of action serves to protect shall interrupt the prescription of the right of action against the person who acknowledges the right (Article 3:318).

In general private law, a prescription period is not interrupted by negotiations between the debtor and the creditor.[100] However, invoking prescription by a debtor during negotiations or immediately after breaking-off negotiations may be unacceptable according to standards of reasonableness and fairness.[101]

After the interruption of the prescription, a new prescription period starts to run. In general, the starting time is the day following the day of the interruption (Article 3:319, paragraph 1). The new period is equal to the original one but may not exceed five years. Nevertheless, the prescription shall in no event be complete until the moment when the original period would have expired without interruption (Article 3:319, paragraph 2).

In some cases there is ground for the extension of the prescription period. Article 3:321 briefly sums up the grounds for extension. For example, a cause for extension

98. HR 20-10-2000, ECLI:NL:HR:2000:AA7688, NJ 2001/268. *See* outside the law of damages HR 20-6-2014, ECLI:NL:HR:2014:1492, NJ 2014/335.
99. HR 14-2-1997, ECLI:NL:HR:1997:ZC2274, NJ 1997/244.
100. There exist some special provisions to this effect relating to insurance covering liability for accidents; *see* Art. 10 of the Act on the insurance relating to motor car accidents and Art. 7:942 para. 3.
101. HR 1-2-2002, ECLI:NL:PHR:2002:AD5811, NJ 2002/195; HR 9-4-2010, ECLI:NL:HR:2010:BL3866, NJ 2010/214; HR 26-1-2018, ECLI:NL:HR:2018:111.

exists between spouses not separated from bed and board (sub a) and between registered partners (sub g), between a legal representative and the incapable person whom he represents (sub b) and between legal persons and their directors[102] (sub d).

The legal effect of extension is that where a prescription period would otherwise expire during the existence of a ground of extension or within six months after the cessation of such a ground, the period continues to run for six months from the cessation of such ground (Article 3:320).

V. Lapse

201. Some statutory periods are not meant as periods of prescription but as periods of lapse (‘*déchéance*’). These also have the result that after the period has run, the debtor is prevented from exercising his right. Nevertheless, a statutory period of lapse must be distinguished from prescription. There are several differences:

(a) in case of prescription, the right of action perishes; in case of lapse, the right itself perishes;
(b) the passing of a prescription period only has effects when the prescription is invoked by the interested party, while the passing of a lapse period *ipso iure* causes the extinction of the right. But an exception to this rule may be accepted in cases where the period of lapse is clearly prescribed in the interest of a party (as opposed to the public interest);
(c) a period of lapse normally is not subject to interruption or extension.

Dutch patrimonial law does know some statutory periods of lapse, but this kind of period is more usual in other fields of the law, such as the law of civil procedure or family law, where often short lapse periods are prescribed in the general interest. The periods prescribed, for example, exercising the right to appeal, may be characterized as periods of lapse. In only one part of patrimonial law, transport law, periods of lapse abound. The sting is taken from these by a special statutory provision (Article 8:1701), giving the parties the right to contractually extend such a period.

Periods of lapse can in general not be interrupted or extended. A statutory period of lapse may not be extended by the parties, but they are free to shorten it. If such a stipulation for one reason or another is ineffective (e.g., in case of annulment of the contractual stipulation or in case it would be unacceptable according to standards of reasonableness and fairness to invoke the stipulation), the statutory period resumes its force.

It must be noted that parties may also agree on a period of lapse in order to shorten a statutory period of *prescription.* Such a contractual period of lapse presents certain differences from a statutory period, which cannot be dealt with here.

102. HR 11-9-2020, ECLI:NL:HR:2020:1413, NJ 2021/295.

Chapter 2. Damages and Exemption Clauses

§1. Damages: Introduction

202. The section on damages (Article 6:95–110) applies to all legal obligations to repair damage, including liability arising from non-performance of an obligation (contractual or otherwise), from an unlawful act, and from unjustified enrichment. It does not relate to damages which form the object of contractual provisions, such as liquidated damages and insurance.

The term 'damage' refers to the actual harm that has been caused by, for example, the non-performance of an obligation or an unlawful act.

The damage which must be repaired pursuant to a legal obligation to pay damages consists of patrimonial loss and any other prejudice, the latter to the extent that the law confers a right to damages therefor (Article 6:95). Pursuing that subject, Article 6:106 provides for a provision on moral damage (*see* further *infra*, paragraph 216).

§2. Way of Reparation

203. Damages must in general be paid by paying money. In some cases, however, factual reparation is more natural than the payment of money; for example, a damaged object may be repaired or replaced by the person who caused the damage, or a previous lawful situation may be re-established. For these cases, Article 6:103 states that the judge may award reparation in a form other than the payment of a sum of money. Reparation of damage *in natura* may only be awarded upon the demand of the victim. It is at the discretion of the court to grant it. Under the old Code, the Supreme Court has allowed reparation other than by paying money only in cases of unlawful acts. Apart from factual acts, a debtor may also be ordered to perform a juridical act, such as the transfer of ownership of property or the taking-up of negotiations. In a 1967 landmark case, the defendant accepted a house as a gift from a very old lady who was under his influence while knowing that the plaintiff had a right to buy the house. This was judged to be an unlawful act. As a remedy, the court ordered the defendant to transfer the house to the plaintiff for a reasonable price.[103]

§3. Sustained Loss and Lost Profits

204. Patrimonial damage comprises both the loss incurred by the creditor and the profit sustained (Article 6:96, paragraph 1). Article 6:69, paragraph 2, lists some categories of costs that may be claimed as patrimonial damage but which could be open to doubt without legal provision:

---

103. HR 17-11-1967, ECLI:NL:HR:1967:AC4789, NJ 1968/42. Cf. HR 14-1-2011, ECLI:NL:HR:2011:BO3521, NJ 2012/88.

(a) reasonable costs to prevent or mitigate damage which could be expected as a result of the event giving rise to liability. From Article 6:101 it follows that the victim is obliged to take measures to prevent or mitigate the damage. Article 6:96, paragraph 2, sub a, guarantees that the victim may claim the costs of these measures – provided that they are reasonable – from the person who is liable;
(b) reasonable costs incurred in assessing damage and liability;
(c) reasonable costs incurred in obtaining extrajudicial payment.

In a controversial judgment, the Supreme Court held that the costs of raising a child that was born because the sterilization of the mother was conducted inadequately can be recovered as patrimonial loss. Even the loss of earnings of the mother, if she reasonably chooses not to work for a while because of the child, can be recovered as such.[104]

§4. Determination of Damages

205. With regard to the determination of the extent of the damage that must be repaired, the basic principle is that the victim must be placed as much as possible in the same situation as the one he would have been in if the event that caused the damage had not taken place. From this principle it follows that only the damage actually suffered must be repaired and that this damage must be fully repaired.

There are exceptions to both rules. An exception to the first rule is the calculation of the damage according to the abstract method. This is a method of assessing damages according to objective criteria, that is, irrespective of whether the plaintiff in the case at hand really suffered these damages. Another exception to the first rule is found in Article 6:104: if a person who is liable to another has derived profit from the fact for which he is liable, the court may assess the damage at the amount of such profit or a part thereof. An exception to the second rule is the reduction of the obligation to pay damages by the judge on the grounds of reasonableness. All these exceptions will be discussed *infra* in more detail.

The court shall assess the damage in a manner most appropriate to its nature. Where the extent of the damage cannot be determined precisely, it is estimated (Article 6:97).

§5. Abstract Method

206. With regard to some cases, the Supreme Court has ruled that the extent of the damages should be determined according to objective criteria (the so-called abstract method of calculation). If the abstract method is applied, the judge does not take into account the special and subjective circumstances of the case and the victim, but he calculates the damages which a victim in a similar position as the present debtor would generally suffer as a result of the failure in the performance or the unlawful act in question. This method of calculation was, for example, used in a

104. HR 21-2-1997, ECLI:NL:HR:1997:ZC2286, NJ 1999/145.

case of non-performance of an obligation to deliver goods with a market price. The damage was calculated on the basis of difference between the purchase price and the market price at the moment when the default of the seller commenced. The fact that the buyer had already resold the goods for a price below the market price was not taken into account. This rule on the method of calculation is codified in Article 7:36 and 7:38 (*see infra*, paragraph 260).

The most important cases in which the abstract method was used until now were the reparation of damages caused by the damaging of a thing (e.g., the owner of a car unlawfully damaged is entitled to compensation for the costs of repair, objectively calculated, irrespective of actual repair) or by failure in the performance of a contract of sale, consisting in non-delivery of goods or delivery of inferior goods (*see also infra*, paragraph 260). It certainly isn't so, however, that the court always awards a plaintiff's request for abstract damages. In a case, for instance, where a lessor asked for abstract damages (the costs of repair) because the lessee had not complied with his duty to abandon the rented space in the same state as he rented it, these abstract damages were not awarded because the lessor did not suffer any actual damages because he was going to thoroughly renovate the object anyway.[105]

This means that the use of the abstract method must not be seen as a rule of law but more as a practical help that may be used in some cases. In general, the outcome of the abstract method is seen as a minimum amount. If the plaintiff can prove that his actual damage surpasses the damage determined according to the abstract method, he may claim the damage he actually suffered.

§6. Benefit Enjoyed by the Liable Person

207. The benefit that the liable person has enjoyed as a result of his failure in the performance or unlawful act is not a part of the damage suffered by the victim. Nevertheless, in some cases, this benefit may be claimed by the victim. Article 6:104 – already shortly mentioned above – states that if a person who is liable towards another on the basis of an unlawful act or a failure in the performance of an obligation has derived profit from that act or failure, the judge may evaluate the damage, upon the demand of this other person, according to the amount of that profit or part thereof. For this rule to apply it is required that the victim proves that he has suffered any damage, but he need not prove its extent.[106] The rule will have its main importance in the field of violations of rights of intellectual property and related areas.

§7. Future Damages

208. The victim may claim reparation not only for the damage he has already suffered but also for the damage he will suffer in the future as a result of the failure

105. HR 6-6-1997, ECLI:NL:HR:1997:ZC2387, NJ 1997/612.
106. HR 24-12-1993, ECLI:NL:HR:1993:ZC1202, NJ 1995/421; HR 18-6-2010, ECLI:NL:HR:2010:BM0893, NJ 2015/32.

in the performance of an obligation or an unlawful act. This future damage must be assessed on the basis of what may reasonably be expected. The court may wholly or partially postpone the assessment of damage which has not yet occurred; it may also immediately assess future damage after an evaluation of the probabilities. In the latter case, the court may order the debtor either to pay a lump sum or to make periodic instalment payments, accompanied or not by an obligation to provide security (Article 6:105, paragraph 1). The court may determine in its judgment that the periodic instalment payments can be modified in case of unforeseen circumstances (Article 6:105, paragraph 2).

§8. Legal Interest

209. The debtor is *ipso iure* obliged to pay legal interest on the amount to be paid by way of reparation of damages if the liability is based on failure in the performance of an obligation or if it is based on an unlawful act (Article 6:119 *jo* 6:83, sub b; *see* paragraph 183 above).

§9. Causal Relation

210. The obligation to pay compensation naturally presupposes that the failure in the performance or the unlawful act is the cause of the damage suffered by the plaintiff. This normally presupposes that the failure or the unlawful act is the '*condicio sine qua non*' of the damage; that is to say that without it, the damage would not have occurred. But this test in itself is not sufficient; there must be an additional criterion. Otherwise, too broad a range of consequences of a certain event (a certain breach of contract or unlawful act) would be listed as consequences for which the debtor should pay damages. A classic example to illustrate this is found in the case of the old lady who sees a car accident caused by someone ignoring a traffic light. At seeing this, she suffers a heart attack. In such a case, it is generally accepted the person who ignored the traffic light is not liable for the damages the old lady suffers because of her heart attack. This, however, cannot be explained by the '*condicio sine qua non*' principle since, without the negligence of the driver, she would not have had the attack. How to account for this? On this point in Dutch law an interesting development has taken place. Between 1927 and 1970, the Supreme Court adhered to the theory of adequate causation. Under this theory, the court would construe Articles 1283 and 1284 of the old Code in such a way as to require that the debtor could reasonably foresee the damage (including its extent) at the time of the conclusion of the contract or, in the case of wilful breach, at the time of the breach. The same test used to be applied with regard to unlawful acts, in which case, of course, only the time when the unlawful act was committed could be decisive. This opinion was followed by the draft Code (published in 1961).

In the 1960s, a new current in legal doctrine criticized the test of foreseeability, contending that the degree of probability required would vary according to the nature of the liability and the nature of the damage, so that one should rather concentrate upon those factors which make it reasonable (or not reasonable) to attribute the damage to the event for which the defendant is responsible, as its cause.

In 1970, the Supreme Court departed from the formula of foreseeability for the first time, apparently under the influence of the new trend, but without formulating a new criterion in general terms.[107] The present Code accepting this doctrine provides in Article 6:98:

> Reparation of damage can only be claimed for damage which is related to the event giving rise to the liability of the debtor in such a way that, taking into account the nature of the liability and of the damage, it can be attributed to him as a result of such event.

With regard to the question of whether this attribution should or should not take place, all circumstances of the case should be taken into account. Article 6:98 already mentions the nature of the liability (e.g., legal or contractual liability, fault or risk liability, liability based on traffic accidents, professional malpractice, etc.) and the nature of the damage (e.g., injury or damage of things, patrimonial damage or moral damage, easily foreseeable damage or damage that could hardly be expected, etc.).

Circumstances outside these two categories may also play a part, for example, the gravity of the unlawfulness and the fault, the fact that the liable person has done the victim a favour, the question of who has taken out insurance, etc.

In this doctrine, foreseeability remains a factor of importance. In this respect, the knowledge and experience the liable person had – or, according to the standards of a normally developed person, should have had – at the time of the failure in the performance or the unlawful act should be taken into account. The degree of probability which is required depends on the circumstances of the case.

The practical effect of this doctrine seems to be a broad liability for physical injuries, especially in case of traffic and other accidents.[108] In cases of mere patrimonial damage, however, the concept of foreseeability continues to play an important part in legal practice.

Not only the fact that the damage has occurred but also the kind of damage and the extent of the damage should be causally related to the event in the sense that they may be reasonably attributed to the debtor who is liable for the event.

In a controversial series of recent cases, the Supreme Court has further refined the concept of causality by introducing the so-called reversal rule, which is used to alleviate the plaintiff's burden of proof on the point of the causal relationship between the damage and the event for which the defendant is liable. The burden of proof of the causal relationship between the damage and the fact which – allegedly – caused it usually lies with the plaintiff. This has proven to be a serious impediment to success. According to the 'reversal rule', when someone violates a norm that is meant to prevent a specific kind of damage and the plaintiff proves that this

107. HR 20-3-1970, ECLI:NL:HR:1970:AC5007, NJ 1970/251.
108. HR 20-9-2019, ECLI:NL:HR:2019:1409, NJ 2020/233.

kind of damage occurred, a causal relationship between the conduct and the damage is presumed. The burden of proof that the damage was not caused by his conduct then lies with the defendant.[109]

Another way of alleviating the plaintiff's burden of proof is awarding damages in proportion to the chance that the defendant's behaviour has caused the plaintiff's damage. This approach has been adopted in an asbestos case, where it was uncertain whether the damage (lung cancer) was caused by the employer's negligence in taking necessary precautions to protect the employees or by an employee's smoking habit.[110]

§10. More Than One Cause

211. The decision that the damage is related to an event does not mean that the event is the only cause of the damage. To determine liability, it is sufficient that the event is a relevant cause, that is to say, meets the criteria of Article 6:98. For example, if a bicycle left unguarded by the keeper is stolen or two persons simultaneously but independently set a house on fire, the keeper and the thief respectively and the two arsonists are all fully liable.[111] The Supreme Court has made it unequivocally clear that also in the case of an 'overtaking cause', that is, where the damage for which someone is liable would have been caused by a later event all the same, full liability for the liable person remains, except if the overtaking cause would have been attributable to the person suffering the damage. For instance, in a case where a victim of a car accident suffers loss of income for which the person who caused the accident is liable, this liability ceased when the victim suffered an accident-unrelated heart attack, which would have caused his incapacity to work all the same.[112] The heart attack is an overtaking cause attributable to the victim. On the other hand, in a case where a municipality caused loss of income of a snack bar holder by negligently causing the end of his business, its liability did not end when a few boys set the building on fire where the snack bar used to be, even though this would have caused the end of his business all the same. The act of the boys was not attributed to the snack bar holder.[113]

Sometimes, the damage may be a result of two or more events, but it is not clear which event actually caused the damage. For example, two producers introduce a medicine on the market which contains harmful material; a patient takes a capsule of this medicine, which results in damage; the patient is not able to prove which manufacturer produced the capsule that caused the damage.[114] Article 6:99 states that where the damage may have resulted from two or more events, for each of

---

109. HR 29-11-2002, ECLI:NL:HR:2002:AE7345, NJ 2004/304; HR 7-12-2007, ECLI:NL:HR:2007:BB3670, NJ 2007/644; HR 10-1-2020, ECLI:NL:HR:2020:27, NJ 2020/45.
110. HR 31-3-2006, ECLI:NL:HR:2006:AU6092 NJ 2011/250.
111. *See infra*, para. 215 on the question of how the contribution among the liable persons themselves must be determined.
112. HR 2-2-1990, ECLI:NL:HR:1990:AB7897, NJ 1991/292.
113. HR 7-12-2001, ECLI:NL:HR:2001:AB2795, NJ 2002/576.
114. HR 9-10-1992, ECLI:NL:HR:1992:ZC0706, NJ 1994/535. *See also* HR 18-12-2009, ECLI:NL:HR:2009:BK0873, NJ 2012/614.

which a different person is liable, and where it has been established that the damage has arisen from at least one of these events, the obligation to repair the damage falls upon each of such persons, unless one proves that the damage is not the result of an event for which he is liable. This article gives a rule of evidence. It lays the burden of proof on the possible liable persons, whereas, in general, the burden of proof would rest on the victim.

§11. Diminution of the Amount of the Damage: Benefit, Contribution by Victim and Judicial Reduction

212. The amount of the damage, calculated by the methods discussed above, may be diminished because of three reasons:

(1) benefits caused by the event are deducted from the total amount;
(2) the obligation to repair damage is reduced when circumstances imputable to the victim have contributed to the damage;
(3) the court may reduce the obligation to repair damage if reasonableness so requires.

The reasons in sub 1 and 2 will first be discussed. The reason in sub 3 will be dealt with in paragraph 219 *infra.*

§12. Benefit

213. Article 6:100 states that where one and the same event has resulted in both loss and benefit for the person who suffered it, the benefit must, to the extent that this is reasonable, be taken into account in assessing the reparation of the damage to be made.

Examples of such benefits are the replacement of an old thing by a new thing, a tax advantage and some insurance payments. Non-pecuniary (moral) benefits may also be taken into account, but only in the assessment of non-pecuniary (moral) damage (*see infra*, paragraph 216).[115]

Whether the event is the *causa* of the benefit must be answered by applying the same criteria for the determination of a causal relation as discussed above.[116]

§13. Victim's Contribution to Damage

214. Article 6:101 deals with the apportionment between the liable person and the victim in case the latter contributes to the damage by his own negligence or otherwise.

115. HR 21-2-1997, ECLI:NL:HR:1997:ZC2286, NJ 1999/145.
116. HR 8-7-2016, ECLI:NL:HR:2016:1483, NJ 2017/262. *See* on the benefit the liable person has enjoyed as a result of his failure in the performance *supra*, para. 207 on Art. 6:104.

Where circumstances which can be attributed to the person suffering the loss have contributed to the damage, the obligation to repair the damage is reduced by apportioning the damage between the person suffering the loss and the person who must repair the damage in proportion to the degree in which the circumstances which can be attributed to each of them have contributed to the damage. However, a different apportionment shall be made, or the obligation to repair the damage shall be extinguished in its entirety or maintained if it is fair to do so on account of varying degrees of seriousness of the faults committed or any other circumstances of the case (Article 6:101, paragraph 1).

The main rule of this provision is apportionment according to causality, not according to fault. A criterion based on mere fault would not suffice in cases where either the liability of the defendant is based on risk (e.g., the liability of the debtor for acts of the persons mentioned in Article 6:76) or where it is reasonable to attribute certain circumstances to the injured party which are not due to his fault (e.g., the case that an employer suffers damage because of an accident caused both by his employee and by a third party; *see also* Article 6:101, paragraph 2).

The second branch of this rule provides for an exception to the main rule if another way of apportionment is required by the standards of reasonableness. One of the most important applications of this exception in the case law of the Supreme Court is the disregard of the faults of children under 14 years of age who are injured in motorcar accidents.[117]

Article 6:101 does not only refer to circumstances that contribute to the occurrence of damage but also to circumstances that affect the amount of the damage (e.g., the injury suffered by the driver of a motorcar is higher because he did not wear his safety belt).

As mentioned before, Article 6:101 includes the rule that the victim is obliged to reduce the damage as much as is reasonably possible. If he is negligent in taking the necessary measures, the damage caused by his negligence will, in general, be deducted from the amount of the damage that has to be paid by the debtor. As we have seen, *supra*, in paragraph 204, the (reasonable) costs the victim has made to take measures may be claimed as damages.

§14. Liability of Two or More Persons

215. Two or more persons who are each obliged to repair the same damage are solidarily liable (Article 6:102, paragraph 1). An example in the field of contractual liability is the damaging of a thing by two debtors who are obliged to take care of the thing. The debtor who has paid for the damage may take recourse against the other persons; the damage is apportioned among them by applying Article 6:101 *mutatis mutandis* (Article 6:102, paragraph 1, second branch).

---

117. HR 1-6-1990, ECLI:NL:PHR:1990:AB7631, NJ 1991/720.

§15. Moral Damage

216. As was mentioned above, not only patrimonial damage but also moral (non-pecuniary) damage may be claimed, although moral damage can only be claimed to the rather limited extent authorized by law (Article 6:95). Because of the fact that the right to reparation of moral damage has a personal character, it is only to a limited extent capable of transfer or seizure. Article 6:95, paragraph 2 states that the right to moral damages cannot be transmitted and seized unless agreed upon by contract or unless an action for such damages has been instituted. For transmission by general title, it is sufficient that the person entitled has notified the other party that he claims damages. The relevant provision is Article 6:106, paragraph 1. For any prejudice not comprising patrimonial damage, the person suffering the loss has the right to damages to be fairly assessed:

(a) if the person liable intended to (specifically)[118] cause such prejudice. An extreme case is that of a father killing his 7-year-old child in order to cause moral damages to his wife, who wants to divorce him;[119]
(b) if the person suffering the loss sustained physical injury, if his honour or reputation has been impugned or if his person has been otherwise afflicted. Affliction of someone's person includes *inter alia* a serious infringement of his privacy;[120]
(c) if the prejudice consists of the impugnment of the memory of a deceased person inflicted upon his spouse where the spouses were not separated from bed and board, upon his registered partner or upon a blood relative of the deceased to the second degree, provided that impugnment occurred in a manner which would have given the deceased, had he still been alive, the right to damages for injury to his honour or reputation.

The most important of these possibilities is the possibility under b. Under the old Code, which was silent on the subject, the right to moral damages in case of bodily injury had been accepted by the Supreme Court in a famous decision of 1943,[121] in which arguments were drawn from legal history and from the law existing in neighbouring countries. Whereas the scope of application of the decision has long been held as being confined to unlawful acts, in the system of the present Code, the rule of Article 6:106 is clearly also applicable to cases of breach of contract. However, it should be mentioned that Dutch courts have adopted a rather restrictive course in assessing moral damages, both as regards their existence and their amount.

It is generally felt in Dutch society that the law is too strict in creating rights to moral damages. One particular example of this strictness was the fact that near relatives (e.g., parents) were not entitled to moral damages for the death of a beloved (e.g., a child)[122] caused by someone who is liable therefor. Following the example

118. HR 26-5-2020, ECLI:NL:HR:2020:868, NJ 2020/231.
119. HR 26-10-2001, ECLI:NL:HR:2001:AB2775, NJ 2002/216.
120. HR 15-3-2019, ECLI:NL:HR:2019:376, NJ 2019/162.
121. HR 21-5-1943, ECLI:NL:HR:1943:21, NJ 1943/455.
122. *See* for example HR 8-9-2000, ECLI:NL:HR:2000:AA7041, NJ 2000/734.

of English law, Parliament has worked on an act which grants certain types of relatives a fixed amount of moral damages in the case of such deaths. In the meantime, the Supreme Court had to decide several cases in which the plaintiff tried the boundaries of the possibilities. In one particularly gruesome case, for instance, the Supreme Court accepted the possibility of awarding 'shock damage' to a mother who suffered mental injury because of the awful way in which she was confronted with the body of her 5-year-old daughter, killed in a car accident.[123] In another case, the Supreme Court accepted the possibility that an injured person who is lying in a coma is awarded moral damages.[124] On 1 January 2019, the act on (fixed amounts of) moral damages for certain relatives (*Stb.* 2018, 132) came into being and adjusted Article 6:107 and 6:108.

§16. Physical (or Mental) Injury and Death

217. Article 6:107 and 6:108 contain special provisions on the kind of damages which may be awarded in case of acts causing physical (or mental) injury or death and on the persons who may claim them.

In principle, in cases of injury, only the injured person can claim reparation for all physical damages (including costs of medical care and loss of income) and, as we have seen, for his moral damages. Article 6:107 allows one exception to this rule in favour of third persons who have defrayed certain costs because of the injury of the victim. Article 6:107, paragraph 1 sub a, states that where a person suffers physical or mental injury as a result of an event for which another person is liable, that other person must not only compensate the loss of the injured person himself but also defray the costs which a third person, otherwise than pursuant to insurance, has incurred for the benefit of the injured, and which the latter, had he incurred them himself, would have been able to claim from that other person. The Supreme Court has judged that this provision includes in principle the loss incurred by a mother who gives up her job to look after her injured child, at least to the extent that she would otherwise have been compelled to hire the services of somebody else to look after the child.[125] Article 6:107a contains a provision on the right of the injured's employer to claim the sickness allowance he paid the victim (when the victim was entitled to such an allowance). The employer's claim to damages is doubly limited to the amount of money he paid the victim and to the amount of money, the victim could have claimed in the hypothetical situation that he would not have received his employer's sickness allowance.

123. HR 22-2-2002, ECLI:NL:HR:2002:AD5356, NJ 2002/240. *See* on this type of damages also HR 28-6-2022, ECLI:NL:HR:2022:958, NJ 2023/285.

124. HR 20-9-2002, ECLI:NL:HR:2002:AE2149, NJ 2004/112. This used to be quite controversial because of the reasoning that a person who is in a coma is not aware of his situation, while moral damages are meant to ease the (mental) pain caused by being aware of one's loss or injury. The importance of this case should not be overestimated however, because of the rather particular circumstances of the case (the victim had been in a quite conscious state of mind for a while, in which he presumably had been aware of the state he was in).

125. HR 28-5-1999, ECLI:NL:HR:1999:ZC2912, NJ 1999/564.

Article 6:107, paragraph 1 sub b obliges the liable person to compensate an amount of damages determined by a Regulation not relating to patrimonial loss incurred by the close relatives of the injured party. Article 6:107, paragraph 2 defines which close relatives are entitled to such damages, for example, the spouse, a parent or a child.[126]

The defendant may raise the same defences against the third person as he would have had against the injured person (Article 6:107, paragraph 5).

§17. Rights of Third Persons in Case of Death

218. The next provision, Article 6:108, specifies who may claim compensation and what type of loss may be claimed in the case of a death for which another person is liable. As is the case with physical harm, the rights of third persons to claim compensation because of the death of, for example, a relative, were quite restricted, but as of 1 January 2019, close relatives of the deceased are entitled to (fixed) amounts of moral damages. Article 6:108, paragraph 1 states that the liable person must compensate the loss from deprivation of support:

(a) to the spouse where the spouses were not separated from bed and board, the registered partner and the minor children of the deceased, at least up to the amount of the maintenance to which they are entitled by law;
(b) to other relatives by blood or marriage of the deceased, provided that, at the time of his death, the deceased wholly or partly maintained them or was obliged to do so by court order;
(c) to the persons who, before the event giving rise to liability, lived with the deceased as his family and were wholly or largely maintained by the deceased, to the extent that it can be assumed that the situation would have continued had the death not occurred and that these persons cannot reasonably provide adequately for their own maintenance;
(d) to the person who lived together with the deceased as a family and to whose maintenance the deceased contributed by attending to the common household, to the extent that such person suffers loss because, after the death, other arrangements must be made to provide for the household.

Article 6:108, paragraph 1 contains an enumeration of the restricted group of persons who can bring an action. There is also a restriction concerning the nature of the damages suffered: only the loss of support may be compensated. Furthermore, as to the other relatives and members of the household of the deceased, there is a condition that the plaintiff was already supported by the victim during his lifetime.

126. Under the old Art. 6:107, para. 1 (and on the basis of Art. 6:106) a third person was not entitled to reparation of moral damage which the injury of the victim had caused him; *see* para. 216 for the developments prior to this legislative addition granting fixed amounts of damages to close relatives.

There is no right to compensation for other pecuniary loss caused by the death, like costs of a notary or mourning costs;[127] only funeral expenses must be compensated (Article 6:108, paragraph 2). Article 6:108, paragraphs 3 and 4 oblige the liable person to compensate an amount of damages determined by a Regulation not relating to patrimonial loss incurred by the close relatives of the deceased. The restricted group of close relatives entitled to moral damages incurred as a result of the death of a loved one is identical to the persons entitled, pursuant to Article 6:107, paragraph 1 sub b and paragraph 2, to moral damages which the injury of a loved one had caused them; Article 6:108, paragraph 6 states that a person is not entitled to compensation referred to in Article 6:108, paragraph 3 to the extent that this person has already received compensation for the same event based upon Article 6:107, paragraph 1 sub b. In that way, in a case where a loved one eventually dies of his injuries, a close relative is entitled to the fixed amount of moral damages for the death of his loved one minus the fixed amount he already received on the basis of Article 6:107, paragraph 1 sub b as a compensation for the moral damages which the injuries of his loved one had caused him.

The person against whom a claim for damages is made has the same defences as he would have had against the deceased (Article 6:108, paragraph 5). This means that the liable person may invoke an exemption clause (e.g., in transport conditions) that was contractually binding for the deceased.[128]

§18. Judicial Reduction

219. The section on legal obligations to repair damage closes with two articles of particular significance. Article 6:109 was already briefly mentioned above. The article states in paragraph 1 that the court may reduce a legal obligation to pay damages if a full award of damages would lead to clearly unacceptable results in the given circumstances, including the nature of the liability and the juridical relationship between the parties and their financial resources.

One of the grounds for the introduction of a general judicial power to reduce a legal obligation to pay damages was the extension of the cases of risk liability in the law of torts, which cannot be discussed here. The nature of the liability is therefore one of the factors to be considered by the judge. Another factor is the nature of the juridical relationship between the parties, especially the contract. Social inequality of the parties, the proportion between prestation and counter-prestation, etc., may play a part in that respect. The third factor mentioned in Article 6:109, paragraph 1, is the financial resources of the parties. The financial resources of the debtor may be a relevant factor, although this circumstance must always be weighed against the

127. HR 28-5-2019, ECLI:NL:HR:2019:829, NJ 2019/359.

128. In this respect Art. 6:108, para. 5, constitutes a breach with the old law. Under old law the Supreme Court ruled that the right to claim compensation for loss of support caused by the death of a person is not a right that once belonged to the deceased person but a right that immediately arises on behalf of the surviving relative, which meant, according to the Court, that the deceased was not entitled to dispose of this right. Therefore the liable transporter could not invoke his exemption clause against the aggrieved relative; *see* HR 22-12-1950, ECLI:NL:HR:1951:222, NJ 1951/222.

other circumstances of the case, such as the financial situation of the victim (including the question of whether the damage on his part is covered by insurance) and the gravity of the fault.

The list of Article 6:109, paragraph 1, is enunciative. Other relevant factors may be the fact that disinterested help was given, the existence of an obligation to take risks pursuant to an employment contract, the fact that the liable person has himself suffered considerable damage, the gravity of the fault of the liable person, the nature of the damage, etc.

One should realize, however, that reduction of damages should be awarded in only those cases where a full award of damages would lead to *clearly unacceptable* results. The Supreme Court has judged that courts should, therefore, be reluctant to grant such reduction.[129]

Any stipulation in breach of paragraph 1 is null and void (Article 6:109, paragraph 3). The reduction may not be made if it reduces the amount below that for which the debtor has covered his liability by insurance or was obliged to do so (Article 6:109, paragraph 2).

§19. Maximum Liability Amounts

220. Finally, Article 6:110 states that in order that liability which may arise from loss does not exceed that which can reasonably be covered by insurance, a Regulation may set limits on such liability. Separate amounts may be determined, *inter alia*, by reference to the nature of the event and of the loss and the grounds of liability. No Regulation on the basis of this article has come into existence as yet (2024).

The Code contains many forms of contractual and non-contractual risk liability. The general opinion is that especially non-contractual risk liability is only justified if it can be insured. Article 6:110 makes it possible to ensure that liabilities may be covered by insurance, although at present, an exception to this principle is accepted where environmental liability is concerned. The provision of Article 6:110 is not restricted to non-contractual liability nor to risk liability. An example of a case in which limitation of a contractual liability may be justified may be found in the field of transportation law in which contractual limitations are common practice already.

§20. Exemption Clauses

221. See on exemption clauses, *supra*, paragraph 114. Furthermore it must be noted that – apart from the provisions on exemption clauses in general conditions – it may be unacceptable according to standards of reasonableness and fairness to invoke an exemption clause. Whether this is a fact will depend on the circumstances of the case. Relevant circumstances in that respect may, among other things, be the gravity of the fault of the debtor, the nature and importance of the interests involved, the nature and object of the contract, the way the exemption clause was entered into, the degree to which the other party was aware of the meaning of the

129. HR 28-5-1999, ECLI:NL:HR:1999:ZC2913, NJ 1999/510.

clause, the (dis)proportion between the exemption and the damage suffered, the degree of professionalism of the parties and the relations between them.

If the exemption clause has been inserted into the contract as a result of undue influence, Article 3:44, paragraph 4 applies, *see* paragraph 88 *supra.*

Chapter 3. Restitution

222. See on the subject of restitution, paragraph 190 *supra* on the effects of setting aside.

Part VII. Special Topics

Introduction

223. As I discussed in paragraph 22, *supra*, part of the codification process of the present Civil Code is a Book on special contracts, Book 7. The special contracts to be discussed *infra* are enacted in Book 7. Book 7 is filling up gradually. Some topics, like the sale of goods, have been part of it from the beginning, January 1992. Other topics have been added later, such as the employment contract (1997), donation (2003), lease (2003), lease of land (2007), insurance (2006), consumer credit contracts (2011) and loan agreements (2017). Some other topics are expected to be added later, such as the contract of partnership and bills of exchange and cheques.

Not all special contracts of Book 7 will be discussed here, and if so, only in general. I will refrain from discussing the employment contract, for instance, although the provisions on this type of contract form a substantial part of Book 7 (Article 7:610–749). Neither will I discuss the travel contract (Articles 500–513d). An important special contract in Book 7 is the contract of services ('a contract whereby one party, the provider of services, binds himself towards the other, the client, to perform, otherwise than on the basis of a contract of employment, work consisting of something other than the creation of a work of a tangible nature, the safekeeping of things, the publication of work, or the carriage or transportation of persons or things', Article 7:400). The Code specifies quite a number of different types of contracts for services, of which only the commercial agency contract will be discussed. Other types are mandates (Article 7:414–424) and contracts in respect of medical treatment (Article 7:446–499).

Chapter 1. Agency

§1. Definition

224. The regulation on agency, as adapted to Directive 86/653/EC on independent agents, has been inserted in Title 7 of Book 7 of the Civil Code. The 'agency contract' is defined in Article 7:428:

> A commercial agency contract is a contract whereby one party, the principal, instructs the other party, the commercial agent, and whereby the latter binds himself, for a fixed or indeterminate term and for remuneration, to act as an intermediary in the conclusion of contracts, and, as the case may be, to enter into such contracts in the name and for the account of the principal, without being his servant.

In order to be an agent in the sense of Article 7:428, an agent must be an independent intermediary. There is no employee-employer relationship between him and his principal. There must be a steady relationship between the principal and agent; incidental mediation is not enough to constitute an agency contract.

Normally, the agent does not act in his own name but in the name, to the expense and at the risk of his principal. This means that the contract concluded with the third party is binding for the principal, not for the agent. 'In the name of' the principal means that the agent must disclose to the third party that he is acting for a principal. Only in that case, Dutch law accepts the effects of what in continental systems is called 'representation': binding a person on whose behalf one is concluding a legal act. Normally, it is also necessary that the agent is authorized to act in the name of a principal. However, it is not entirely excluded that a principal is bound by a contract which was concluded in his name by an unauthorized person, in particular when the third party in good faith was led to believe by the pseudo-principal that the agent was authorized to act in his name. The doctrine of representation is set out, not in the law of contract but in a separate title in Book 3 (Title 3.3, Article 3:60–79) following Title (3.2) on the law relating to legal acts in general (*see* on Title 3.2 paragraph 36 above). The reason is that the authority to act on behalf of a principal is granted by a separate (unilateral) legal act, which is often combined with a contract (e.g., a contract of mandate, a contract of employment, a contract of commercial agency, etc.), but is not confined to contractual relationships.

The object of the contract can be both goods and services. In that way, the Dutch regulation deviates from the Directive as the latter only applies to agents who deal with goods.

There are no formal requirements for an agency contract. However, each of the parties is obliged to provide the other party, at his request, with a signed document that contains the then-applicable text of the agency contract (Article 7:428, paragraph 3). There are two exceptions to the rule that no formality is required: the stipulation of '*delcredere*' (Article 7:429; *see* on *delcredere* further *infra*, paragraph 225) and stipulations that restrict the liberty of the agent to work after the end of the agency contract (competition clauses; Article 7:443) are only valid if they have been put in writing.

If a contract meets the definition of Article 7:428, Article 7:428–445 are applicable (with the exception of agency contracts governed by the Insurance Mediation Act). The main goal of these articles is to protect the agent in his relationship with the principal. Most articles can therefore not be derogated from (Article 7:445).

§2. Obligations of the Agent

225. The agent must look after the principal's interest with the requisite care and comply with his reasonable instructions. He is obliged to give the principal all the necessary information and, more especially, to notify him forthwith of the contracts in which he has acted as an intermediary or which he has concluded for the principal. This follows from Article 7:401–403 in the general section of contracts concerning activities undertaken by one party on behalf of another.

Article 7:429 concerns the stipulation of *delcredere.* In general, the risk that third persons fail in the performance of obligations resulting from contracts concluded through or by the agent does not lie with the agent but with the principal (unless the agent is to be blamed for the choice of the third person). The agent can, however, make himself liable in writing for such obligations by consenting to a so-called condition of *delcredere.*

By making the condition of *delcredere*, the agent may stipulate a higher commission. Unless otherwise agreed in writing, the commercial agent, under a *delcredere* condition, shall only be liable for the solvency of the third party. This means that the agent is only liable in case of non-payment or late payment of the third party, and not in case of failure in obligations other than the obligation to pay in due time. He cannot make himself liable for any amount exceeding the commission agreed on unless the condition relates to a specified contract or to contracts which he concludes himself in the name of the principal. In the latter case, the court may moderate the amount for which the agent is liable if there is an obvious disproportion between the risk undertaken by the agent and the commission agreed on. All circumstances shall be taken into account, especially the way in which the agent has looked after the interest of the principal.

The Directive does not contain provisions on the condition of *delcredere.* Article 7:429 therefore did not have to be adapted.

§3. Obligations of the Principal: General Obligations

226. Article 7:430, paragraph 1 states that the principal must do all that is necessary on his part under the given circumstances to enable the agent to do his work. This general duty is elaborated in paragraph 2: the principal must put at the disposal of the agent the necessary documentation and information. Furthermore, he must warn the agent if he foresees that contracts will or may be concluded in a considerably lesser degree than the agent was entitled to expect, and he must notify the agent within a reasonable period of his acceptance or refusal or of the non-performance of a contract solicited by the agent (paragraphs 3 and 4).

§4. Commission

227. The most important obligation of the principal is the obligation to pay commission. The main rule is found in Article 7:431. The agent is entitled to commission for the contracts entered into throughout the duration of the commercial agency contract:

(a) if the contract has been entered into through his intervention;
(b) if the contract has been entered into with a person solicited earlier for a similar contract;
(c) if the contract has been entered into with a person who belongs to the clientele assigned to the commercial agent or who is established in the territory assigned to him unless it has been expressly agreed that the commercial agent has no exclusivity to that clientele or in that territory.

Article 7:431, paragraph 1, sub c, creates an assumption of exclusive rights when the agent has been allotted a certain clientele or a certain territory. If the principal does not want the agent to have such exclusive rights, this must be expressly stipulated.

The second paragraph of Article 7:431 states that the agent is entitled to commission for the preparation of contracts entered into after the commercial agency contract has ended: (a) if these contracts are principally due to activities performed by him during the course of the commercial agency contract and if they have been entered into within a reasonable period following the termination of that contract; or (b) if the agent or the principal, pursuant to the conditions specified in the first paragraph, has received the order from the third person before the termination of the commercial agency contract.

The agent is entitled to the commission agreed on. Failing a stipulation on commission, he is entitled to the customary or – if no customs apply – a reasonable commission.

The right to commission exists as soon as the contract with the third party has been entered into (Article 7:426). This is earlier – and therefore considered more favourable for the agent – than the minimum standard of the Directive where the right to commission is linked to the execution of the contract. An order sent by the agent to the principal is – as far as the right to commission is concerned – deemed to have been accepted unless the principal notifies the agent within a reasonable period (one month, unless the contract provides otherwise) that he refuses the order or makes a reservation (Article 7:432, paragraph 1). The parties may agree that the right to commission will be dependent upon the performance of the contract. This stipulation must be expressly made. This condition only withholds commission from the agent if the principal proves that the non-performance cannot be imputed to him (Article 7:432, paragraph 2 *jo* Article 426, paragraph 2). If non-performance results from a fault of the principal or from circumstances he may be held accountable for because they are at his risk (like shortage of raw material or workers), the commission is due.

If the stipulation of paragraph 2 is made, the right to commission arises no later than when the third party has performed his part of the contract or ought to have done so if the principal had performed his part (paragraph 3).

§5. Specification of Commission: Substantiating Documents

228. The mandatory Article 7:433 deals with the obligation of the principal to specify the commission and to allow the agent to inspect the substantiating documents. After the end of each month (or every two or three months if this is agreed upon in writing by the parties), before the end of the following month, the principal is obliged to provide the agent with a written statement of the commission due for that month, stating the information on which the calculation is based (paragraph 1).

This paragraph is more favourable than the Directive, which demands a specification every quarter. The agent has the right to inspect the substantiating documents but cannot demand their surrender. At his cost, the agent may be assisted by an expert, accepted by the principal, or, if not accepted, appointed by the interim provisions judge. The parties may agree in writing that the documents shall be inspected by a third party. The agent and the third persons involved are under a duty of confidentiality.

From case law of the Supreme Court, it follows that the answer to the question as to what extent the substantiating documents should be given for inspection depends on the circumstances of the case and the interests of the parties, which should be reasonably taken into account.[130] The general principle is that the principal is obliged to have these books and documents inspected but only to the extent that is necessary to inform the agent of information not known to him and in the possession of the principal, on which the calculation of the commission depends, so as to enable the agent to verify the calculation of the principal or to make a calculation himself.

§6. Exigibility of Commission

229. The commission becomes exigible no later than at the time when the written statement referred to in Article 7:433 must be provided. Article 7:434 has been adapted to the Directive; the old article provided that the commission was exigible on the eighth day of the month following that in which the agent must be given details. The parties are free to derogate from Article 7:434, however, not to the detriment of the agent.

§7. Remuneration

230. The agent is entitled to remuneration if he is ready to perform or has already performed his obligations pursuant to the agency contract, even if the

130. HR 5-2-1971, ECLI:NL:PHR:1971:AB6985, NJ 1971/222.

principal has not availed himself of his services or has done so considerably less than could normally be expected unless the principal's conduct is the result of circumstances which are not reasonably attributable to him (Article 7:435, paragraph 1).

This paragraph provides for a division of the risk in a situation in which the principal does not make (enough) use of the services of the agent. In general, the refusal of the principal to contract comes at the risk of the agent; if the principal does not contract, the agent is not entitled to commission. Article 7:435 slightly reduces the risk that the activities of the agent are not paid for. In the literature, the provision of this article is compared to the provisions on creditor's default (Article 6:58, *see supra*, paragraphs 158 ff.). The remuneration of Article 7:435 is no real commission because no contracts were concluded.

When determining the remuneration of paragraph 1, the sum of the commission earned in the preceding period and all other relevant factors, such as the expenses saved by the agent by not performing work, should be taken into account (paragraph 2).

§8. Termination of the Contract

231. The agency contract ends after the expiry of the period for which it was concluded. An agency contract which is continued by both parties after the expiry of the period for which it has been entered into, binds the parties for an indeterminate period upon the same conditions (Article 7:436). The parties may derogate from Article 7:436. Under the old rule, a contract was considered to be continued – on the same conditions – for one year at most. Under the present regulation on agency, termination of a continued contract is easier. The termination of an agency contract concluded for a specific time makes the party who terminates the contract without observing its duration in general liable for damages (Article 7:439, *see* paragraph 232 *infra*). A contract concluded for an indefinite time may be terminated (with observance of a period of notice) at any time.

Article 7:437 states that if the agency contract was concluded for an indeterminate period or for a fixed period with a right of early termination, each of the parties may terminate it with due observance of the period of notice agreed on. In the absence of an agreement on this, the period of notice will be four months, extended by one month after the contract has continued for three years and by two months after six years (paragraph 1). Paragraph 2 states that the period of notice may not be shorter than one month in the first year of the contract, two months in the second year and three months in the following years. If any longer periods are agreed on by the parties, these may not be shorter for the principal than for the agent. Notice should be given by the end of a calendar month.

The agency contract is terminated by the death of the agent (Article 7:438, paragraph 1); in the event of the principal's death, the contract does not end in principle, but both his heirs and the agent are entitled to terminate the contract by giving four months' notice, provided this is done within nine months after the death (paragraph 2).

§9. Irregular Termination: Urgent Reasons

232. A party who terminates the contract without respecting its duration or without observing the statutory or contractual period of notice and without the consent of the other party is liable for damages unless he terminates the contract for an urgent reason for which the other party has forthwith been notified (Article 7:439, paragraph 1). Urgent reasons are defined in paragraph 2 as circumstances of such a nature that the party who terminates the contract cannot reasonably be expected to maintain the contract even temporarily. Urgent reasons for the principal may be, for example, bankruptcy of the agent or the fact that the agent works for a competitor; an urgent reason for the agent may be the fact that the principal does not make use of his services. If the termination of the contract for an urgent reason is based on circumstances for which the other party is to blame, the latter is liable for damages (paragraph 3). From this paragraph, it follows that an urgent reason does not always have to be a circumstance for which the other party is to blame. The occurrence of a neutral fact may constitute an urgent reason.

A stipulation that leaves it to one of the parties to decide whether there is an urgent reason is null (paragraph 4).

Article 7:439 is closely similar to the provisions on termination of a contract of employment. One of the deviations of general contract law is that an irregular termination has juridical effects (terminates the contract) but makes the terminating party liable for damages. The reason for this is that an agency contract – like an employment contract – is based on mutual trust, which is assumed to be no longer present after an irregular termination.

The claim for compensation of damages is prescribed by the expiry of one year after the fact that caused the claim (Article 7:444). Article 7:439 is a mandatory provision.

§10. Setting Aside

233. Pursuant to Article 7:440, paragraph 1, each of the parties is entitled to apply to the subdistrict court to set aside the contract on the grounds of:

(a) circumstances giving rise to an urgent reason within the meaning of Article 7:439, paragraph 2; or
(b) a change of circumstances that is of such a nature that fairness requires that the contract be terminated immediately or after a short period.

Also this provision is similar to the corresponding provision on contracts of employment.

In case of circumstances which leave room for doubt whether they constitute an urgent reason or not, the party who wants to terminate the contract may prefer to turn to the court instead of terminating the contract one-sided and thus taking the risk of having to pay damages over a considerable period of time. If the court sets aside the contract on the basis of a circumstance that constitutes an urgent reason and if the defendant can be blamed for this circumstance, he is liable to pay damages (paragraph 2).

If the court sets aside the contract on the basis of a change of circumstances – which may be a change of all kinds of foreseeable and unforeseeable circumstances of an objective nature (e.g., a downswing in the relevant business sector) and of a subjective nature (e.g., the loss of mutual trust) – the court may grant indemnification to one of the parties (paragraph 3).

Article 7:440 is a mandatory provision. Prescription of a claim based on this article takes, as in the case of a claim based on Article 7:439, place after one year (Article 7:444). Article 7:440 leaves intact the right of the parties to set aside the agency contract and claim costs, damages and interests on the basis of the general provisions on failure in the performance of an obligation.

§11. Damages

234. Article 7:441 deals with the damages payable pursuant to Article 7:439 and 7:440. The party liable to pay damages owes the other party a sum equal to the remuneration for the period that the agency contract should have continued in the event of normal termination. In determining such amount account shall be taken of the commission earned in the preceding period and of all other factors to be considered in the case (paragraph 1). In this sense, the amount of damages is fixed by Article 7:441, paragraph 1; no proof of actual damage is needed. In general, the amount will be fixed on the commission earned in a period of twelve months preceding the termination. The period of twelve months was laid down in the old regulation on agency but was not maintained because applications of such a fixed period may, in some cases, lead to unreasonable results (e.g., if only occasionally a contract with very high value is concluded, and this has taken place shortly before twelve months preceding the termination).

If the sum appears too high in view of the circumstances, the court may reduce the sum (paragraph 2). This provision has lost part of its interest because Article 6:109 BW contains a general judicial power to reduce legal obligations to repair damage, *see supra*, paragraph 219.

Instead of the fixed amount of the remuneration, the party who has suffered a loss can claim full damages. In that case, he must prove the amount of damages (paragraph 3).

Article 7:441 contains mandatory rules.

§12. Goodwill Compensation

235. Upon the termination of the agency contract, the agent will in general be entitled to goodwill compensation. Goodwill compensation is based on reasonableness and fairness; the agent has increased the value of the business of the principal and it is considered reasonable that he receives a remuneration for that.[131] Goodwill compensation was introduced in 1977 when the Dutch provisions on agency were adapted to the Common Provisions annexed to the Benelux Convention of 1973. In 1989, Article 7:442 was adapted to the EC directive. Before the adaptation, the claim to goodwill compensation came into being at the end of the agency contract, no matter how it ended. Also, when the termination of the contract could be blamed on the agent, the agent was in principle entitled to goodwill compensation. However, if the courts judged such a claim unreasonable, they could dismiss the claim. In the present Article 7:442, this system has changed.

Article 7:442, paragraph 1 states that the agent will – irrespective of the right to claim damages – at the end of the contract be entitled to clientele compensation, to the extent:

(a) that he has brought the principal new clients or that he has considerably extended the contracts with existing clients and that the contracts with these clients still yield considerable advantages for the principal; and
(b) that payment of this compensation is fair, taking into account all circumstances, especially the commission lost from the contracts with these clients.

Another circumstance that may be taken into account when determining which compensation is fair is the possible restriction for the agent to work after the end of the contract, resulting from a competition clause.

The amount of the compensation shall not exceed that of the remuneration for one year, calculated according to the average of the past five years or, if the contract lasted a shorter period, according to the average of the entire duration thereof (paragraph 2). The right to compensation lapses if the commercial agent has not notified the principal within one year after the end of the contract that he demands compensation (paragraph 3).

Paragraph 4 states three – restrictive – cases in which the remuneration shall not be due:

(a) if the contract has been terminated by the principal under circumstances that make the agent liable for damages pursuant to Article 439, paragraph 3;
(b) if the contract has been terminated by the agent unless such termination is justified by circumstances attributable to the principal or is justified by the age, disability or illness of the agent on the basis of which he can no longer reasonably be expected to continue his work;
(c) if the contract has been terminated by the agent who, pursuant to an agreement with the principal, transfers his rights and obligations under the agency contract to a third person.

131. HR 19-5-2017, ECLI:NL:HR:2017:935, NJ 2017/227.

In these three cases, the agent is not entitled to goodwill compensation even if it would be reasonable to grant him such compensation. In all other cases compensation is in general due, but the amount of the compensation may be influenced by the standards of reasonableness and fairness.

Before the termination of the contract, Article 7:442 may not be derogated to the detriment of the agent.

§13. Competition Clauses

236. A stipulation limiting the agent in his freedom to work after the end of the contract is – as we have seen – only valid if it has been put in writing. Another condition for validity is that it has to relate to the kinds of goods or services for which the agent was a representative and to the territory or the clientele and the territory entrusted to him (Article 7:443, paragraph 1).

A competition clause is only valid for a maximum of two years after the end of the contract (paragraph 2).

In general, the principal cannot derive rights from such a stipulation if the agency contract has been terminated in a way that makes the principal liable for damages. This rule is contained in paragraph 3. If the contract has ended:

(a) because the principal terminated it without the agent's consent, without having observed the legal or contractual period of notice and without an urgent reason of which the agent has forthwith been notified;
(b) because the agent terminated the contract for an urgent reason of which the principal was forthwith notified and for which the latter can be blamed;
(c) by a judicial decision based on circumstances for which the principal can be blamed.

Moreover, at the request of the agent, the court may annul such a clause, wholly or partly, on the basis that the agent is unfairly prejudiced, thereby, in proportion to the interest of the principal to be protected (paragraph 4).

The parties are not free to derogate from Article 7:443.

Chapter 2. Deposit

§1. Definition

237. Title 9 of Book 7 of the Civil Code deals with the contract of deposit. Article 7:600 contains the definition:

> Deposit is a contract whereby one party, the depositary, obliges himself towards the other party, the depositor, to keep safe and return a thing which the latter entrusts or will entrust to him.

Title 7.9 is also – with one exception – applicable in case of judicial deposit, provided that the contract has not derogated from Articles 7:600 ff. or the judge who has ordered deposit has determined otherwise.

Under the old Code, deposit was a 'real' contract. From the definition of Article 7:600, it follows that, under the present Code, this is no longer the case. The contract comes into being when consensus is reached; the handing over of the thing is no longer a constitutive requirement.

Article 7:600 does not include the so-called *depositum irregulare*, a contract of deposit with regard to replaceable things, on the basis of which the depositary is not obliged to return the same things he received but may return the same amount of things of the same kind.

§2. Obligations of the Depositor

238. The depositor owes remuneration to the depositary if the latter has entered into the contract in the course of his profession or business (Article 7:601, paragraph 1). The obligation to pay remuneration is the main obligation of the depositor.

Contrary to the old Code, the basic assumption of the present Code is that deposit is not, in general, a favour among friends but that it is mostly performed on a commercial basis.

If remuneration is owed but the amount has not been fixed by the parties, the depositor owes remuneration as customarily calculated or, in the absence thereof, a reasonable remuneration (Article 7:601, paragraph 2). In assessing what is reasonable, it is important to take into account the amount generally asked by fellow depositaries as remuneration for the same kind of services.[132] To the extent that they are not included in the remuneration, the depositor must reimburse the depositary for the expenses related to the deposit, as well as for loss which the depositary has incurred as a result of the deposit (Article 7:601, paragraph 3). The second and third paragraphs of Article 7:601 are applicable both to the professional and non-professional depositary, although in case of a non-professional depositary, the main rule is that no remuneration is due.

---

132. HR 6-6-1997, ECLI:NL:HR:2001:AB2020, NJ 1998/723.

The depositary is entitled to suspend the return of the thing until the remuneration is paid or the expenses or damage are reimbursed, *see* paragraphs 192 ff. *supra* on rights to suspend performance.

If the depositor fails in the performance of his obligations the depositary is entitled to set aside the contract, *see* paragraphs 190 ff.

§3. Obligations of the Depositary

239. The main obligation of the depositary is to safekeep the thing. In the conduct of the deposit, the depositary must exercise the care of a good depositary (Article 7:602). Safekeeping is not only passive; it includes active care. The degree of care required depends first of all on the contents of the contract but also on the special circumstances of the case, such as the nature of the thing (e.g., a horse must be fed, a car must be protected against theft), the nature of the contract in question (e.g., whether the depositary is a commercial company or a private person who gives disinterested help), usage, and reasonableness and fairness. The duty of care of a professional depository includes a responsibility for the things used in safekeeping the goods; thus, a depository who had been storing cheese powder in a defective cooling system was held liable for damages, even though the defects in the system were not his fault.[133]

The depositary may only use the thing to the extent that the depositor has given permission thereto or that use is necessary to maintain or restore the thing in good condition (Article 7:603, paragraph 1).[134] An example of a case in which use is necessary is the case of a riding horse that must have exercise.

Paragraphs 2 and 3 of Article 7:603 deal with subdeposit. The depositary may not deposit, without permission of the depositor, the thing with a third person unless this is necessary in the interest of the depositor. The latter situation may occur if the depositary is not able to take care of the deposited thing himself. In general, the depositary is – in accordance with the main rule of Article 6:76 – liable for the acts of the sub-depositary as if they were his own acts. An exception to this rule is made in case the deposit was not for remuneration and the depositary was forced to sub-deposit as a result of circumstances not attributable to him. In that case there is still a possibility that the depositary may be liable for other reasons, for example, if he is to blame for the choice of the sub-depositary.

The depositary must remit to the depositor the fruits which the thing yields in the period between its receipt and its return (Article 7:604). The depositor may demand that the thing be returned without delay and the depositary that it be taken back without delay (Article 7:605, paragraph 1); on account of serious reasons, the court may determine otherwise (paragraph 2). The return must be made at the place where, pursuant to the contract, the thing must be kept unless a different place has been indicated in the contract for the return (paragraph 3). The depositary must

133. HR 28-11-1997, ECLI:NL:HR:1997:ZC2511, NJ 1998/168.
134. HR 10-7-2015, ECLI:NL:HR:2015:1830, NJ 2015/321.

return the thing in the condition in which he has received it (paragraph 4). If there are two or more depositaries, they are solidarily liable for the return and compensation of damages (Article 7:606).

§4. Deposit and Third Persons

240. In paragraphs 137 ff. *supra*, it was pointed out that a contract and especially exemption clauses in a contract sometimes may be invoked by or against a third person. Article 7:608 contains an elaboration of this principle in the case of subdeposit. If a sub-depositary is sued extra-contractually by a depositor for damage suffered with respect to the thing, the former is liable towards the latter no further than he would be as a co-contacting party to the contract by which the depositor has deposited the thing (paragraph 1).

This is reasonable since the depositor has agreed to the deposit on certain conditions. The fact that the contract is executed by a subcontractor does not free him from the conditions he has accepted.

If a depositary is sued extra-contractually for damage suffered with respect to the thing by a third person who is not a depositor, he is liable no further than he would be as co-contracting party of the depositor, pursuant to the contract entered into with this person (paragraph 2).

If a sub-depositary is sued by such a third person, he is liable no further than he would be as a depositary pursuant to the preceding paragraph (paragraph 3).

Paragraph 4 contains an exception to the rules of the preceding paragraphs: they cannot be invoked by a depositary or sub-depositary who, when entering into the contract on the basis of which he received the thing, knew or should have known that his co-contracting party was not entitled to deposit the thing with him.

With respect to paragraph 1 we may think of the case in which the depositary was not allowed to subdeposit and with respect to paragraphs 2 and 3 of the case in which the depositor has stolen the thing from the owner.

The provision of paragraph 4 is similar to that of Article 3:291, paragraph 2, *see supra*, paragraph 30 on the right of retention.

Chapter 3. Sale of Goods

§1. Introduction and Definition

241. Dutch law of sale has its roots in the Roman concept of '*emptio-venditio*', a consensual contract which created for the parties obligations to transfer possession (and, in practice, the ownership) of the thing respectively to pay the agreed price. In this concept, contract and transfer of ownership are not the same thing but have to be distinguished sharply. German, Austrian and Swiss law have the same type of contract of sale, unlike French law, in which the contract itself already effects the transfer of ownership. In English law, the two types of contracts of sale can be found. The Sale of Goods Act distinguishes between 'sale' (the contract by which ownership is transferred) and 'agreement to sell' (the contract on the basis of which ownership is transferred later).

In the Dutch Civil Code, the contract of sale is the first special contract provided for in Book 7. Article 7:1 defines sale as a contract whereby one person undertakes to give a thing and the other to pay a price therefor in money. To give a thing means, in this respect, both to transfer the ownership and to deliver the thing. This definition illustrates the purely consensual and obligatory character of the contract.

Not only a thing (in the sense of a corporeal object) but also patrimonial rights can be the object of a contract of sale. Article 7:47 explicitly states so. The provisions on sale of things apply to the extent that this is in conformity with the nature of the right.

Generalities such as successions and companies can be sold but cannot be transferred as a whole. Each part must be transferred individually. It depends on the contract which property and, possibly, debts are involved in the sale.

A contract of sale must have an object that exists in the present or will exist in the future. Sale of future things frequently happens. Furthermore, the object of the contract must be determined or determinable. A contract of sale does not require that the seller is the owner of the thing. The seller may perform his obligation by transferring the thing after having become owner or by bringing about direct transfer by a third person who is the owner. In general, the buyer only has an interest in becoming owner of the thing. If the seller, because of the fact that he is not the owner, fails in the performance of his obligation, the buyer is entitled to regular remedies for breach of contract.

Apart from the object of sale, the price is an important element. If the price is not determined explicitly or tacitly, according to the old Code, there is no sale. The present Code states, however, that where a sale has been entered into without a determination of the price, the buyer owes a reasonable price; in determining that price, one takes account of the prices usually stipulated by the seller at the time of entering into the contract (Article 7:4). In this (technical) sense the price is no longer an *essentiale* of the contract. This Article is written for cases in which parties did not concern themselves about the price of the thing sold, but not for cases in which parties had been negotiating a sale but could not reach an agreement on the price.[135]

135. HR 10-12-1999, ECLI:NL:HR:1999:AA3839, NJ 2000/5.

The contract of sale is a synallagmatic contract and is governed by the general rules on juridical acts in Book 3, by the relevant parts of Book 6 concerning the law of obligations, including the general rules on contracts and by the first title of Book 7.

Title 7.1 is largely based on the general part of the Code (Title 3.2, Book 6). It contains mainly provisions that can be considered a supplement to or derogation from the general rules. Some provisions of the regulation on sale were adapted or added pursuant to several Directives, for example, Directive 2011/83/EU on consumer rights.

§2. Sale with Regard to Things Certain and Determinate and Sale with Regard to Things Determined only as to Kind

242. Under the old Code, the distinction between *contracts with regard to things certain and determinate* and *contracts with regard to things determined only as to kind* was important because of the fact that the Code created different consequences for the two types. For example, on sale of things, certain and determined, a special regulation on 'hidden defects' was applicable, which derogated from the general rules on failure in performance. Another important consequence was that there was a difference in the moment at which the risk of loss or damage to the thing was transferred to the buyer. The distinction has lost much of its importance under the present Code, where the provisions on sale almost always apply equally to both kinds of contracts. Only in Article 7:10, paragraph 2, which deals with the transfer of the risk, a special provision for things determined as to kind is found. *See* further *infra*, paragraph 250.

§3. Consumer Sale

243. The Code contains special provisions on consumer sale. These provisions have a mandatory character and are inserted in order to strengthen the position of consumers. Next to legal regulations on product liability, general terms and conditions and misleading publicity, special provisions on consumer sale were also deemed necessary. These provisions have undergone several changes over the years because of the implementation of different directives, most lately Directive 2011/83/EU on consumer rights, Directive 2019/771/EU on certain aspects concerning contracts for the sale of goods and Directive 2019/770/EU on certain aspects concerning contracts for the supply of digital content and digital services.

Consumer sale, as derived from the old Directive 1999/44/EC, is defined in Article 7:5, paragraph 1, sub a. In Title 1 of Book 7, a consumer sale means the sale of a moveable thing entered into by a seller acting in the conduct of commerce, business, craft or acting in a professional activity and by a buyer who is a natural person acting for purposes outside his business or professional activity.

Paragraph 3 makes an exception with regard to contracts pertaining to water supplied to the user by pipelines, whereas paragraph 5 explicitly states that the provisions on consumer sale apply to deliveries to a natural person acting for purposes outside his commercial, business, craft or outside his professional activities, of electricity, heating, cooling and gas. The implementation statute in paragraph 4 of Article 7:5 provides for the application of the provisions on consumer sale to contracts for work regarding a moveable thing (such as a dental plate, for instance) where the contractor is acting in the course of a business or profession and the 'buyer' is a consumer.

In a consumer sale, there may be no derogations which are to the detriment of the buyer from sections 1–7 of Title 1 (to be discussed *infra*), and there may be no limitations on or exclusions of the rights and actions which the law (i.e., general contract law in Book 6 of the Code) grants to the buyer for failure in the performance of the obligations of the seller (Article 7:6, paragraph 1).

With regard to rights and actions for failure in the performance, we must especially think of the general provisions on non-performance (*see supra*, paragraphs 177 ff.), damages (paragraphs 202 ff. *supra*) and setting aside (paragraphs 190 ff.). The implementation of the Directives (in particular the old Directive 1999/44/EC on consumer sale) also provides for the possibility to reduce the price if the good sold does not conform to the contract, but only when repair or replacement is impossible or may not reasonably be asked of the seller or when the seller has failed in the performance of his obligation to replace or repair (Article 7:22, paragraph 1, sub b *jo* paragraph 2). This is dogmatically construed as a partial setting aside of the contract. The provisions also concern limitations of rights and actions other than limiting the rights and actions themselves. For example, a stipulation reversing the apportionment of the burden of proof to the detriment of the consumer. Stipulations, as in Article 7:6, paragraph 1, are annullable; this flows from Article 3:40, paragraph 2 (*see supra*, paragraph 97).

Article 7:6, paragraph 2 mentions some articles to which paragraph 1 does not apply but states that stipulations in general terms and conditions derogating from those articles to the detriment of the buyer are considered to be unreasonably onerous.

In the following, while discussing the contract of sale in general, I will pay some more attention to consumer sale contracts.

Article 7:7, paragraph 1 (applicable to all types of sale) contains a special provision for the case in which a thing is sent to a person without his request. The person to whom a thing has been sent and who may reasonably assume that this has been done in order to induce him to buy is, irrespective of any contrary communication by the sender, entitled in his relationship with the sender to keep the thing by gratuitous title unless it can be attributed to the recipient that the sending has taken place. If the recipient sends the thing back, the costs thereof are borne by the sender. Similarly, Article 7:7, paragraph 2 states that a consumer shall have no obligation to pay for the unsolicited delivery of things, financial products, water, gas, electricity, district heating or digital content not delivered on a physical carrier.

The provisions on consumer sale regard moveable things only. A widely felt wish to protect prospective buyers of immoveable property (houses) against overly rash decisions, however, has led to an addition of two articles to Title 1 of Book 7 (Article 7:2 and 7:3). Article 7:2 prescribes the written form for the sale of a house to a consumer and gives the buyer the right to set aside the sale within three days after he has received the document in which the sale is laid down. Article 7:3 allows the buyer to register the contract of sale in the public registers of immovable property in order to protect his personal right against persons acquiring rights from the seller before the buyer eventually acquires the right of property from the seller. The registration requires a notarial deed; the protection lasts for six months.[136]

§4. Sale on Trial

244. A *sale on trial* is a sale whereby the buyer has accepted the offer of the seller provisionally under the reservation that he will decide definitely after testing the thing. Article 7:45 states that a sale upon trial is considered to have been entered into under the suspensive condition that the thing satisfies the buyer. Where the buyer allows to pass a period sufficient to assess the thing without notifying the seller of his decision, he can no longer reject the thing. As long as the sale is not definitive, the seller bears the risk of the thing (Article 7:46).

§5. Formation of the Contract of Sale

245. Formation of the contract of sale is entirely governed by the general rules on formation of contracts (*see supra*, paragraphs 38 ff.). With regard to the determinability of the obligations (Article 6:227), the validity of a contract of sale does, as mentioned, not depend on the question of whether a price is determined. A contract of sale may be entered into without determining the price. In such cases, a reasonable price must be paid (Article 7:4).

§6. Obligations of the Seller

246. The main obligations of the seller are:

(1) to transfer ownership of the thing sold (Article 7:9, paragraph 1 and Article 7:15);
(2) to deliver the thing with its accessories, including the title deeds and other records. Delivery means giving the buyer possession of the thing (Article 7:9, paragraphs 1 and 2). In the case of sale subject to reservation of title, delivery means bringing the thing under the control of the buyer (paragraph 3);
(3) to deliver a thing that conforms to the contract (Article 7:17).

136. This regulation leads to complicated questions. *See* HR 6-2-2009, ECLI:NL:HR:2009:BG5850, NJ 2009/344; HR 8-10-2010, ECLI:NL:HR:2010:BN1252, NJ 2012/211; HR 12-7-2013, ECLI:NL:HR:2013:BZ9959, NJ 2014/273.

§7. Transfer of Ownership

247. The obligation to transfer ownership has an obligatory character and means that the seller has to perform all acts, necessary to bring about the transfer. The obligation is fulfilled when the buyer has become the owner. This result can be reached not only by transfer of ownership by the seller but also in other ways, like direct transfer by a third party.

The obligation to transfer ownership may be a conditional obligation; for example, the obligation may be subject to the condition that the thing sold will be paid for first. In this case, the seller retains his title to the thing sold until payment has been made; upon payment, ownership passes *ipso iure* to the buyer (Article 3:92).

If a seller is not the owner and lacks the right to dispose of the property, a transfer of a moveable thing, unregistered property or a right payable to bearer or order is valid if the acquirer is in good faith (Article 3:86). In case of moveable things this means that the buyer becomes the owner anyway, despite the fact that the seller lacked the right to dispose of the thing. Only if the owner of the thing has lost its possession through theft, he may reclaim it during a period of three years unless the acquirer is a natural person who has bought the thing in a shop or unless money or documents payable to bearer or order are involved.

Furthermore, from Article 6:42 (*see supra*, paragraph 153), it follows that in case of a thing determined as to kind, the seller who lacked the right to dispose of the thing may require that it be given to the person to whom it belongs, provided that, at the same time, he offers to deliver another thing corresponding to the obligation and that the interest of the buyer is not opposed to the thing being given back.

Transfer of ownership will, in most cases, require cooperation of the buyer. If the buyer does not cooperate, he normally will come into creditor's default. *See* on default of the buyer further *infra*, paragraph 252.

The seller is not only obliged to transfer the ownership of the thing sold but also to transfer the ownership free of all charges and encumbrances except for those which the buyer has expressly accepted (Article 7:15, paragraph 1). Notwithstanding any contrary stipulation, the seller guarantees the absence of charges and encumbrances resulting from matters capable of being registered in the public registers, which were not so registered at the time when the contract was entered into (Article 7:15, paragraph 2).

Where an action is brought against the buyer for eviction or for the recognition of a right which should not have encumbered the thing, the seller must be joined in the action in order to defend the interests of the buyer (Article 7:16).

Only in the case of sale for the purpose of execution, the buyer may not invoke the fact that the thing is subject to a charge or encumbrance which should not have encumbered it (Article 7:19).

§8. DELIVERY

248. Apart from transfer of ownership, the seller is obliged to deliver the thing to the buyer in the sense of putting him into possession of the thing or, in case of sale with reservation, bringing the thing under the control of the buyer.

Possession is the detention of property for oneself (Article 3:107). Whether somebody detains property and whether he does so for himself or for another is determined according to common opinion, taking into account, among other things, the facts as they appear (Article 3:108). Transfer of possession takes place when the possessor enables the acquirer to exercise such control over the property as he himself was able to exercise over it (Article 3:114). In some cases, a bilateral declaration without material acts is sufficient (Article 3:115).

Delivery requires cooperation of the buyer. If the buyer does not cooperate, creditor's default on his side will be the result (*see infra*, paragraph 252).

On the one hand, delivery is a condition for the transfer of ownership of moveable things (*see* Article 3:84). On the other hand, delivery is independent of the transfer of ownership, which is important because the moment of delivery determines the transfer of the risk (*see* further *infra*, paragraph 250). Furthermore, the fruits belong to the buyer as of the day of delivery, upon the understanding that civil fruits (such as rent or interest) are calculated from day to day (Article 7:14).

§9. PLACE, TIME AND COSTS OF DELIVERY

249. Place and time of delivery are determined by the general rules of the law of obligations, *see supra*, paragraphs 155 and 156. As mentioned in paragraph 156, *supra*, delivery does not imply that the thing sold must be brought to the domicile of the creditor, that is, the buyer.

The seller bears the costs of delivery, including those of weighing and counting. The buyer bears the costs of removal, of a deed of sale and of transfer (Article 7:12). If in a consumer sale other than a distance or off-premises agreement, the seller or a carrier designated by him delivers the thing to the buyer, costs can only be claimed to the extent that the seller, at the time of entering into the contract, has indicated them separately or that he has provided data on the basis of which he calculates them. The same applies to costs owed for other work by the seller in connection with the sale (Article 7:13).

§10. RISK

250. From the general Article 6:265 (*see supra* paragraphs 190 ff.), it follows that in case of force majeure on the side of the debtor, the debtor has to bear the risk with regard to the counter-prestation: the debtor who is unable to perform loses his right to the counter-prestation if and when the creditor sets aside the contract (as he will normally do). Article 7:10, paragraph 1 confirms this general rule and determines the moment at which the risk is transferred to the buyer as the moment of delivery. The article states that the thing is at the risk of the buyer from the delivery, even if the title has not been transferred at that time. As a consequence, the purchase price remains due, irrespective of the loss or deterioration of the thing by a cause which cannot be attributed to the seller.

Paragraph 2 corresponds with Article 6:266 on the creditor's default: the same rule as in paragraph 1 applies as of the time when the buyer is in default in performing an act by which he must cooperate in the delivery. In the case of sale of things determined as to kind, the default of the buyer does not transfer the risk to him until the seller has specified the things destined for the performance of the contract and has notified the buyer thereof. Specification does not mean, however, that the seller is not entitled to deliver other things corresponding to the obligation (this follows from Article 6:65 *in fine*, *see* paragraph 160 *supra*).

Paragraphs 3 and 4 correspond to Article 6:265, 6:271 and 6:273. The thing remains at the risk of the seller if, on good grounds, the buyer invokes the right to set aside the sale or the right to have the thing replaced. This implies that the risk is transferred to the buyer if he decides to keep a thing which is defect. Where, after delivery, the thing has remained at the risk of the seller, the seller is also responsible for the thing's loss or deterioration by the act of the buyer. However, as of the time when the buyer must reasonably foresee that he must give the thing back, he is obliged to look after the safe keeping of the thing as a prudent debtor. If he fails to do so, his right to replacement lapses (Article 7:21, paragraph 1 sub c), but his right to set aside the contract still stands in principle, although the buyer must pay damages in so far as he is not able to give the thing back unharmed.

Article 7:11 contains a special provision for the consumer sale. If the seller or a carrier designated by him delivers the thing at the buyer's, the thing is only at the risk of the buyer as of that time.

Transfer of the risk takes place independently of the fact of whether the thing delivered is in conformity with the contract. If in case of sale of a thing certain and determinate, this thing is delivered, and if in case of sale of a thing determined only as to kind, a thing that meets the generic description is delivered, the risk is transferred by the mere delivery of the thing.

§11. Conformity

251. As mentioned, the obligation of the seller to deliver a thing that conforms to the contract must be distinguished from the obligation to deliver the thing. The latter obligation is mentioned separately in Article 7:17, paragraph 1.

A thing does not conform to the contract if it does not possess the qualities which the buyer was entitled to expect on the basis of the contract. The buyer may expect that the thing possesses the qualities which are necessary for a normal use thereof and the presence of which he did not have to doubt, as well as the qualities which are necessary for special use, provided for in the contract (paragraph 2). One of the factors which should be taken into account in order to determine what the buyer was entitled to expect is the knowledge of the seller (or what he should have known) about the use the buyer intended to make of the thing and the information the seller gave about the thing. Other relevant factors may be, for example, the nature of the thing (new or used), the price (normal or reduced) and the kind of shop in which the thing was sold.

A thing other than the one agreed to or a thing of a different character does not conform to the contract either (paragraph 3). The same applies if what has been delivered varies in quantity, size or weight from what has been agreed (paragraph 3). With regard to a contract of sale of a thing determined only as to kind, Article 6:28 already provides that the debtor (i.e., the seller) may not deliver a thing of less than average quality (*see supra* paragraph 153).

Where a sample or model has been shown or given to the buyer, the thing must conform thereto unless it has only been given by way of indication without the necessity of the thing conforming thereto (paragraph 4).

On the sale of an immovable thing, the statement of surface dimensions is presumed to be meant only as an indication, without the thing having to conform thereto (paragraph 6). This provision is in keeping with the prevailing view. However, if it follows from the contract that the mention of surface dimensions is not just an indication of the size but an essential element, deviation may mean that the thing does not conform to the contract in the sense of Article 7:17, paragraph 3.

In determining whether a thing delivered pursuant to a consumer sale conforms to the contract, information regarding the thing made public by or on behalf of the previous seller of that thing, acting in the course of a profession or business, is deemed to be information from the seller, except to the extent that the latter was neither aware nor ought to have been aware of such specific information or that he has clearly contradicted it (Article 7:18, paragraph 2 sub d). As a result of this article, the consumer may invoke advertising by the producer or the importer against the seller.

Deviation of marginal importance will not lead to the conclusion that the thing does not conform to the contract. This kind of deviation must not be confused with deviation, which constitutes non-conformity but the character of which is too minor to justify replacement of the thing delivered (one of the remedies the buyer has at his disposal, *see infra*, paragraph 254).

In the case of a sale for the purpose of execution, the buyer may not invoke the fact that the thing does not conform to the contract unless the seller is aware of this (Article 7:19).

§12. Default of the Buyer

252. On default of the buyer, first of all, the general rules apply, *see supra*, paragraphs 180 ff. Title 7 contains in section 5 some special provisions on default of the buyer. If the contract gives the buyer the power to specify the thing by indicating its measure, its form or otherwise and where the buyer is in default in so doing, the seller may proceed to do so himself, taking into account the needs of the buyer of which he is aware (Article 7:31). Furthermore, if the buyer is in default in taking delivery, and the thing is subject to rapid loss or deterioration or if its safekeeping would cause serious inconvenience or unreasonable cost, the seller must have the thing sold in an appropriate manner (Article 7:32).

§13. Remedies for the Buyer

253. If the seller fails in the performance of his obligation and the failure may be attributed to him, the buyer has the rights and actions mentioned *supra* in paragraph 177: the right to claim performance, damages and partially setting aside the contract. Title 7.1 contains further provisions on each of these remedies.

First of all, it should be mentioned that if the buyer wants to invoke the fact that what has been delivered does not conform to the contract, he may no longer do so if he has not notified the seller thereof within a reasonable period after he has or reasonably should have discovered this; where the thing proves to lack a quality which according to the seller it possessed, or where the deviation pertains to facts which the seller knew or ought to have known but has not communicated, the notification must take place within a reasonable period after the discovery (Article 7:23, paragraph 1). The main intention of Article 7:23, paragraph 1, is to protect the interest of the seller to be made aware of any complaints within a reasonable period. Which period is fair depends of course on the circumstances of the case. The provisions on consumer sale deem a two-month period reasonable (Article 7:23, paragraph 1, last sentence). Rights of action and defences based on non-conformity are prescribed by the expiry of two years from the notification; however, the buyer retains as a defence against an action for payment the right to claim a reduction in the purchase price through a partial setting aside of the sale or his right to damages (Article 7:23, paragraph 2).

§14. The Right to Performance

254. Article 7:20 and 7:21 grant the buyer – without prejudice to all other rights or actions (Article 7:22, paragraph 4) – some special claims for performance.

Where the thing is subject to a charge or an encumbrance which should not have encumbered it, the buyer may demand that the charge or encumbrance be removed, provided that the seller can reasonably comply therewith (Article 7:20).

Where the thing delivered does not conform to the contract, the buyer may, pursuant to Article 7:21, paragraph 1, demand:

(a) delivery of what is lacking;
(b) repair of the thing delivered, provided that the seller can reasonably comply therewith. This exception concerns both the technical and the economical capacities of the seller. If, in a consumer sale, the seller has not performed his obligation to repair the thing delivered within a reasonable period after written notice to that effect from the buyer, the latter is entitled to have the thing repaired by a third person and to claim the costs thereof from the seller. This is a deviation from Article 3:299, which provides that effectuation of the result of an obligation by the creditor of the obligation requires judicial authorization;
(c) replacement of the thing delivered unless the variance from what was agreed to is too insignificant to justify this, or unless, after the buyer should reasonably have taken into account the right to set it aside, the thing has been lost or has deteriorated because the buyer has not ensured its safekeeping as a prudent

debtor. Things determined as to kind are replaceable because of their nature; replacement of things certain and determinate is sometimes also possible, for example, if they are the subject of an alternative obligation (where the debtor must perform one of several different prestations of his choice, the choice of the creditor or of a third party).

The buyer may choose which of his rights he wants to effectuate. However, in exercising this choice, for instance, between demanding specific performance and demanding damages, the buyer will have to act according to standards of reasonableness and fairness, which means that he will have to take into account the justified interests of the seller.[137] Also, if, in case of a consumer sale, the buyer demands the repair or the replacement of a thing capable of replacement, the seller is entitled to choose between a replacement or the reimbursement of the purchase price. This provision is meant to accommodate the seller, who may not derogate from Title 7.1, which is mandatory in case of a consumer sale (*see supra*, paragraph 243). The seller must make this choice within a short period and, subsequently, he must perform his obligations within a reasonable period, failing which the buyer may enforce his rights to repair or replacement.

The enforcement of these rights is, however, restricted. Pursuant to Article 7:22, paragraph 1 *jo* 2, the buyer in a consumer sale may set aside the contract or reduce the price only when repair or replacement is impossible (or may not be asked of the seller) or when the seller did not do so (deliver, repair or replace) within a reasonable period and in a not too troublesome way.

§15. Damages

255. With regard to damages, the general provisions apply (*see supra*, paragraphs 202 ff.), but section 7 also contains some special rules. Where a sale is set aside, and the thing has a current price, damages shall equal the difference between the price provided for in the contract and the price current on the day of non-performance (Article 7:36). Where the buyer or the seller has entered into a replacement sale and, in doing so, has acted reasonably, he is entitled to the difference between the agreed price and that of the replacement sale (Article 7:37). This means that in these cases an 'abstract' method of calculation is standard, although a higher amount of damages are not precluded in the event that the damage suffered is greater (Article 7:38).

In case of consumer sale, there are some restrictive provisions in Article 7:24 and 7:25, again because of the fact that Title 7.1 may not be derogated from, which would sometimes lead to onerous results for the seller. Where the failure of the seller consists of a defect in his product, the seller is not liable for the damage by death or bodily injury and damage to other things (as referred to in section 6.3.3 on product liability, which is in conformity with the relevant EC directive) unless: (a) he was aware or ought to have been aware of the defect, (b) he has promised the

137. HR 5-1-2001, ECLI:NL:HR:2001:AA9311, NJ 2001/79.

absence of the defect, or (c) it concerns damage to things for which the consumer has no right to compensation from the producer because of the franchise provided for in section 6.3.3.

If, in the first two cases, the seller repairs the buyer's damage, the buyer must transfer his rights flowing from section 6.3.3 to the seller. Where the buyer has exercised one or more of his rights against the seller, the latter is, in principle, entitled to reparation of damage with respect to the person from whom he has bought the thing.

§16. The Right of the Buyer to Set Aside the Contract

256. The only special provision – with the exception of the provisions on risk, already discussed above, which are important in this respect because they influence the obligations to undo which result from the setting aside – is again a provision on the consumer sale. If, pursuant to a stipulation made in the contract, the seller increases the price after the conclusion of the sale, the buyer is entitled to cancel the contract by a written declaration unless it was stipulated that the delivery would take place more than three months after the sale (Article 7:35, paragraph 1). Price in this respect includes the amount that was provisionally indicated as purchase price at the time the contract was entered into, subject to price modifications (Article 7:35, paragraph 2).

§17. Obligations of the Buyer

257. The buyer is obliged to pay the price (Article 7:26, paragraph 1) or part of it when he is entitled to reduce the price according to Article 7:22, paragraph 1, sub b. This is the main obligation of the buyer. Payment must take place at the time and place of delivery; in a consumer sale, the buyer cannot be obliged to prepay more than half the purchase price (Article 7:26, paragraph 2). The provision on the place of payment is a deviation from the general rules (Article 6:116 and 6:118, *see supra*, paragraph 156), according to which payment must be made at the creditor's domicile. However, in practice, the place of delivery will often be the creditor's domicile.

Where the buyer has received the thing but intends to reject it, he must look after its safekeeping as a prudent debtor. He has a right of retention over the thing until the seller has indemnified him against the costs he has reasonably incurred (Article 7:29, paragraph 1); *see supra*, paragraph 30 on the right of retention. Where a buyer intends to reject a thing sent to him and delivered at the appropriate place for delivery, he must take delivery of this thing unless payment of the purchase price is required, serious inconvenience or unreasonable cost ensues, or unless the seller is present at the place of delivery or a person who is entitled, at that place and on his behalf, to charge himself with the care of the thing (Article 7:29, paragraph 2). Where the thing is subject to rapid loss or deterioration or when its safekeeping would entail serious inconvenience or unreasonable cost, the buyer must have the thing sold in an appropriate manner (Article 7:30).

In general, the buyer has no obligation to take delivery of the thing. However, if he does not cooperate, he comes into creditor's default, with all its consequences. Moreover lack of cooperation provides the seller with some special rights to cancel the contract (*see infra*, paragraph 259).

§18. Remedies of the Seller

258. In case of failure in the performance of the buyer, the seller may claim, in accordance with the general provisions, performance (in a consumer sale, the right of action for payment of the purchase price is prescribed by two years (Article 7:28), in other cases by five years (Article 3:307)), damages and he may set aside the contract.

§19. The Right of the Seller to Set Aside the Contract

259. Article 7:33 and 7:34 contain two special provisions.

Article 7:33 states that if it is of essence that a moveable thing is delivered on a certain day and if the buyer does not take delivery on that day, this constitutes a ground to set aside the contract. According to Article 7:34, the seller may set aside the sale by a written declaration if the fact that no delivery is taken gives him good reason to expect that the price will not be paid.

The setting aside creates the obligation for the buyer to restitute the thing to the seller. The seller may, however, reclaim the thing as owner if he has reserved the title of ownership or if he exercises the right to reclaim ('revendicate') under Article 7:39 (*see infra*, paragraph 260).

§20. The Right of Revendication

260. Article 7:39 states that the seller of a moveable thing, other than registered property, which has been delivered to the buyer can revendicate the thing by a written declaration addressed to the buyer if the price has not been paid and if in connection therewith the requirements to set aside the contract have been met. By exercising the right of revendication, the seller regains the ownership of the thing. Furthermore, the declaration sets aside the sale and terminates the rights of the buyer and of third parties to whom he may have sold the thing. In case of partial payment, only the unpaid part or a part that corresponds to the unpaid price (if what is delivered is susceptible to such division) may be revendicated.

The right of revendication cannot be exercised:

(a) if the thing delivered is no longer in the same condition as it was when delivered (Article 7:41);

(b) if the thing has been transferred, given in *usufruct* or pledged, otherwise than by gratuitous title, to a third person who did not reasonably have to expect that the right of revendication would be exercised, unless the thing has remained in the hands of the buyer (Article 7:42);
(c) if the buyer has accepted a negotiable deed for the full purchase price (Article 7:43); and
(d) when, simultaneously, six weeks have passed since the right to payment of the purchase price has become exigible and sixty days counted from the day on which the thing was deposited with the buyer or with someone on his behalf (Article 7:44).

§21. International Sale

261. Until 1992, international sales were governed by the Hague Uniform Laws on International Sales of 1964. On the first of January 1992, the Vienna Convention on the International Sale of Goods (CISG) entered into force for the Netherlands.

The implementation into Dutch law of the old Directive 1999/44/EC on certain aspects of the sale of consumer goods and associated guarantees, aiming at a minimum level of protection of consumers in international consumer sales, was effectuated by 1 May 2003. Several provisions have been discussed in the preceding paragraphs.

Chapter 4. Building Contracts

§1. Introduction and Definition

262. Building contracts are a species of contracts for work. The present Civil Code, as it entered into force in 1992, did not contain new provisions on contracts for work. The provisions of the old Civil Code were inserted into Book 7A unchanged. In 2003, new provisions have been inserted in Title 12 of Book 7.

In the Code, the contract to undertake work is defined in Article 7:750, paragraph 1 as the contract whereby one party, the contractor, obliges himself towards the other party, the principal, to bring about and deliver a work of material nature, not in an employer-employee relationship, and the principal has to pay the price in money.

With regard to building contracts, not only the provisions of the Code are important, but also general conditions, such as the so-called *Uniforme Administratieve Voorwaarden* (UAV), and the so-called Model sale/construction contract.

§2. The *Uniforme Administratieve Voorwaarden*

263. With regard to building contracts, general conditions have always been widely used. The UAV have been decreed by a common decision of several ministers. However, the UAV were not drawn up unilaterally by those ministers. The organization of unions in the building industry and other organizations and institutions concerned with building have been consulted. The last version of the UAV was decreed in 2012. Although the UAV are laid down in a ministerial decision, their status is the same as other general conditions in civil law. The UAV are widely used by parties to building contracts in which the design of the object of the work originates from the principal, and during construction, the work is supervised by or on behalf of the principal by a professional person, mostly an architect or an engineer. The UAV contain an arbitration clause in which the settlement of disputes is submitted to the Board of Arbitration for the building industry. If this arbitration clause is used in a construction contract with a principal that is a non-professional private person, a consumer, it is considered unreasonably onerous pursuant to Article 6:233, sub a *jo* 6:236, sub n (*see supra*, paragraph 114).

§3. The Model Sale/Construction Contract

264. There is also an important category of contracts in which the design of the object of the work originates from the contractor himself and in which the work is not supervised during construction. With regard to these kinds of contracts, the principal is usually a consumer. In 1974, a 'model sale/construction contract' with annexed 'general conditions for the sale and building of houses' was brought about with the cooperation of, among others, the Consumers Union, the Organisation of Public Notaries and the Union of Building Contractors. The Model contract was most recently revised in 2023. The model is compulsory in case of subsidized house-buildings. The Model contract also contains an arbitration clause.

The construction of a building is in general a rather complicated affair. The building is therefore described accurately in the so-called specifications. The work must be executed according to the specifications. The specifications contain not only the technical side of the project, but other conditions as well, and they often contain a reference to general conditions. The juridical relationship of the parties is largely determined by the specifications.

§4. Obligation of Result?

265. The contract for work is generally considered as a contract which creates an obligation of result. The contractor is – except in the case of force majeure – obliged to bring about the agreed result. If the work is constructed according to the instructions and under supervision of someone on behalf of the principal, some circumstances may, however, be attributed to the principal. For example, the contractor will, in that case, not be responsible for mistakes in the design or for the suitability of building material prescribed by the principal. *See* further *infra*, paragraph 269.

§5. Formation of the Contract

266. A principal who wants to find a contractor who offers the lowest price may invite tenders for the work.[138] In this respect, the so-called Aanbestedingsreglement Werken (ARW) 2016, a uniform regulation on tenders, is often used; if the national government is involved, the use of the ARW is even required. This very detailed regulation will not be discussed here.

§6. Risk

267. Title 7.12 does not contain a special provision on the perishing of works under construction and the risk for damage thus suffered. From the commentary on the text, it follows, however, that the contractor bears the risk in such a case. The Code does contain in Article 7:757 a provision on the perishing of a thing with regard to which the work has to be done. If the thing is in the hands of the constructor (which it will mostly be in the case of building contracts), he bears the risk. If the thing is not in the hands of the constructor, he is entitled to a proportional part of the contract sum (corresponding to the labour which has already been accomplished and the costs made) unless the perishing of the thing must be attributed to him. If the principal has caused the perishing on purpose or as a result of his gross fault, the contractor may claim the full contract sum after deduction of the costs he saved.

138. I will leave aside possible complications resulting from relevant EU regulations.

§7. Liability for Things and for Subcontractors

268. Article 7:760, paragraph 1 contains a rule that is in accordance with Article 6:77 (*see supra*, paragraph 167). The consequences of defective construction of the work resulting from materials or things used by and originating from the contractor which are faulty or unfit for the purpose, are attributed to the contractor. If the materials or things are prescribed by and originate from the principal, liability will in general lie with him unless the contractor has failed in his duty to warn the principal or has otherwise failed in professionalism or care (paragraph 2). According to the commentary, the principal is not responsible for consequences of the use of faulty material that is generically fit for the purpose in question but is only unfit in this specific case. This solution is in accordance with the UAV but differs from the current doctrine, based on a Supreme Court decision of 1966[139] that places the liability with the principal in such cases.

The contractor is in general allowed to call in subcontractors to carry out (a part of) the work (Article 7:751). Under the UAV, the contractor needs permission in writing if he wants to make use of subcontractors.

According to Article 7:751 *jo* Article 6:76, the contractor remains, in that case, responsible for the acts of his subcontractor (*see supra*, paragraph 167). It is a controversial point whether the contractor is also responsible if he was not free in his choice of subcontractor, but followed the directions of the principal in this respect. According to the UAV, the contractor may claim from the principal the 'additional construction costs' caused by the faulty performance of the subcontractor, although the contractor has to do what he can to minimize the damages for the principal.

§8. Obligations of the Contractor

269. The main obligation of the contractor is to complete the work.

If the building plan is designed by or on behalf of the principal, the constructor has to work according to that building plan, and he has to follow the instructions of the principal.

The contractor who discovers (or should have discovered) faults in the design has the duty – based on the principles of reasonableness and fairness – to warn the principal even when the principal is himself a professional (Article 7:754). In such a case the fact that the principal is a professional might be a ground for dividing the damage on the basis of Article 6:101 (*see* paragraph 214 *supra*).[140] He may only proceed with the work after consultation with the principal.

The contractor has to complete the work for the contract sum agreed on. Article 7:753, paragraph 1 provides that the court may change the agreed sum in case of

139. HR 25-3-1966, ECLI:NL:HR:1966:AC4642, NJ 1966/279.

140. HR 25-11-1994, ECLI:NL:HR:1994:ZC1555, NJ 1995/154; HR 18-9-1998, ECLI:NL:HR:1998:ZC2705, NJ 1998/818; HR 8-10-2004, ECLI:NL:HR:2004:AP0954, NJ 2005/52; HR 8-9-2006, ECLI:NL:HR:2006:AX9511, NJ 2006/494.

the occurrence of price-increasing circumstances after the conclusion of the contract, which cannot be attributed to the contractor. This provision is a species of the general provision of Article 6:258 on unforeseen circumstances, *see supra*, paragraphs 172 ff.

The UAV also contain a provision on unforeseen circumstances at the time of the conclusion of the contract that cannot be attributed to the contractor and increases the costs of the work considerably. Unlike Article 7:753, the UAV do, in these cases, not provide for a change of the agreed sum, but instead, the contractor can claim the additional costs from the principal.

If no contract sum has been fixed, or if the contractor has only given a price indication, the principal shall owe a reasonable price pursuant to Article 7:752, paragraph 1. If the contractor has given a price indication, he may not exceed the indicated sum by more than about 10% unless he warns the principal first in order to let him decide if he wants the work to be limited (Article 7:752, paragraph 2).

Often during construction, there occurs a request for surplus work. The contractor is not obliged to perform all alterations and additions to the work desired by the principal. However, it would be often contrary to reasonableness and fairness to refuse. Under the UAV, the contractor is in general obliged to perform surplus work; this obligation is, however, limited to 15% of the contract sum.

The contractor has to complete the work by the agreed date. The UAV determine that the principal may deduct a certain amount from the contract sum if the work has not been delivered in time. These kinds of contractual provisions are generally used in the building business. However, if the real damage is much higher than the sum to be deducted, such a provision may turn out to be unreasonable. Under Article 6:94, paragraph 2, the court may grant supplementary damages in extraordinary cases.

§9. Obligations of the Principal

270. If the construction is initiated by the principal (which will not always be the case, *see supra*, paragraph 264), he must do what is necessary to render the construction of the work possible, also with regard to the legal aspects. He must, for example, see to it that the building lot may be entered, and if he is obliged to provide building materials, he must take care that this is available in time. If a building permit is required, he will generally be the one that has to provide for this permission.

The opinions differ on the question as to whether the principal is obliged or merely authorized to inspect and, after approval, accept the work. At any rate, negligence of the principal to inspect, etc., must not cause prejudice to the position of the contractor. In that respect, Article 7:758 provides that if the contractor has indicated that the work is ready to be delivered and the principal does not inspect the work within a reasonable period and accepts it, whether or not subject to a reservation, or does not reject it indicating the defects, the principal is presumed to have tacitly accepted the works. The UAV contain a provision that if the principal does not react within eight days after inspection, the work is considered to be approved on the eighth day. The same kind of fictitious approval is construed if the principal refuses to inspect the work after he has been invited to do so in writing. Under the UAV, the day of approval is also the day on which the work is considered to be delivered.

Approval and acceptance have juridical effects, such as, among other things, change of risk, exigibility of the contract sum, no more damages based on late delivery, release of the contractor liability for defects the principal should have discovered on inspection and the start of the prescription period of Article 7:761, paragraph 1.

The main obligation of the principal is to pay the agreed contract sum.

As mentioned, in many cases, surplus work is involved, requested by the principal or required by the actual developments. The old Code aimed to protect the unprofessional principal and granted the contractor only a right to an increase of the contract sum if two conditions were met: (1) the alterations in the work must have been commissioned in writing by the principal, and (2) there must have been consensus about the price of the surplus work. There was a controversy about the nature of the condition that the commission must be in writing. Some writers state that this was a constitutive condition (no contract without writing); others say it was only a matter of proof. In case of an oral commission to perform surplus work, the article could lead to unreasonable results. The present Article 7:755 therefore lays down that the contractor may claim an increase of the contract sum on the grounds of additions or changes desired by the principal, provided that he has warned the principal in time that this would necessarily lead to an increase of the price (this warning does not have to be in writing), unless the principal should have understood this necessity. This provision takes as a starting point that surplus work does not always imply a price increase. In this respect, the degree of professionalism of the principal with regard to the necessity of a price increase (and not so much the extent of the price increase) due to surplus work will play an important role.[141]

Under the UAV, there is no need to protect the principal against the contractor: both parties are professionals or assisted by professionals.

In some cases the sum to be paid consists of the costs of labour and material increased with a percentage of these costs as profit for the contractor and taxes. The provisions on surplus work are naturally not applicable to these kinds of contracts.

The principal has to pay the agreed sum when the work is finished and delivered unless otherwise stipulated. In the building business, payment in instalments is rather customary (*see* in this regard also the mandatory Article 7:767 and 7:678).

§10. Termination of the Contract

271. A building contract ends in the usual way all contracts end. There are, however, three remarks to be made.

Both parties are entitled to set aside the contract in case of failure in the performance of the other party. Article 7:756 contains some additional rules. If, before the determined date of delivery, it is probable that the work will not be delivered in time or in a proper way, that the principal will not perform in time or in a proper way or

141. HR 1-7-2022, ECLI:NL:HR:2022:989.

that the contractor will not be able to perform as a result of circumstances which may not be attributed to him, the contract may be set aside by the court. Because of the fact that there is only a probability of future failure, judicial interference will, in this case, always be required.

According to Article 7:764, the principal has the right to end the contract at any time (even before the work has started), in which case he must pay the contract sum under deduction of the saved costs of the contractor. There is no obligation to pay damages. The provision will never be invoked by the principal in case of failure in the performance of the contractor because this would lead to the obligation to pay damages. In case of failure in the performance, the principal will resort to regular remedies.

The old Code considered the building contract as a contract with a personal element, that is, a contract that is concluded with a view to the person of the contractor. For this reason, the death of the contractor led to termination of the contract. Under the present Code, the contract no longer terminates automatically if the contractor dies. Article 7:763 states, however, that each one of the parties may terminate the contract if they have a reasonable interest in termination, considering the nature of the contract. If the contract is terminated, the principal must pay a compensation fee for the labour and costs, determined according to the standards of reasonableness and taking into consideration all circumstances. According to the commentary, the principal will never have to pay more than in case of termination dealt with in Article 7:764. Article 7:763 also applies in case of invalidity of the contractor. Under the UAV, the contract does not end in the event of the death of the contractor. The heirs acquire the rights and obligations of the deceased and, therefore, have to finish the work or bear the costs involved in completion.

§11. Remedies: Liability for Defects

272. If, during construction or on the occasion of the final inspection (Article 7:759), the principal protests against defects, the contractor will have to repair these defects. In general, the principal is entitled to reparation in kind.

If the contractor has been given the opportunity to repair the defects but has not done so, the principal may claim the costs related to reparation. He may also demand judicial authorization (Article 3:299, *see supra*, paragraph 188) to have the work repaired or finished at the expense of the contractor. The principal may also stipulate that no judicial authorization will be required. The UAV demand that first, the contractor is summoned to comply with his obligations and that the principal is entitled to have the work finished at the expense of the contractor if the contractor remains passive. The contractor is, in that case, only entitled to payment once it has become clear what the costs involved were.

273. The contractor is released from liability for defects the principal should have discovered (Article 7:758, paragraph 3). The contractor must in general be given the opportunity to repair defects for which he is liable. The right of action with regard to defects prescribes two years after the moment on which the principal has protested against the defect or twenty years after the moment of delivery

(Article 7:761). The contractor may not be exonerated of liability for hidden defects that were known to him but on which he has remained silent. Rights of action with regard to these defects may not be subjected to shorter prescription periods than the ones just mentioned (Article 7:762).

The UAV state the principle that the contractor is no longer liable for defects after the day of delivery, with the exception of a hidden defect.

Chapter 5. Lease

§1. Introduction and Definition

274. The contract of lease is a contract of great social importance. It is a civil contract and, for a large part, provided for in the Civil Code, but it also has a public element. The regulation of the contract is, to a large extent, dominated by the urge to protect the economically weak party. This is done, among other things, by regulation of the lease prices and a strict regime on the termination of lease contracts with regard to residential and commercial space. The law on lease – both in the Code and in the special acts that modify the civil regulation – is, therefore, largely mandatory law.

The Civil Code, as it entered into force in 1992, did not yet contain new provisions on lease. The provisions of the old Civil Code were inserted into Book 7A unchanged. In 1998, however, a draft of Title 7.4 was proposed based on a draft that was made as early as 1972. Title 7.4 has replaced the old provisions in 2003. Although Title 7.4 does contain some changes to the old law, these are not of a fundamental nature. The same is true for the contract of lease of land (agricultural lease), which followed in 2007.

The contract of lease and rent may be defined as a contract whereby the lessor puts the enjoyment of a thing – in whole or in part – at the disposal of the lessee (Article 7:201).

Lease is a consensual contract which does not require a special form, although the law sometimes attaches different consequences to an oral contract and a contract in writing.

All things and patrimonial rights may be the object of lease unless the law provides otherwise, or it would be contrary to the nature of the right.

Title 7.4 starts with general provisions (Article 7:201–202), then continues with the obligations of the lessor (Article 7:203–211) and those of the lessee (Article 7:212–225). Provisions on the transfer of the lease contract in case of transfer of the leased object and provisions on the termination of lease follow (Article 7:226–231). The provisions on lease of residential space are inserted as Article 7:232–282 and those on lease of commercial space as Article 7:290–7:310.

§2. General Provisions on the Lease of Things: Obligations of the Lessor

275. The lessor has the following main obligations (Articles 7:203). The lessor must put the leased object at the disposal of the lessee. Where the lessee so requires, the lessor must, pursuant to Article 7:706, repair any defects of the leased object unless this is impossible or requires expenses which could not reasonably be asked from the lessor. Only minor repairs have to be made by the lessee (Article 7:206, paragraph 2 *jo* 7:217). Article 7:204, paragraph 2 gives the following definition of a defect: a defect is a state or property of the thing or any other circumstance (which is not attributable to the lessee) which causes the thing not to provide the enjoyment to the lessee which he is entitled to expect of a well-maintained thing of this kind at the conclusion of the contract.

§3. General Provisions on the Lease of Things: Obligations of the Lessee

276. The lessee has the following main obligations (Articles 7:212 ff.):

(1) The lessee has to pay the rent. The rent has in general to be paid in instalments. It depends on the contract whether the rent has to be paid in advance or not and whether the rent has to be paid by the week, month, quarter or other time limit. In the absence of a contractual stipulation, the local custom is decisive. The general provisions to the obligations to pay a sum of money are also applicable to the obligation to pay rent, *see supra*, paragraphs 154 ff. Terms which have been set for the payment of rent are generally set with the intention of bringing about default of the lessee if the rent is not paid on time unless the lessee can make plausible that the term has another purpose (*see supra*, paragraph 181, on Article 6:83, sub a).

(2) The lessee must use the thing in a proper way and according to its purpose. In general, the lessee must use the thing himself. But if the sublease concerns a part of a house while the house is and remains the lessee's main residence, the opposite rule applies: sublease is permitted unless the contract provides otherwise. *See*, on the position of the sub-lessee of residential space further *infra*, paragraph 284.

The lessee is liable for all damage inflicted to the thing during the period of lease, unless the event that caused the damage may not be attributed to him. He is liable for damage caused by himself, his house-mates (including the persons he permits in the house) and his sub-lessees.

(3) The lessor must give the thing back at the end of the contract. There are, however, exceptions to this rule; these will be discussed *infra*, when the protection for lessees against cancellation by the lessor will be dealt with. The lessee must in principle leave the house behind in the same condition as it was when the contract of lease was concluded. On leaving the house, the lessee may take with him the things he has installed in the house – such as floor covering or built-in kitchen material – unless this would cause damage to the house.

The lessee has the right to make changes to the leased object if the lessor consents; in case of lease of residential space, the lessor must consent if the changes will not influence the possibilities of leasing the space or its value (Article 7:215, paragraphs 1 and 2). If the lessor nevertheless does not consent, the lessee may ask for judicial authorization (Article 7:215, paragraphs 3–5). This is mandatory law, except with regard to changes to the outside of the leased object. At the end of the lease, the lessee may claim compensation from the lessor for the value of improvements made to the extent that the lessor would be enriched by these improvements according to the standards of Article 6:212, *see* paragraph 329 *infra* (Article 7:216, paragraph 3, which is, by the way, not mandatory law). Article 7:221 permits sublease unless the lessor has reasonable objections to it. However, Article 7:221 is not mandatory, and most lease contracts forbid sublease. Article 7:244 stipulates for lease of residential space that the lessee may only sublease part of the house (the right to sublet rooms). This provision is not of a mandatory character.

§4. Termination of the Contract: General Provisions

277. The contract of lease may be terminated in the usual way. There are, however, quite a lot of additional specific provisions on lease. In this paragraph a few remarks will be made on the general rules on termination of contracts of lease. Later on, attention will be paid to the special provisions on the termination of lease contracts with regard to residential space, commercial space and agricultural leases. In this respect, it should be mentioned that where I use the term 'cancellation', this term refers to the unilateral termination of the contract for the future by a notice of one of the parties.

If, during the period of lease, the object perishes by coincidence, the contract lapses *ipso iure*.

All contracts for a certain and determinate period end after expiration of that period; special cancellation notice is not needed (Article 7:228, paragraph 1).

The contract of lease does not end when one of the parties dies (Article 7:229, paragraph 1).

In case of bankruptcy of the lessee both the trustee in bankruptcy and the lessor are entitled to terminate the contract prematurely (Article 39 of the Bankruptcy Act).

The contract of lease also ends in case of compulsory purchase by the administration (Article 42 of the Compulsory Purchase Act).

If the contract of lease concerns registered property on which a right of hypothec is established, the deed of hypothec may contain an express stipulation that limits the grantor of the hypothec in his power to lease the encumbered property without the consent of the hypothecary creditor or to determine the manner in which or the time during which the property can be leased. Such a stipulation may be invoked against the lessee by the hypothecary creditor (or – under certain conditions – by the buyer after a forced sale) (Article 3:264). If the grantor of the hypothec has acted contrary to the stipulation and the creditor invokes the stipulation, this may lead to termination of the contract. Furthermore, if in the case of lease of residential space invoking the stipulation would result in the lessee of a dwelling to whom Article 7:271–277 (*see infra*, paragraphs 280 and 282) applies, having to vacate the space, permission of the interim provisions judge is in general required. This permission will be given unless, even when maintaining the contract, it is obvious that sufficient proceeds will be obtained to satisfy the hypothecary creditor(s). Where the lessee loses his right by annulment pursuant to Article 3:264, compensation is paid to him for the damage which he suffers as a consequence of the annulment out of the proceeds of the property produced by the execution (after the hypothecary creditor has been fully paid).

§5. Alienation of the Leased Thing

278. A contract of lease does not end if the leased thing is sold or alienated unless this is stipulated otherwise in the contract (Article 7:226). In case of lease of residential, commercial or agricultural space derogation of this rule is not allowed. At the moment of transfer, the original lessor is replaced by the transferee; the latter acquires all rights and obligations resulting from the contract. He will in general also have to respect the contract of lease concluded after the alienation but before the actual transfer, provided that the lessee did not know that the thing was alienated already.

§6. Lease of Residential Space

279. Lessees of residential space are protected by the provisions of Article 7:232–282. Since the end of World War I, there has been much demand for houses but only a limited supply. Especially after World War II, there has been a permanent housing shortage. This has led to high rents and a vulnerable position of the lessees. Since 1950, the legal protection of lessees has been increased; in 1979, the protective regulations were inserted into the Code, supplemented by provisions in separate Acts. As of 2021, the lease of residential space has gradually become more (publicly) regulated in separate Acts to protect lessees of both subsidized dwellings and houses on the (current) free market against the shortage and expensiveness of housing. Acts to, for example, limit the amount with which the lease price can annually increase (as implemented in Article 7:248, paragraphs 2 and 3) and to enforce a (transparent) maximum lease price for certain (not only subsidized) dwellings came into effect or are prepared by the government (*see*, *infra*, paragraphs 286 ff. on the regulations on lease prices and change of rent).

§7. Definition of Residential Space

280. In Article 7:233, a residential space is defined as a built immovable thing leased as independent accommodation or a dependent part thereof leased as accommodation, including the immovable accessories.

Independent accommodation means that the dwelling must have its own entrance and basic facilities (Article 7:234).

The definition is broad. Outside the scope of the definition fall, for example, traditional houseboats (these are not immoveable) and houses owned by a company and occupied by employees of that company in connection with their work, such as houses for wardens or gardeners (these are not used on the basis of a contract of lease). Rooms are covered by the definition, but the protection of lessees of non-independent residential space is less far-reaching (Article 7:233).

§8. Protection Against Cancellation by the Lessor of Residential Space

281. The main purport of Article 7:271–282 is to protect the lessee against cancellation of the contract by the lessor. According to the legal system as laid down in Article 272, cancellation does not have effect until it has been sanctioned by judicial permission.

Cancellation of a contract of lease of residential space – no matter if the contract has been concluded in writing or orally, for a determinate or indeterminate period – must be notified by means of a writ or a registered letter. The legal terms in Article 7:271, paragraph 5, sub b have to be taken into account: the minimum term is three months, increased with one month for every year the lessee has enjoyed the use of the space, up to a maximum of six months. The notice of cancellation must mention the reason for cancellation. If no reason is mentioned or another reason than the ones allowed by the law is mentioned, the cancellation is null. Furthermore, in the notice, the lessee must be asked to let the lessor know in writing within six weeks if he consents to the termination of the contract. If the lessee does not consent or does not respond, the lessor must turn to the subdistrict court and demand termination of the contract. The subdistrict court may only terminate the contract if one of the five grounds for termination that are summed up in the Code applies. The grounds are not only limitative but also imperative; if there is a ground for termination, the court must terminate the contract.

§9. Grounds for Termination of Lease of Residential Space

282. The grounds for termination in Article 7:274, paragraph 1 are the following:

(a) The lessee has not behaved as a good lessee. This ground includes, among other things, improper use of the space, the inducement of serious inconvenience and non-payment. If the lessee does not behave as a good lessee, the lessor may also demand the setting aside of the contract. Although the setting aside of a contract of lease of residential space also requires a judicial decision, there are some advantages: the overall procedure is less complicated, the judicial decision may be executed by anticipation and the lessor may also demand damages.

(b) The contract is concluded for a certain and determinate period, and the lessor has expressly stipulated that the dwelling must be vacated after expiration of that period. This ground may not be invoked if the lessor no longer has an interest in vacation. The stipulation may only be made in a few limited cases, among others, if the lessor lived himself in the dwelling and will move there again after expiration of the period.

(c) The lessor shows that he needs the leased space so urgently for his own use – not including alienation – that it cannot be required from him, taking into account the interests and needs of both parties and the sub-lessees (if any), that he continues the contract, provided that the lessee may acquire other suitable residential space. 'Own use' may be other use than for residential purposes, for example, use as business accommodation or for renovation (Article 7:274, paragraph 3). It may also include use by another person if this use serves an own interest of the lessor. A 'suitable' other space does not have to be equivalent. It depends on the special circumstances of the case and especially on the personal circumstances of the lessee (such as his income) and whether another available dwelling is suitable for him. A lessor who acquired the dwelling – including the lease contract – less than three years ago may not invoke this ground.

(d) The lessee does not consent in a reasonable offer to conclude a new contract with regard to the same space, provided that this offer does not concern a raise of rent or additional costs (such as costs for water, electricity, use of furniture, etc.). Disputes about rent and costs must be dealt with in the way provided for in the Act on lease prices of residential space. This ground refers to the situation that the lessee does not agree with changes or improvements (and the raise of rent and costs connected with these changes or improvements) the lessor wants to bring about.

(e) The lessor wants to realize a purpose attributed to the space by the prevailing zoning plan.

(f) The lessee makes plausible that his interest in ending the lease agreement relating to a dependent residential space, which forms a part of the dwelling in which the lessor has his main residence, weighs more heavily than the interest of the lessee in continuing it.

(g) The lease of an independent home in a building for which an environmental permit has been granted for a maximum period of fifteen years, and the lease has been terminated on the day on which that environmental permit is issued to expire. The written rental agreement must state the environmental permit referred to in the first sentence and the period for which it was granted.

If the lessor demands termination on grounds (a) or (d), the judge may grant the lessee a term of one month to comply with his obligations or to accept the offer (Article 7:274, paragraph 6). If the contract is terminated on grounds (c) or (e), the judge may determine a contribution to the moving expenses of the lessee to be paid by the lessor (Article 7:275).

In exceptional cases, the lessee may act contrary to reasonableness and fairness if he invokes the protection of Articles 7:271 ff. (*see supra*, paragraph 32).

If the court decides to terminate the contract, the contract remains in force until the decision has become irreversible.

§10. Co-Lease

283. If the lessee is married or has a registered partner or lives together with another person, these persons are also protected by the Code.

The spouse or registered partner of the lessee is co-lessee *ipso iure*. Lessee and co-lessee are jointly and severally responsible for performance of the obligations resulting from the contract. If the contract with the lessee terminates, the spouse becomes lessee. In case of divorce, the court may determine which one of the spouses will be lessee of the marital home. His decision has effects against the lessor (Article 7:266).

According to Article 7:267, paragraph 1, the person who lives together with the lessee may become co-lessee by permission of the lessor or – if the lessor refuses his permission – by a judicial decision, given at the joint request of the lessee and the other person. The court only rejects the request if the other person has lived less than two years in the dwelling or the common household does not have a long-lasting character, if the request was made with the sole intention that the other person will obtain the position of (main) lessee in the near future or if the other person does not offer enough guarantees from a financial point of view for proper performance of the obligations resulting from the lease contract (Article 7:267, paragraph 3). If the contract terminates with regard to the lessee, the co-lessee continues the contract as lessee pursuant to Article 7:267, paragraph 5. Only if a public residence permit is needed for the dwelling, a judicial decision is required. Lessees and co-lessees/non-spouses may ask the court to determine that one of them will not continue to be a party to the contract (Article 7:267, paragraph 7). The decision effects the lessor.[142] Article 7:267, paragraph 7, is especially of interest in case of the breaking-off of a non-marital relationship.

If the main lessee dies, the co-lessee becomes lessee. He may cancel the contract within six months. The person who lived together with the lessee but did not have the status of co-lessee may also continue the contract, first for six months and longer, if the court permits continuation. The court must deny permission if there is no common household with a long-lasting character, if the other person does not offer sufficient financial guarantees or if he does not dispose of a public residence permit (Article 7:268, paragraphs 1–3).

§11. Sublease

284. Pursuant to Article 7:269, a contract of sublease with regard to independent residential space in which the sub-lessee has his main residence is, in case of termination of the contract between the lessor and the lessee, *ipso iure* continued by the main lessor. The sub-lessee therefore acquires his own right against the lessor, irrespective of the fact of whether the lessee had permission or not to conclude a contract of sublease. The lessor may, within six months, demand termination of the contract on the ground that the lessee/former sub-lessee does not offer sufficient financial guarantees, that the sublease was concluded with the intention that the sub-lessee will obtain the position of lessee, that continuation of the contract cannot reasonably be imposed upon the lessor considering the circumstances of the case or if the sub-lessee does not dispose of a public residence permit.

142. HR 24-12-2021, ECLI:NL:HR:2021:1964, NJ 2022/206.

§12. Replacement

285. If the lessee wants to exchange his rented dwelling with another person, he may, on the grounds of Article 7:270, demand judicial authorization to put that other person in his position as lessee. This other person must possess a public residence permit if required. The court considers the circumstances of the case and may only grant the request if lessee has a weighty interest in the house exchange. If the proposed lessee does not offer sufficient financial guarantees, the request must always be dismissed.

§13. Lease Prices of Residential Space (Article 7:246–257)

286. For some categories of residential space, there is no freedom of lease prices at all (e.g., some subsidized dwellings, houses that are declared uninhabitable); for other residential spaces, there is, in principle, freedom of contract with regard to the rents. However, the Code gives both parties the opportunity to turn to one of the 'rent tribunals' (of which the composition and method of working are regulated by a special Act) within three months after the commencement of the contract and demand a decision on the reasonableness of the rent. Under the terms of this regulation an elaborate system of housing assessment is developed in order to measure the quality of leased residential space. In this system the space acquires a certain amount of points on the basis of objective criteria; linked to this system, criteria for the reasonableness of rents (and changes of rents) are formulated. If the parties do not appeal to the subdistrict court within two months after the decision of the tribunal, the parties are deemed to have contracted in accordance with the decision of the rent tribunal.

§14. Change of Rent

287. If the leased space is improved during the lease period, an increase of the rent must, in principle, be agreed on beforehand, and the increase must be in a reasonable proportion to the costs the lessor has paid. The amount of the increase becomes part of the lease price, and both parties may demand advice from the rent tribunal about that price (Article 7:255 (subsidized dwellings) and 7:255a).

The parties may also (once a year) propose a unilateral change in rent as laid down in Article 7:248. This includes the usual annual rent increase. If the lease does not provide for such a rent increase, the proposal must comply with certain conditions as to term, form, information to be given, among other things, the percentage or amount of the change, the concrete proposed rent, the proposed day of commencement, the way in which the lessee may lodge objections to the proposal and the consequences of non-reaction (Article 7:252). If the lessee pays the proposed rent, he is deemed to have agreed with the proposal. If the lessee does not react, the lessor may ask the rent tribunal to send a second notice to the lessee; the lessee is bound to the proposal unless he demands a decision from the tribunal within six weeks after the notice has been dispatched. If the lessee rejects the proposal in the proper way, the lessor must turn to the tribunal (Article 7:253).

A contractual stipulation that the rent will be increased annually with the highest percentage that is permitted by the public authorities is valid. If, in that case, the lessee has objections against the rise, he must propose a reduction. If, in case of a proposal of reduction, the lessor does not agree with the proposal, the lessee may demand a decision of the tribunal within six weeks after the proposed commencing date (Article 7:254).

§15. Additional Costs and Extra Charges

288. Article 7:259 stipulates that the lessee has to pay the service costs which the parties have agreed upon, and if they have not reached an agreement on this topic, an amount conforming to statutory criteria or reasonable service costs. The provision applies to subsidized dwellings and houses on the free market on the basis of Article 7:247 *jo* 7:265.[143] Service costs will have to regard the goods or services connected to the fact that the lessee is living in the leased object. Other kinds of services, like medical services given to elderly people living in a so-called service flat, do not fall under the definition of 'service costs' given in Article 7:237, paragraph 3. With regard to additional costs and extra charges other than rent, service costs or costs for utilities, Article 7:264 stipulates that any contractual provision by which one of the parties gains an unreasonable advantage is null.[144]

§16. Lease of Commercial Space

289. The provisions on lease of commercial space (Article 7:290–310) are more or less tailored after the provisions on lease of residential space, but there are some considerable differences.

§17. Definition of Commercial Space

290. Article 7:290, paragraph 2, sub a defines commercial space as a built immovable thing or a part thereof which is on the basis of the contract of lease intended to be used for the practice of:

(a) a retail business;
(b) a restaurant or cafeteria;
(c) a takeaway or delivery service;
(d) a trade.

143. HR 24-4-2020, ECLI:NL:HR:2020:808, NJ 2020/290.
144. HR 24-4-2020, ECLI:NL:HR:2020:808, NJ 2020/290; HR 16-7-2021, ECLI:NL:HR:2021:1157, NJ 2022/74.

In the leased space there must be a room for direct delivery of moveable things or services, which is open to the public. Furthermore, space for a hotel or camping business is considered to be commercial space in the sense of Article 7:290, paragraph 2, sub b and sub c. The commercial space includes the land and independent dwelling that belong to the space.

The definition does not cover all space that would be considered commercial space in common parlance. The purport of the regulation is to protect businesses that are tied to a particular space because of customers, goodwill, investments, etc.

On '290-space', Article 7:291–310 is applicable; on other commercial space – which will not be discussed here – Article 7:230a, which also contains a system of protection against termination and vacation, applies.

§18. Protection Against Cancellation by the Lessor of Commercial Space

291. First of all, the possibility to cancel the contract is severely restricted during the first ten years. The contract is considered to be concluded for five years – unless another period, longer than five years and shorter than ten years, has been agreed upon and is extended *ipso iure* until a term of ten years has been reached (Article 7:292). Extension may be prevented by cancellation with observance of a term of at least one year (Article 7:293, paragraph 2) and the other formalities summed up in the Code which are comparable to the formalities required for the cancellation of a contract of lease of residential space (Articles 7:294 ff.), but only bad management of the lessee and urgent need of the lessor to use the space personally (or have it used by his spouse or a close relative)[145] constitute grounds for cancellation (Article 7:296, paragraph 1). If it appears afterwards that the lessor did not really have the intention to use the space – which is presumed to be the case if he does not move into the space within one year – the lessee is entitled to damages (Article 7:299). After cancellation, the contract remains in force until the subdistrict court has terminated the contract at the request of the lessor. The above-mentioned regulation has an imperative character, but the parties may demand judicial permission to insert derogating stipulations in their contract. However, such permission – which will only be given in case of special circumstances – is not often demanded. After the contract has taken effect, judicial permission for a contract by which the lease is terminated is no longer required.

No judicial permission is required for a contract for the duration of two years or shorter. To such a contract, the protective provisions of Articles 7:292 ff. do not apply (Article 7:301, paragraph 1). If the parties have concluded a contract for less than two years but the lessee keeps using the space after expiration of this period, the contract is *ipso iure* converted into a contract for – in total – five years (Article 7:301, paragraph 2) unless the parties have concluded another contract before the date of expiration, in which case judicial permission is needed for a contract shorter than five years.

145. HR 13-6-2008, ECLI:NL:HR:2008:BC6116, NJ 2008/338; HR 1-4-2022, ECLI:NL:HR:2022:494, NJ 2022/152.

The extended contract (Article 7:300) does not terminate *ipso iure* after ten years. Cancellation is required. Both parties may cancel the contract with a term of one year and in accordance with the other formalities. The contract is terminated by the cancellation if the cancellation comes from the lessee or if the lessee consents in writing to the cancellation of the lessor (Article 7:295, paragraph 1). In the other cases, the lessor must demand termination by the court and the contract continues until the court has decided irreversibly that the contract will terminate. The request will, pursuant to Article 7:296, paragraphs 3 and 4, be dismissed if the lessee, if his interests in extension are weighed in a reasonable way against the interests of the lessor in termination, cannot be required to vacate the leased space. The request must always be granted on one of the following grounds:

(a) bad management;
(b) urgent need for personal use as commercial space;
(c) refusal to consent in a reasonable offer to conclude a new contract with regard to the same space provided that this offer does not concern an increase of rent or additional costs;
(d) realization of a purpose attributed to the space by the prevailing zoning plan.

The court is obliged to grant the lessee a term of one month to accept a reasonable offer (Article 7:296, paragraph 4 sub c *jo* 7:298).

After extension of the contract by the court – unless the period of extension is less than one year – the lessor may again cancel the contract at the end of the term and demand the court to terminate the contract. The same rules apply as described above.

If a contract is not cancelled at the end of the first term of ten years, the contract continues as a contract for an indeterminate period unless the parties agree otherwise. Such a contract must be cancelled with observance of a period of at least one year. Contracts that continue as contracts for a determinate period or contracts that are concluded for more than ten years in the first place must be cancelled towards the end of the period, with observance of a term of at least one year. Furthermore, the same rules as discussed above apply here.

If, during the lease period, the lessee fails in the performance of his contractual obligations, the lessor may demand the setting aside of the contract. As in the case of the lease of residential space (Articles 7:231 *jo* 6:265 ff.), a judicial decision is needed in that respect.[146] The court may grant the lessee a period to comply with his obligations.

§19. Goodwill

292. If the contract ends as a result of cancellation by the lessor and the lessor derives profit from the fact that the space, after the termination of the contract, is

146. HR 28-9-2018, ECLI:NL:HR:2018:1810, NJ 2019/446.

used for a similar business as the one the lessee conducted, the former lessee is, pursuant to Article 7:308, entitled to a compensation for goodwill, determined according to reasonable standards. No goodwill compensation is granted if more than a year has passed before a similar business is established in the space. The provision of goodwill compensation is a mandatory law.

§20. Death of the Lessee of Commercial Space and Replacement of the Lessee

293. The heirs of a lessee who has concluded a contract for a determinate period may cancel the contract within six months after the death of the lessee unless they are entitled to sublet the commercial space (Article 7:302 *jo* 7:293 paragraphs 2 and 3).

If the lessee wants to transfer to another person the business he runs in the leased space, he may demand judicial authorization to place that other person into his position as lessee. The parties may not exclude this power of the lessee. The court considers the circumstances of the case, but he may only grant the request if the lessee has at least a weighty interest in transferring the business and if the proposed lessee offers enough guarantees for performance of the contractual obligations and for good management (Article 7:307).

§21. Lease Prices of Commercial Space

294. There are no strict price regulations for leased commercial space. In principle, the parties are therefore free to determine any price. However, if the price does not correspond (anymore) to the price of comparable commercial space, the parties may request that the subdistrict court adapt the price they agreed on. If the contract is concluded for a determinate period, the parties may do so after expiration of that period; if the contract is concluded for an indeterminate period, the parties may do so once in five years (Article 7:303, paragraph 1). Furthermore, there may be a judicial adaptation on the occasion of the extension *ipso iure* of a contract originally concluded for two years and of the extension of the contract after five and/or ten years, either as a result of a judicial decision or as a result of the fact that the contract has not been cancelled. The court must take into account the average of the prices of comparable commercial space in the neighbourhood or if non-present, else were on a comparable location in the preceding five years (Article 7:303, paragraph 2). This system of price assessment aims to prevent high price increases in the area (e.g., as a result of the conclusion of new contracts) from having immediate effects on the prices of current contracts. Furthermore, the prices of comparable space must be corrected in the sense that the effects of inflation are neutralized. If the request to increase the rent is based on improvements made by the lessee, the request will be dismissed on the basis of Article 7:303, paragraph 3.

§22. Agricultural Lease

295. The contract of agricultural lease (both with regard to farmsteads and with regard to agricultural land) was codified in Book 7 Title 5 in 2007; until that time, it was regulated by a separate act, the Agricultural Holdings Act. Agricultural lease is a civil contract, but there is a large amount of public intervention in the contract. Land Chambers (entrusted with supervision of contracts of agricultural lease) and the agricultural chamber of the district courts (entrusted with jurisdiction in conflicts about agricultural lease) play an important role.

The position of most leaseholders is vulnerable, especially when they depend on a leased farmstead for their income and housing. The main purpose of the statutory regulation is to protect the leaseholder. The instruments are – as in the case of lease of residential and commercial space – a strict regime of termination and price regulation. Most of the provisions of Title 7.5 are mandatory laws.

Agricultural lease is defined in Article 7:311 as a contract whereby one party undertakes to give the other party an immovable property (farmstead or land) in use in order to practice agriculture, against payment of a counter-prestation.[147] The counter-prestation may only be a lease price, which is a price in money determined by a period of time (Article 7:328). This means that the price may not depend on other factors, such as the price of products, unless the Land Chamber allows such a price.

A contract of agricultural lease must be laid down in writing (Article 7:317) and must be approved by the Land Chamber (Article 7:318). Until the contract has been approved, the lessor does not have a right of action for the price and the contract is deemed to be a contract for an indeterminate period which may not be cancelled (Article 7:322). A contract to change or end the original contract must also be laid down in writing and be approved by the Land Chamber. The Land Chamber may approve the contract, adapt the contract to bring about conformity with the legal standards or declare the contract null.

A contract of lease of a farmstead is concluded for twelve years, and a contract of lease of land for six years (Article 7:325). The contract may also be concluded for a longer period, provided that a date of termination is determined; a contract for a shorter period needs approval from the Land Chamber, which is given only in special circumstances and if no harm is done to the interests of agriculture.

296. The strict regime of termination and price regulation in the Agricultural Holdings Act has led to the undesirable result that less and less land owners are willing to lease their land and farmsteads. It is generally felt to be necessary to introduce a more liberal regime. This has led to the introduction, in 1995, of two new forms of lease of agricultural land (these forms are not applicable to farmsteads): the so-called harvest lease (lease for the duration of a one- or two-year crop) and the once-only lease (single lease for the duration of at least one but at most twelve years). With regard to these forms of agricultural lease, many mandatory provisions

147. *See also* HR 20-12-2019, ECLI:NL:HR:2019:2034, NJ 2020/43.

are not applicable. In Title 7:5, the 'once-only lease' has been replaced by the 'liberalised lease'(*see* Articles 7:397 ff.). These forms of agricultural lease therefore give the lessor and lessee the freedom to arrange their contract according to their own views.

§23. Obligations of the Parties to a Contract of Agricultural Lease

297. The main obligations of the lessor (*see* Articles 7:336 ff.) are to put the leased farmstead or land in good condition at the actual disposal of the leaseholder, to provide the leaseholder with the undisturbed enjoyment of the leased farmstead or land, to guarantee the leaseholder the absence of defects, to make the necessary reparations with the exception of the small and daily ones, to rebuild buildings perished by fire or storm – unless the Land Chamber releases him from this obligation or the contract was concluded for a shorter period than the legal term or rebuilding cannot be reasonably asked from the lessor, to pay the leaseholder at the end of the contract compensation for improvements the latter was authorized to make (Article 7:350) and, as a rule, to give the leaseholder the opportunity to obtain the leased farmstead or land in ownership if he intends to alienate them (*see* Articles 7:378 ff.).

The main obligations of the leaseholder are laid down in Articles 7:346 ff. and include: to pay the price, which may under certain circumstances be adapted by the Land Chamber or the agricultural chamber of the court, to use the leased farmstead or land as a good leaseholder meaning among other things to use the farmstead or land according to its purpose, not to make unauthorized changes and to properly exploit it, and to return the leased farmstead or land in good condition at the end of the contract.

§24. The Setting Aside of the Contract

298. If one of the parties fails in the performance of his obligations the Land Chamber may, depending on the circumstances, set aside the contract at the request of the other party. Apart from the right to claim setting aside, the lessor is entitled to request an investigation (Article 7:376). If the chamber finds negligence on the part of the leaseholder, this may result in instructions given by the chamber to the leaseholder.

§25. Extension of the Contract

299. In principle, the contract of agricultural lease is extended each time *ipso iure* for a period of six years (Article 7:325, paragraph 5). Both parties can terminate the contract, but if a termination by the lessor is opposed by the leaseholder, it can only become effective if accepted by the court on one of the grounds specified by Article 7:370. The court will accept the request for termination if the leaseholder has breached his obligations, if the lessor, his spouse or a close relative needs the farmstead or land personally for agricultural use, if the leaseholder does not accept a reasonable offer to conclude a new contract or if the interest of the lessor to terminate the contract prevails over the interest of the leaseholder to maintain and extend the contract.

Furthermore, the court may set aside the contract if the lessor wants the farmstead or land to have a non-agricultural purpose in accordance with the general interest (Article 7:377). In this case, the leaseholder has a right to compensation.

§26. Replacement

300. The leaseholder may request at any time that the agricultural chamber will replace him as leaseholder by his spouse, close relatives or co-leaseholders (Article 7:363). The most important ground for refusal is that the proposed leaseholder does not offer sufficient guarantees for proper exploitation and management. The leaseholder may also request that his spouse or close relatives be considered co-leaseholders (Article 7:364).

§27. Other Ways of Termination of Agricultural Lease

301. The contract of lease terminates if the leased farmstead or land perishes by coincidence or if the use thereof becomes permanently impossible.

The contract does not terminate with the death of one of the parties (Article 7:366). However, the contract may be set aside after the death of the leaseholder by the lessor or the surviving relatives of the leaseholder. The relatives of the leaseholder may also request that one of them take the place of the leaseholder and that the others be discharged from the lease.

As was already pointed out in paragraph 278, a contract of lease does not end if the leased thing is sold or alienated (Article 7:361).

Chapter 6. The Settlement Contract

§1. The Settlement Contract

302. Articles 7:900 ff. are devoted to the settlement contract, a contract whereby the parties determine their juridical relationship in mutual agreement in order to end or to prevent an uncertainty or dispute.

The settlement contract must be distinguished from a contract merely concerning evidence. The difference between a contract concerning evidence and a settlement contract in the material sense shows procedurally: if the parties take a standpoint different from the contract, the judge must, in the case of a contract of evidence, base his judgment on the statements of the parties while in the case of a settlement contract, he must stick to the contract in which the juridical relationship of the parties was determined. In the present Code, the contract of evidence, which excludes counterevidence, is assumed to be a settlement contract (Article 7:900, paragraph 3). Article 7:900 states that in the case of a settlement contract, the parties accept a settlement of their legal relationship, which is meant to have a binding effect also if it should differ from the juridical situation existing in reality.

303. The settlement contract may be concluded both with a view to existing uncertainties as to future uncertainties. A settlement contract which is not at all based on an uncertain state of affairs is no settlement contract in the proper sense. Objective uncertainty is not required; subjective uncertainty (i.e., that in the opinion of the parties, there is uncertainty between them) is, in general, sufficient.

A settlement contract with regard to an uncertain state of affairs or dispute in the field of patrimonial law is valid, even if the settlement should appear to be contrary to mandatory law. Only if the settlement is by content or necessary implication contrary to good morals or public order, such a contract is null (Article 7:902).[148] The settlement contract, as provided for in the Code, also comprises the binding party decision and the binding advice. In case of a binding party decision, the settlement is brought about by one of the parties; in case of a binding advice, the settlement is brought about by a third person, not by way of arbitration (Article 7:900, paragraphs 2 and 4). A party is not bound by a binding party decision if the party who had to take the decision has used his power in a way contrary to reasonableness and fairness or has taken a decision that no reasonable person would have taken. If a binding advice is unreasonable as to the way it came into being or as to its contents, the party who wants to hold the other party to the advice will act contrary to reasonableness and fairness. The Code provides for annullability in such cases (Article 7:904).

148. HR 21-4-1995, ECLI:NL:HR:1995:ZC1711, NJ 1997/570; HR 27-3-2009, ECLI:NL:HR:2009:BH1544, NJ 2009/579; HR 6-1-2017, ECLI:NL:HR:2017:19, NJ 2017/37.

§2. Nature and Effects of the Settlement Contract and the Compromise

304. There has been much discussion about the nature and effects of settlement contracts.

Some authors consider these contracts to have a declaratory effect; that is, the parties do not create a new juridical situation but only settle what has to be considered already from the beginning as the existing juridical situation between them. In this theory, which is based on fiction, no additional juridical acts are required to transform the old juridical situation into a new one.

Other authors assume that the parties do create a new situation ('dispositive theory'). The parties leave the old situation aside and bind themselves to uphold the settlement even if afterwards, it would appear that the settled situation does not correspond to the real pre-existing situation. According to this theory, the contract may create obligations for the parties in order to bring about the new situation. For example, in case of a settlement contract with regard to the ownership of registered property, transfer by entry into the public registers is required.

The declaratory theory has been prevailing for a long time. Originally, the draft Code also took the declaratory view as a starting point, even though some exceptions were formulated. The relevant provisions in the draft have been changed, however, after a discussion about the desirability of the declaratory theory. In the provisions as they stand now, the dispositive theory has been adopted, even though the possibility that a settlement may have declaratory aspects is not ruled out (Article 7:901).

§3. The Setting Aside of the Contract

305. The controversy about the declaratory or dispositive theory also bore on the possibility of setting aside the contract. After all, in the declaratory theory, the compromise is not a synallagmatic obligatory contract, and to such a contract, the provisions on setting aside are not applicable (*see supra*, paragraph 190).

A more general argument against the possibility of setting aside the contract was that a settlement contract intends to definitely put an end to an unsecure situation or (in case of a compromise) a dispute. It would therefore not be attractive to bring about a revival of the pre-existing unsecure situation.

In the Code, setting aside is, in principle, possible. However, if the setting aside would affect a decision already taken by a party or third person, the setting aside may not be brought about by a unilateral declaration and may be refused by the court on the ground that the party who wants the contract to be set aside, has sufficient means to obtain redress of or compensation for the failure in the performance (Article 7:905).

§4. Influence of Defects of Consent

306. Because of the fact that the purpose of the settlement contract is to create security with respect to the juridical situation between the parties, the question also arises if the parties may invoke error, threat, fraud or abuse of circumstances.

With regard to the unsecure circumstances which caused the contract to be concluded, the parties may not invoke error. They have taken the risk that the real situation was different from the situation about which consensus was reached.[149] With regard to other circumstances which the parties assumed to be certain, error may be invoked.[150]

The Code does neither contain specific provisions on fraud, threat or abuse of circumstances in the section on settlement contracts. The general provisions apply. On application, the special nature of the settlement contract has of course to be taken into account.[151]

§5. Settlement of Mass Claims

307. In 2005, the Title on the contract of settlement was supplemented with Article 7:907–910 on collective settlements. This article allows the court (the Amsterdam Court of Appeal) to facilitate the settlement of mass claims for damages by declaring a collective settlement, created by parties liable for the damage caused and organizations of interested parties, binding for all parties concerned, subject to the possibility for persons who have suffered damage to opt out of the settlement. The details of the regulation, which is rather complicated and technical, cannot be described here. The regulation has proven to be a success; it has been applied in cases of physical harm,[152] but also in cases of damages suffered by shareholders as a result of, e.g., a misleading prospectus or a liquidation of financial institutions.[153]

149. HR 15-11-1985, ECLI:NL:HR:1985:AC4400, NJ 1986/228; HR 20-2-2015, ECLI:NL:HR:2015:394.
150. *See* HR 29-9-1995, ECLI:NL:HR:1995:ZC1825, NJ 1998/81; HR 1-2-2013, ECLI:NL:HR:2013:BY3129, NJ 2013/84.
151. *See* HR 27-1-2017, ECLI:NL:HR:2017:95 and HR 12-10-2018, ECLI:NL:HR:2018:1903 on the application of abuse of circumstances.
152. Court of Appeal Amsterdam 1-6-2006, ECLI:NL:GHAMS:2006:AX6440, NJ 2006/461.
153. E.g., Court of Appeal Amsterdam 25-1-2007, ECLI:NL: GHAMS:2007:AZ7033, NJ 2007/427; Court of Appeal Amsterdam 29-5-2009, ECLI:NL:GHAMS:2009:BI5744, NJ 2009/506; Court of Appeal Amsterdam 17-1-2012, ECLI:NL: GHAMS:2012:BV1026, NJ 2012/355; Court of Appeal Amsterdam 13-7-2018, ECLI:NL:GHAMS:2018:2422.

Chapter 7. Suretyship

§1. Introduction and Definition

308. Since January 1992, Title 14 of Book 7 of the Civil Code deals with suretyship.

An essential element of the contract of suretyship is that the prestations of the parties to the contract are not the main element of the contract, but the fact that the surety guarantees the performance of the obligation of another. Article 7:850, paragraph 1, defines suretyship as a contract whereby one party, the surety, obliges himself towards the other party, the creditor, to perform an obligation to which a third person, the principal debtor, is or will be bound towards the creditor. Where the obligation of the principal debtor has an object other than the payment of a sum of money, the suretyship is – unless explicitly stipulated otherwise – for the claim for damages owed on the basis of non-performance of that obligation (Article 7:854).[154]

Suretyship is a form of solidary liability. This follows from Article 6:6, paragraph 2, which states, among other things, that where two or more debtors are each liable for the whole of the same debt, they are solidarily liable. Article 7:850, paragraph 3 provides that the provisions regarding solidary obligations apply to suretyship to the extent that this title does not derogate therefrom. The difference between suretyship and other forms of solidary liability is that the surety presents himself towards the creditor as someone who only wants to provide security and that – in his relationship towards the principal debtor – the debt does not concern him.

Suretyship is a species of the genus guarantee contracts. There are many guarantee contracts which are not sureties. An example is the bank guarantee on the basis of which a bank is obliged to pay as soon as the creditor demands payment. An essential difference with suretyship is that the bank guarantee is detached from the underlying juridical relationship. In the case of suretyship, there is always a link between the obligation of the principal debtor and the surety.

The principal obligation for which the suretyship is given need not exist at the moment the suretyship is entered into. Article 7:851, paragraph 2 states that suretyship can be entered into for future obligations of the principal debtor to the extent that they are sufficiently determinable. Suretyship for future obligations is common practice, mostly in the form of suretyship towards a creditor (often a bank) for all or certain kinds of claims this creditor will have in the future against a certain debtor.

Suretyship is a contract between creditor and surety, and therefore the validity of suretyship does not require that the principal debtor be aware of it (Article 7:850, paragraph 2).

154. HR 8-1-2021, ECLI:NL:HR:2021:38, NJ 2021/178.

§2. Consumer Suretyship

309. The provisions on suretyship are in general not of a mandatory character. Suretyship is an important element in the credit system and the interests of the creditors require flexibility and a minimum of impediments. On the other hand, a need was felt to prevent private persons from entering rashly into a contract of suretyship. For this reason, some special provisions are inserted in section 2 of Title 14 to protect the private surety. A private surety is defined in Article 7:857 as a natural person acting neither in the conduct of a profession or business nor for the benefit of the normal exploitation of the business of a company limited by shares or a private company with limited liability of which he is a director and in which, alone or with his co-directors, he holds the majority of the shares. As a result of the last part of this definition, sureties given by directors' major shareholders – often required by banks as an extra security for the debts of the company – miss the protection of section 2.[155]

Section 2 applies *mutatis mutandis* to contracts by which a private surety obliges himself to a certain specific prestation in the event that a third person does not perform towards the creditor a certain specific obligation with a different content (Article 7:863). For example, someone obliges himself to deliver a thing of some kind to the creditor in case the principal debtor fails in his obligation to deliver a thing of that kind.

The mandatory provisions of section 2 may neither be evaded by a construction in which a private person does not enter into a surety or similar contract himself but gives an order to a non-private person to do so on behalf of a third person but to the account of the private person. Article 7:864, paragraph 1, provides that in such a case, the person receiving the order is not entitled towards the person giving the order to reimbursement of what he has paid to the creditor, to the extent that the present section would have been a bar to the liability, as surety, of the person giving the order. Paragraph 1 may only be derogated from if this is done in writing and signed by the person giving the order in which the nature of the derogation is described and if it involves an order to a bank or another institution which is in the business of granting suretyships (paragraph 2).

The provisions of section 2 will be further discussed *infra.*

§3. Nature of the Contract

310. Suretyship has a subsidiary nature. The surety is not obliged to perform until such time as the principal debtor has failed in the performance of his obligation; the creditor who puts the principal debtor into default according to Article 6:82 (*see supra*, paragraphs 180 ff.) must at the same time notify the surety thereof (Article 7:855).

Suretyship also has an accessory nature; from the definition given above it already follows that there is no suretyship without a principal obligation. Article

155. HR 26 -1-2007, ECLI:NL:HR:2007:AY9678, NJ 2007/74.

7:851, paragraph 1, explicitly states that suretyship is dependent upon the obligation of the principal debtor for which it has been entered into.

There is no suretyship if the principal obligation is not valid. When the principal obligation comes to an end, the suretyship will, in general, also come to an end. According to Article 7:853, suretyship is extinguished on the expiry of the period of prescription of the right of action to claim performance of the obligation by the principal debtor. Suretyship generally follows the principal obligation; if the claim for which the suretyship is given is transferred, the new creditor acquires *ipso iure* the rights resulting from the suretyship (Article 6:142, paragraph 1, *see also supra*, paragraph 142). Another consequence of the accessory character is that – contrary to other cases of solidarity and to the independent guarantee – the surety has most of the defences connected with the principal obligation (*see* further *infra*, paragraph 312).

§4. Form

311. In general there are no formal requirements for contracts of suretyship. In case of consumer-suretyships, however, there are some special provisions.

Article 7:858 states that if, at the time the suretyship is entered into, the amount of the obligation of the principal debtor is not determined, the suretyship is only valid to the extent that a maximum amount, expressed in money, has been agreed to;[156] interest and costs owed according to Article 7:856 (*see infra*, paragraph 312) can be claimed irrespective of this maximum.

Article 7:859 contains some special rules on proof. The suretyship can only be proven against the surety by a document signed by him (paragraph 1). The suretyship can be proven by all means if it has been established that the surety has performed the obligation of the principal debtor in whole or in part (paragraph 2). The same requirement, as referred to in paragraph 1, and the same latitude as referred to in paragraph 2, apply to the proof of the contract which obliges to enter into the suretyship.

There may be no derogations from these provisions to the detriment of the surety (Article 7:862). It should be stressed that validity itself does not depend on the existence of a writing.

In case of a married person who acts as a private surety, the permission of his spouse is required (Article 1:88). If no permission is given, the suretyship is subject to annulment.

§5. Relation Creditor-Surety: Influence of the Relation Creditor-Principal Debtor

312. The relation creditor-surety is, of course, first of all, influenced by the relation creditor-principal debtor. As we have seen, the surety must perform the obligation the principal debtor has towards the creditor if the principal debtor fails to do

156. HR 19-9-2008, ECLI:NL:HR:2008:BD5520, NJ 2008/508.

so, or the surety must pay the damages owed on the basis of non-performance by the debtor where the obligation consists of something else than the payment of a sum of money. From the moment the principal obligation is exigible, the surety has an obligation towards the debtor, even though he is not obliged to perform until the principal debtor has failed in the performance of his obligation.

The surety owes legal interest only over the period that he himself is in default unless the principal debtor is in default pursuant to Article 6:83, sub b (*see supra*, paragraph 181);[157] the surety must reimburse the costs of the lawsuit against the principal debtor if, by timely notification of the intention to bring an action, he has been given the opportunity to avoid such costs (Article 7:856, paragraph 2).

In cases of consumer surety, the surety is not bound to the extent that more onerous conditions would apply to his obligations than those under which the principal debtor is bound, except to the extent that they concern the manner in which proof of the existence and extent of the obligation of the principal debtor can be made against the surety (Article 7:860).

The surety may, in general, invoke the defences the principal debtor has against the creditor. Article 7:852 states that defences which the principal debtor has against the creditor can also be invoked by the surety if they relate to the existence, the content or the time of performance of the obligation of the principal debtor (paragraph 1). Paragraph 1 intends to exclude the defences that concern the personal circumstances of the principal debtor. If the principal debtor is entitled to invoke a ground of annulment in order to annul the juridical act from which the obligation arises, and if the surety or the creditor has given him a reasonable period to exercise that right, the surety is entitled to suspend the performance of his obligation during that period (paragraph 2); as long as the principal debtor rightfully suspends the performance of his obligation towards the creditor, the surety too is entitled to suspend the performance of his obligation (paragraph 3). The last two paragraphs are meant to protect the surety in situations which otherwise might lead to unreasonable results.[158]

§6. Protection of the Interests of the Surety

313. As in all contractual relationships, the creditor has to take into account the reasonable interests of the other party, in this case, the surety. It is difficult to say how far this obligation goes; it all depends on the circumstances of the case. In general, the creditor must act in the way which is best for the surety to the extent that this is possible without detriment to his own interests. The creditor must also inform the surety about the situation and enable him to protect his own interests. In general, the failure of the creditor to take reasonable care of the interests of the surety will lead to an obligation to pay damages, which may be compensated with the obligation of the surety to pay the creditor.

In case of consumer sureties, the Code specifically protects the surety against lack of care on the part of the creditor in two cases.

157. HR 14-12-2018, ECLI:NL:HR:2018:2301.
158. HR 6-6-2008, ECLI:NL:HR:2008:BC8690, NJ 2010/12.

Article 7:861, paragraph 3, states that a surety is not bound for future obligations to repair damage for which the principal debtor is liable towards the creditor, to the extent that the creditor could have prevented the damage by such supervision as could reasonably be expected from him; and paragraph 4 states that a surety is not bound for future obligations arising from a juridical act which the creditor has performed without being obliged to do so (e.g., credit voluntarily granted by a bank) after he had become aware of circumstances which have considerably diminished the possibility of recovering against the principal debtor, and this unless the surety has explicitly consented to the juridical act or unless this act could not be postponed.

Furthermore, the creditor must abstain from any act that would prejudice the rights which a surety may expect to receive pursuant to subrogation pursuant to Article 6:154 if, by his payment, he would be subrogated. In case of consumer sureties, there may be no derogations from this rule (Article 7:862, sub b). The sanction is not that the surety will be released from his obligations but that the creditor is obliged to pay damages.

§7. Cancellation

314. In case of suretyship for future obligations, the question arises if such a suretyship may be cancelled by the surety. The Code contains, in this respect, provisions on the cancellation of a consumer suretyship, which may not be derogated from to the detriment of the surety. Article 7:861, paragraph 1 states that a suretyship entered into for future obligations may:

(a) be cancelled at all times if it is not for a certain and determinate period;
(b) be cancelled after five years if it is for a certain and determinate period.

After cancellation the suretyship continues for obligations which have already arisen (paragraph 2). In other cases of suretyship with regard to which the contract does not contain provisions on cancellation, it depends on the circumstances of the case as to whether the contract may be cancelled. In general, a suretyship for a certain and determinate period may not be cancelled, and a suretyship may be cancelled if no period is fixed. If a suretyship for an indeterminate period may not be cancelled according to the provisions of the contract, a creditor will sometimes nevertheless act contrary to the principles of reasonableness and fairness if he opposes cancellation by the surety (e.g., after a considerable period of time). It is a matter of course that in cases of professional suretyship, the suretyship continues after cancellation for obligations that have already risen.

§8. Relationship Principal Debtor-Surety

315. Article 7:865 makes explicitly sure that the juridical relationship between the principal debtor and the surety (which is not always based on a contract) is governed by the principles of reasonableness and fairness by declaring Article 6:2 (*see supra*, paragraphs 31 ff.) applicable *mutatis mutandis* to these relations.

The most important effect that the suretyship has between the principal debtor and the surety is that the surety has, pursuant to Article 6:10, a claim against the principal debtor for the entire amount that he has had to pay to the creditor in principal sum, interest and costs (Article 7:866, paragraph 1). Article 6:10, paragraph 1, states that solidary debtors must contribute to the debt and the expenses, each for the share which concerns him according to their mutual relationship. In case of suretyship, the debt and expenses concern the principal debtor, and he is the one who has to bear them in the end. The obligation of the principal debtor towards the surety comes into being at the moment when the contract of suretyship is concluded; it is an obligation under the suspensive condition that the surety will pay the debt of the principal debtor.

The right of the surety flowing from Article 7:866, paragraph 1, is not derived from the creditor and therefore stands apart from possible subrogation (*see* on subrogation *supra*, paragraph 140). Subrogation has as advantage that the surety will also acquire the accessory rights connected to the claim of the creditor, but recourse has the advantage that it includes interest and costs.

The principal debtor only has to pay the interest that really concerns him; from Article 7:866, paragraph 2, it follows that the surety cannot derive a claim against the principal debtor from Article 6:10 nor from Article 6:12 for legal interest over the period in which he was in default due to personal circumstances, or for costs which are personal to him or which he did not reasonably have to make.

Where a person has granted suretyship in respect to one and the same obligation for two or more solidary principal debtors, the latter are solidarily liable towards the surety for what the latter can recover from them in principal sum, interest and costs (Article 7:866, paragraph 3). This is a derogation from the general provisions on solidary obligations (Article 6:10, paragraph 1).

The juridical relationship between the surety and one or more principal debtors may produce a result other than that which would flow from paragraphs 1–3 (Article 7:866, paragraph 4).

If the surety has performed the obligation without notifying the principal debtor thereof, and thereafter, the latter, in turn, has paid the creditor, it will suffice for the principal debtor, as regards the surety, to transfer to the latter his claim against the creditor for undue payment (Article 7:867).

A principal debtor who has been sued pursuant to Article 6:10 may also, against the surety, invoke the defences which he had against the creditor at the time the claim for recovery has arisen (Article 7:868).

§9. Relationship Between Sureties and Non-debtors Liable for the Obligation

316. On the relations between sureties and non-debtors liable for the obligation (e.g., a third person who has granted a pledge or a hypothec), the principles of reasonableness and fairness also apply. Article 7:865 declares Article 6:2 applicable *mutatis mutandis* to these relationships.

The co-sureties and non-debtors are, in principle, free to regulate their relationships as they wish. The law has as a starting point that the surety, first of all, has to take recourse against the principal debtor. If this is impossible, Article 7:869 states that under the corresponding application of Article 6:152, the surety at whose expense the obligation has been discharged may apportion the part which has proved to be irrecoverable between himself, his co-sureties and the non-debtors who were liable for the obligation. Article 6:152 states that the unpaid part is apportioned between the parties in proportion to the amounts for which each party was liable to the creditor at the time of payment (*see supra*, paragraph 140).

§10. Subsurety

317. Finally, Title 14 contains a provision on the subsurety. A subsurety is a person who guarantees the principal creditor that the first surety will perform his obligations. The subsurety must be distinguished from the second surety, a surety for the principal debtor, but only if the first surety fails in his performance. This is a surety for the principal debtor but under a suspensive condition. Article 7:870 states that the subsurety who has performed the obligation of the surety can, in his own interest, exercise the recourse which the surety, if he had performed the obligation himself, would have had against the principal debtor, against co-sureties, or against non-debtors who were liable for the obligation. Article 7:870 protects the subsurety against the consequences of bankruptcy of the main surety.

Chapter 8. Pledge

§1. Pledge

318. The right of pledge is defined in Article 3:227, paragraph 1, as a dismembered right intended to provide recourse against the property subjected thereto for a claim for the payment of a sum of money, with preference over other creditors. In case of pledge, the property concerned must be other than registered property.

Pledge plays an important role in the granting of credits, especially to the business community.

The Code contains in section 2 of Title 9 of Book 3 detailed provisions on, among other things, the way in which the right of pledge is established, consequences of the lack of the right of disposal on the part of the grantor of the pledge and the right of the pledgee to sell the pledged property.

There are, however, no special provisions on the contract of pledge (viz. the contract upon which the establishment of the right of pledge is based). The contract of pledge is a regular synallagmatic obligatory contract, which does not give rise to specific difficulties. The general provisions on contracts, therefore, apply.

Chapter 9. Contracts with the Government and Other Public Administrations

§1. Introduction

319. With regard to this subject, something has already been said *supra*, in paragraphs 8 ff. Here, I will take a closer look at the special position of the government and other public administrations when they enter into a civil contract.

In principle, the general rules of contract law also apply to contracts with the administration (this term is used to indicate both the central administration and other public authorities, *see* further *infra*, paragraph 320), but the fact that the administration exercises public tasks and looks after the general interest bears on the position of the administration as a contracting party. Sometimes, as a consequence of this special position, the administration enjoys more freedom, sometimes less.

When performing juridical acts (either of a public law or of a private law nature), the administration must take into account the 'general principles of proper administration' (*see also* paragraph 8), which include among other things such concepts as equality, legal security and fair play, the reliance principle, the duty to account for a decision and the prohibition on '*détournement de pouvoir*' (the use of power for another purpose than for which it has been granted). Article 3:14 explicitly states that a right which a person – and this includes the administration – has pursuant to private law may not be exercised contrary to the written or unwritten rules of public law.

§2. 'Administration'

320. Article 1 of Book 2 of the Code (the Book on Legal Persons) lists a number of public bodies and grants these bodies legal personality in order to enable them to perform patrimonial acts. The public bodies mentioned are the State (the central administration), the provinces, the municipalities, the district water boards, peat districts and peat polders and those bodies to which legislative powers are granted by virtue of the Constitution. All these bodies certainly belong to the administration. There are of course many more bodies which have public tasks and are instituted and organized by rules of public law, but these bodies are only legal persons in the civil sense if their legal personality is determined by Statute. This often happens; examples are the universities and the general civil pension fund. Sometimes civil legal persons are invested with public tasks or tasks which are aimed at the general interest, for example, the public utilities or the railways. These bodies may – as far as their public tasks are concerned – sometimes also be considered to belong to the administration.

§3. Freedom of Contract

321. The concept of freedom of contract (*see supra*, paragraph 14) applies to a somewhat lesser extent to the administration than to private persons. As we have seen in paragraph 9 *supra*, the administration is not allowed to use an instrument of private law if this would frustrate a public regulation. But also where the administration is free to choose a private law alternative, there are sometimes restrictions to its freedom to choose its contracting partner or to determine the contents of the contract.

The choice of the contracting party is, first of all, subject to the general principles of proper administration. From these principles it follows, among other things, that the administration has to treat potential candidates equally, has to choose on the basis of relevant and objective criteria and must (be able to) account for its decision.[159] Furthermore, there are some statutory restrictions to the freedom of the administration to choose its contracting partner. For example, EU directives and implementing acts on contracts for work contain rules on the selection of contractors.

Sometimes, the administration has no choice at all. Most legal writers hold the view that with regard to some things or services (especially essential provisions like the supply of water or electricity), the administration – including in this respect the public utilities – is in general obliged to contract with everybody.[160] Nowadays this is often regulated in EU legislation. If the administration refuses to contract, there may be abuse of right in the sense of Article 3:13, which states in paragraph 2 that instances of abuse of right are the exercise of a right with the sole purpose of harming another or for a purpose other than that for which it was granted or where its exercise was unreasonable, given the disproportion between the interest in its exercise and the harm caused thereby. Moreover, the refusal to contract will be an unlawful act if this refusal is contrary to the principles of proper administration, especially the principle of equality. An example is the case where the (then) National Telephone Corporation refused to contract with a group of applicants for asylum unless they paid a deposit, while it did not ask for a deposit from others.[161]

The contents of a contract must also be in accordance with the general principles of proper administration. In this respect, the principles of equality and legal security will play an important role: contracts with regard to the same (kind of) things or services must in general be equal as to the contents unless the administration has a valid reason to treat one contracting party differently from another. *See also infra*, paragraphs 99–100 on null contracts and contracts subject to annulment.

The Code contains two provisions which are specifically relevant for contracts with public utilities. Article 6:236 (the 'black list', *see supra*, paragraph 113) states under j that a stipulation in general conditions leading to the tacit prolongation or renewal for more than one year of a contract for the regular delivery of things, including electricity, or for the regular performance of services is deemed to be unreasonably onerous. According to Article 7:5, paragraph 3, the provisions on consumer sale (*see* paragraph 248 *supra*) do not apply to contracts pertaining to water supplied to the user by pipelines.

159. *See* HR 26-11-2021, ECLI:NL:HR:2021:1778, NJB 2021/3180.
160. HR 5-11-2021, ECLI:NL:HR:2021:1652, NJ 2021/352.
161. HR 3-9-1993, ECLI:NL:HR:1993:ZC1050, NJ 1993/714. It should be noted however, that the Supreme Court did not get to decide on this point, because the decision already had to be reversed for reasons not related to the subject. *See* for a case in which the Supreme Court did decide on this point, HR 5-11-2021, ECLI:NL:HR:2021:1652, NJ 2021/352.

§4. Approval

322. If the contracting party is a lower administrative body, approval of the decision to conclude the contract by a body higher in hierarchy will often be required. Without approval, the decision will lack juridical effects. Such a requirement may be considered a 'statutory condition' to which the provisions on stipulated conditions (*see supra*, paragraph 129) may be applied *per analogiam* unless a statutory provision produces a different result.

If approval has been granted before the actual conclusion of the contract, no special problems arise.

If the contract has been concluded before the decision to enter into the contract has been approved, it follows from the provisions on conditional obligations that – during the period in which the decision on approval is pending – the parties are bound to each other (in the sense that they may not withdraw from the contract unilaterally), although the obligations do not yet produce effects. From Article 3:57 it follows that the contracting party or another directly interested person can give notice to the contracting administrative body that the act shall have no effects if the approval will not be obtained within a reasonable period indicated in the notice. Approval of the decision will, in general, not have retroactive effects (*see* paragraph 126 on Article 6:24).

§5. Null Contracts and Contracts Subject to Annulment

323. The general rules of contract law determine whether a contract with the administration is null or may be annulled. Due to the special position of the administration, three grounds for nullity/annulment are especially important: contracts contrary to imperative statutory provisions, contracts contrary to the general principles of proper administration and abuse of circumstances on the part of the administration.

Contracts with regard to public rights or powers of the administration may be null or subject to annulment if such contracts are incompatible with statutory provisions (Article 3:40, paragraph 2, *see* paragraph 97). This may, among other things, be the case if public law prescribes an exclusive public way in which the rights or powers concerned must be exercised.

Furthermore, a contract may be contrary to the general principles of proper administration. Depending on the circumstances, such as the nature and the degree of the infringement and the nature of the principle in question, it is not impossible that such a contract is contrary to good morals or public order and, therefore, null (Article 3:40, paragraph 1). *See also* paragraph 96. It is also conceivable that the derogating function of reasonableness and fairness (*see supra*, paragraph 32) may prevent the administration from invoking the stipulations concerned.

If the administration abuses its rights or its special position in order to induce a person to enter into a contract, there may be abuse of circumstances in the sense as dealt with in Article 3:44, paragraph 4 (undue influence; *see* paragraph 88). As a consequence, the contract which has resulted from the abuse of circumstances may be annulled. Article 3:44, paragraph 4 may, for example, be invoked successfully if the administration has abused a monopoly position.

Finally, it should be noted that general conditions used by the administration with regard to civil contracts are, of course, subject to the provisions on general conditions, *see supra*, paragraphs 112 ff.

§6. Performance and Breach

324. Also, with regard to questions of performance and breach, the general rules of contract law, in principle, apply. The view has been upheld that the administration should always be free with regard to the exercise of its public powers in order to be able to serve the public interest in the best way and that the administration may, therefore, withdraw from a contract; it is, however, the current opinion that the administration is in principle bound to a contract in the same way as a private person. And if the administration fails in the performance of an obligation and this failure may be attributed to the administration, the other party will, in general, be entitled to damages.

Although the general rules apply, the application of these rules may, to a certain extent, be influenced by the fact that the administration is one of the contracting parties and that, therefore, not only the interests of the parties but also the general interest is involved. With regard to contracts concerning the public rights and powers of the administration, the general rules of contract law sometimes lead to somewhat different results than with regard to regular private contracts.

In general, the co-contracting party may claim performance of the contract. However, depending on the circumstances of the case (such as the nature of the public body, the nature of the public interest concerned, the expectations based on the contract, the contents of the contract, etc.), it may be contrary to reasonableness and fairness for the other party to claim performance.

The general interest must be balanced against the individual interest of the other party, although it must be emphasized that it is also a matter of general interest that a party may rely on a contract concluded with the administration. Weighty public interests will block performance if this would lead to serious and irreparable harm to an important public interest.

The situation that the other party may not be able to claim performance by the administration will, in general, be limited to the situation that unforeseen circumstances have occurred. In this case, Article 6:258 applies (*see supra*, paragraphs 172 ff.). In a decision of 1989[162] concerning a public contract but equally applicable to private contracts with regard to public rights and powers, the Supreme Court has anticipated on Article 6:258 and has decided that it is not to be excluded that a claim for performance must be denied and the other party must content himself with damages on the ground of unforeseen circumstances of such a nature that the other party may, according to the criteria of reasonableness and fairness, not expect that the contract be maintained in an unmodified form. This may especially be assumed

162. HR 23-6-1989, ECLI:NL:HR:1989:AD0834, NJ 1991/673.

when there is sufficient justification for this outcome in the light of the circumstances, including new considerations on the side of the public body that led to a change of its policies. In this respect, the nature of the contract, the nature of the public task to the exercise of which the administration refers, and – in case of a change of policy – the nature and the weight of the societal interests served by the change of policy should be taken into account.

Finally it should also be noted that in the phase of performance, the administration will have to observe the general principles of proper administration.

Chapter 10. Quasi-Contracts

§1. Quasi-Contracts: Introduction

325. Title 4 of Book 6 contains Articles 198–212 provisions on obligations arising from other sources than unlawful acts or contracts. Some general remarks on the so-called 'quasi-contracts' have already been made in paragraph 27 *supra.* Here I will discuss the provisions of Title 4 in some more detail.

Section 1 (Articles 198–202) deals with the management of the affairs of another, section 2 (Articles 203–211) contains provisions on undue payment, and the only article of section 3 (Article 212) tackles the subject of unjustified enrichment.

§2. Management of the Affairs of Another

326. Article 6:198 contains a definition of management of the affairs of another (*negotiorum gestio*). Management of another's affairs occurs when a person consciously and with good reason undertakes to look after the interest of another person without having the power to do so pursuant to a juridical act or another juridical relationship provided for elsewhere by law. Examples of *negotiorum gestio* provided for by law can be found in Article 6:30, paragraph 1 (a person other than the debtor can perform an obligation) and in Articles 5:5 ff. on finding and taking care of vacant things.

There is *negotiorum gestio* if someone manages the affairs of *another* person. However, the management may, at the same time, include looking after the manager's own interests. For example, a child of a deceased who takes care of the funeral may manage both his own affairs and the affairs of his siblings. It is not necessary that the person whose affairs are managed already exists, the 'person' may be an unborn child or a company not yet incorporated.

The manager undertakes to look after the *interests* of another. If the intended result is not reached, the act still remains *negotiorum gestio.*

The management of the affairs of another may consist of the performance of juridical acts but also of material acts such as towing away a car after an accident.

There is no *negotiorum gestio* if the power (or the obligation) to act is based on a juridical act or the law. The old Code contained in this respect the condition that there had to be a 'voluntary' act, but this term was considered rather vague. It often happens that the manager acts because he morally feels obliged to do so or because he feels obliged by the rules of proper social conduct. It is doubtful if these are really voluntary acts. In the present Code, this term is therefore no longer used and replaced by the requirement that the manager may not have the power to act 'pursuant to a juridical act or another juridical relationship provided for by law'.

A further condition is that the management has to be undertaken consciously. This means that the manager must have the intention to look after the affairs of another. It is not necessary that the manager knows who the other is. This would lead to unreasonable results in cases of emergency.

Finally, there must be a good reason to act. Management of the affairs of another has an exceptional character. In general, a person is not allowed to enter another person's legal sphere. This means that there must be a special justification to do so. This condition is necessary to avoid meddlesomeness and unwanted interference in other people's affairs.

In general, *negotiorum gestio* against the will of the interested person is not possible. This follows from the nature of *negotiorum gestio.*

A manager is entitled to perform juridical acts in the name of the interested party to the extent that the latter's interest is properly looked after (Article 6:201). Examples of juridical acts which may be performed by way of *negotiorum gestio* are the opening of a bank account or the conclusion of an insurance policy. If the manager has acted in the name of the interested person, a direct juridical relationship between the interested person and the third person will come into being. A manager may also act in his own name. In that case, the result will be a juridical relationship between him and the third person.

Where a person who has acted with a view to looking after the interest of another has done so without good reason or has not acted properly, the interested party may, by approving the acts, renounce the right to invoke the defect against the manager. The interested party can be given a reasonable period for approval (Article 6:202).

§3. Rights and Obligations of the Manager and the Interested Person

327. Article 6:199 and 6:200 deal with the rights and obligations of the manager and the interested person. Almost all obligations of the parties result from the principle that the manager acts at the expense and risk of the interested person.

Article 6:199 deals with the obligations of the manager. The manager must exercise the necessary care in his management and, to the extent that this can be required from him, he must continue the management which he has begun.

As soon as is reasonably possible, the manager reports to the interested party on what he has done. He must render an account of the funds which he has spent or received on behalf of the interested party.

If the manager fails in his obligations, he may – on the basis of the general provisions of Articles 6:74 ff. (*see supra*, paragraphs 160 ff.) – be held accountable for the damage resulting from his failure.

Article 6:200, paragraph 1, states that the interested party must compensate the manager for damage which he has suffered as a result of the management, to the extent that his interest has been properly looked after. This means that not only expenses which caused actual enrichment of the interested person have to be compensated for, but all expenses incurred by the manager, provided that he acted properly and could assume that the expenses would serve the interest of the person concerned. The extent of the obligation to compensate is determined on the basis of the general Articles 6:95 ff. (*see supra*, paragraphs 202 ff.).

Where the manager has acted in the course of a business or profession, he has, to the extent that this is reasonable, the further right to be paid for his activities in accordance with the prices usually charged for such activities at the time of the management (Article 6:200, paragraph 2).

§4. Undue Payment

328. Article 6:203–211 contains provisions on undue payment. Article 6:203 states:

(1) A person who has transferred property to another without basis in law is entitled to reclaim it from the recipient as payment not due.
(2) Where the undue payment consists of a sum of money, the claim for restitution is for the same amount.
(3) A person who, without basis in law, has performed a prestation of a different nature also has the right to demand its reversal from the recipient.

The provisions on undue payment have already been mentioned in paragraph 105, which dealt with, among other things, the effects of nullity and annulment. I will, therefore, confine myself here to a few more general remarks and a short survey of the relevant provisions.

A notable feature of Dutch law is the absence of the requirement that the person who has paid unduly should have paid by mistake. Thus, a person who pays under pressure – for example, threatened with a lawsuit – does not lose his rights, though he may know that the debt does not exist; for the sake of clarity, he may pay 'under protest' and claim restitution afterwards.

As in France, payments not due are understood to comprise not only payments of money but the performance of any act which may be made in the execution of an obligation.

If restitution *in natura* is not possible, the Code distinguishes the case where restitution has become impossible by later events (e.g., the recipient has disposed of the thing delivered to him) from the case where restitution is impossible due to the nature of the performance (a house has been rented for a year). In the first case, the obligation to make restitution is treated according to the general rules on non-performance contained in Articles 6:74 ff. (*see* paragraphs 160 ff.) supplemented by Article 6:204 and 6:205. This means, for example, that the recipient is not liable if he disposed of the thing before he knew or ought to have known that he was or would be under an obligation to make restitution.[163] In the second case, restitution of the performance is normally replaced by reimbursement of the value, even in the case of an act forbidden by law, e.g., in case of the lease of a licence to sell liquor, the use of the licence could be set off against the rent paid.[164]

Under the old Code, the Supreme Court has rejected the principle expressed in the adage '*nemo auditur suam turpitudinem allegans*' (according to which a claim based on improper behaviour on the part of the claimant may not be allowed). The present Code adopts the same view, but with a certain refinement: where the court

163. HR 12-02-2016, ECLI:NL:HR:2016:236, NJ 2017/282. *See* for a case on the recipient acting in bad faith, HR 5-4-2019, ECLI:NL:HR:2019:506, NJ 2019/212.
164. HR 7-11-1935, ECLI:NL:HR:1935:63, NJ 1936/239; HR 28-6-1991, ECLI:NL:HR:1991:ZC0305, NJ 1992/787; HR 12-12-2003, ECLI:NL:HR:2003:AL8443, NJ 2005/431; HR 5-12-2014, ECLI:NL:HR:2014:3532, NJ 2016/159; HR 28-06-2019, ECLI:NL:HR:2019:1046, NJ 2020/257; HR 4-10-2019, ECLI:NL:HR:2019:1500, NJ 2020/259.

finds that it is morally unacceptable to assess the value of a particular act or performance, recovery will be excluded, not only as regards that act but also as regards what the other party has given or done in return, at least in so far as the existence of a unilateral claim for recovery would be unjust between the parties (Article 6:211). The purpose of the Code in this field is to remove any remaining penal element from the civil law of restitution; the commentary declares that where punishment is required, it ought to be inflicted in the ordinary way prescribed by criminal law. The experience with civil sanctions in this field is discouraging.

§5. Unjustified Enrichment

329. Unlike the old Code, the present Code contains – in Article 6:212, paragraph 1 – the general rule that a person who has been unjustly enriched at the expense of another must, to the extent that this is reasonable, repair the damage suffered by that other person up to the amount of his enrichment.

Under the old Code, the Supreme Court has denied the existence of such a general rule and only accepted a claim based on unjustified enrichment in a restricted way, namely if the case was not provided for by the law fitted in the system of the law and was in line with rules already laid down for similar situations (*see also* paragraph 27 *supra*).

Article 6:212, paragraph 1, shows in the first place that the obligation, unlike the one resulting from undue payment, relates to the payment of damages, which means that it is governed by the general provisions on damages in Articles 6:95 ff. (*see* paragraphs 202 ff.). Furthermore, the article makes clear that there has to be an enrichment and that the enrichment must be brought about at the expense of another. Enrichment is every increase in property. The condition that the enrichment has to be brought about at the expense of another means that the enrichment of the defendant has to correspond with a loss of the plaintiff.[165] The plaintiff's right to compensation for his loss does not exceed the amount of the defendant's enrichment. Moreover, the claim for damages can be dismissed if it would lead to an unreasonable result, which may be the case if the enrichment has been inflicted upon the defendant without his consent.

The action is not restricted to cases of 'immediate enrichment'. For example, a mandator, to whose expense an undue payment was made by the mandatary, may claim compensation from the person who received the undue payment.

The key condition of the general rule of Article 6:212, paragraph 1, is that the enrichment has to be unjustified, that is, without reasonable ground. If the enrichment is based on a juridical act, it will almost always be justified. More difficult to answer is the question of whether enrichment based on a legal provision is justified or not. All will depend on the nature of the relevant provision. For example, enrichment caused by prescription or lapse of a period of time will not be unjustified; enrichment caused by accession, amalgamation or creation of a new thing (specification) in the absence of a contractual basis will in general be unjustified.

165. HR 10-5-2019, ECLI:NL:HR:2019:707, NJ 2019/248.

The action based on unjustified enrichment does not have a subsidiary nature. In principle, it may also be instituted if the plaintiff could have based his action for compensation on another juridical ground or against another person.[166] In this respect, Dutch law differs from most other systems of law.

The enrichment is not taken into consideration to the extent that it has decreased as a result of circumstances which cannot be attributed to the enriched person (Article 6:212, paragraph 2). A decrease in the enrichment during the period in which the enriched person did not reasonably have to foresee the existence of an obligation to make reparation for damage shall not be attributed to him. In determining this decrease, the expenses which would not have been made had there been no enrichment, are also taken into account (Article 6:212, paragraph 3). These two provisions are an elaboration of the words 'to the extent that this is reasonable' in the first paragraph.[167]

166. HR 29-1-1993, ECLI:NL:HR:1993:ZC0845, NJ 1994/172; HR 27-6-1997, ECLI:NL:HR:1997:AG7249, NJ 1997/719; HR 30-9-2005, ECLI:NL:HR:2005:AR7928, NJ 2007/154.

167. *See* for another application of this condition, HR 12-2-2016, ECLI:NL:HR:2016:236, NJ 2017/282.

Selected Bibliography

In Languages Other than Dutch

J. Basedow. 'Grundfragen der Vertragsrechtreform, Niederländische Erfahrungen'. *Zeitschrift für vergleichende Rechtswissenschaft* 79 (1980): 132–148.

A.R. Bloembergen. 'Schadenersatz im neuen niederländischen Zivilgesetzbuch'. *Versicherungsrecht* (25 Karlsruher Forum, Jubiläumausgabe 1983), 4 ff.

J. Dainow. 'Civil Code Revision in the Netherlands: The Fifty Questions'. *Am. Comp. L.* 5 (1956): 595–610.

J. Dainow. 'Civil Code Revision in the Netherlands: General Problems'. *Louisiana Law Review* 17 (1957): 273, 293.

J. Dainow. 'Civil Code Revision in the Netherlands: Some New Developments in Obligations and Property'. In *XXth Century Comparative and Conflicts Law* (Legal Essays in honour of Hessel E. Yntema) (1961): 172–189.

A.S. Hartkamp. 'Civil Code Revision in the Netherlands': A Survey of Its System and Contents and Its Influence on Dutch Legal Practice'. *Louisiana Law Review* (1975) (Special Issue): 1059–1090.

A.S. Hartkamp. 'Vers un nouveau Code Civil Néerlandais'. *Revue internationale de droit comparé* (1982), 319 ff.

A.S. Hartkamp. 'Civil Code Revision in the Netherlands'. In *Netherlands Business Legislation*, trans. by Haanappel et al. (looseleaf ed.), prelims 7–23.

A.S. Hartkamp. 'Einführung in das neue Niederländische Schuldrecht'. Teil I, *Archiv für die Civilistische Praxis* 191 (1991): 396–410.

A.S. Hartkamp. 'The Binding Force of Contract in Dutch Law'. In *The Binding Force of Contract,* Budapest, 1991, 41–48.

A.S. Hartkamp. 'Judicial Discretion under the New Netherlands Civil Code'. *American Journal of Comparative Law* 40 (1992): blz. 551–571.

A.S. Hartkamp. 'Das neue niederländische Bürgerliche Gesetzbuch aus europäischer Sicht'. *Rabelsz* 57 (1993): 664–684.

A.S. Hartkamp & M.M.M. Tillema. 'Mass Torts'. *Netherlands Reports for the XIVth International Congress of Comparative Law*, Athens 1994 (1995), 51–69.

A.S. Hartkamp. 'Statutory law Making: The New Civil Code of The Netherlands'. In *Towards Universal Laws. Trends in National, European and International Lawmaking* (Uppsala 22–26 March 1995), in *De lege Juridiska Fakulteten i Uppsala* (Arsbok, Argang 1995), 151–178.

Selected Bibliography

A.S. Hartkamp. 'Interplay Between Judges, Legislators and Academics. The Case of the New Civil Code of The Netherlands'. In *Law Making, Law Finding, and Law Shaping. The Diverse Influences*, ed. Basil S. Markesinis. Oxford University Press, 1997, 91–112.

A.S. Hartkamp. *Indirect Representation according to the Principles of European Contract Law, the Unidroit Agency Convention and the Dutch Civil Code.* Festschrift Drobnig, 1998, 45–56.

A.S. Hartkamp. *Deutsche Einflüsse auf das niederländische Privatrecht.* AcP 200 (2000), 507–510.

A.S. Hartkamp. 'Unjust Enrichment alongside Contracts and Torts'. In *Unjust Enrichment and the Law of Contract*, ed. E.J.H. Schrage. Kluwer Law International, 2001, 25–32.

A.S. Hartkamp. 'Comparative Law before the Dutch Courts'. In *Comparative Law before the Courts,* eds Canivet, Andenas & Fairgrieve. BIICL London, 2004, 229–233.

M.M.C. van de Moosdijk. 'Law of Obligations'. In *Introduction to Dutch Law*, eds L. van den Herik et al. 6th ed., Kluwer Law International, 2022, 135–162.

E.H. Hondius. 'Recodification of the Law in the Netherlands'. *Neth. Int. Law Review* (1982): 348 ff.

E.H. Hondius. 'Neukodifikation des niederländischen Zivilrechts'. *Versicherungsrecht* (25 Karsruher Forum Jubiläumausgabe 1983), 41 ff.

E.H. Hondius. 'Das neue niederländische Zivilgesetzbuch'. *Archiv für die Civilistische Praxis 191* (1991): 378–395.

E.H. Hondius & W.Th. Braams. 'Auf dem Wege zu einem neuen europäischen Haftungsrecht-Beitrag der Niederlande'. *Vorträge Universität des Saarlandes* 1989, Saarbrücken 1990.

E. Ioriatti, 'Il nuovo codice civile dei Paesi Bassi fra soluzioni originali e circolazione dei modelli'. *Rivista di diritto civile* (1992): 117–180.

J.G. Jonas. *Die verschuldensunabhängige ausservertragliche Haftung für Sachen im Entwurf zum Nieuw Burgerlijk Wetboek der Niederlande.* München, 1987.

E.M. Meijers. 'La reforme du Code Civil neérlandais'. *Verzamelde Privaatrechtelijke Opstellen* (VPO) I (1954), 150–273.

E.M. Meijers. 'Case Law and Codified Systems of Private Law'. VPO I, 181–193.

E.M. Meijers. 'La révision du Code Civil neérlandais'. VPO I, 194–204.

F. Nieper c.s. *Niederländisches Bürgerliches Gesetzbuch* (1995).

The Principles of European Contract Law and Dutch Law, A commentary, I. Edited by Danny Busch, Ewoud Hondius, Hugo van Kooten, Harriët Schelhaas (general editor) and Wendy Schrama. Ars Aequi/Kluwer Law International, 2002, 471 p.

The Principles of European Contract Law and Dutch Law, A Commentary, II. Edited by Danny Busch Ewoud Hondius, Hugo van Kooten, Harriët Schelhaas ((general editor). Ars Aequi/Kluwer Law International, 2006, 292 p.

T.B. Smith. 'The Influence Abroad of the Modern Dutch Movement for Code Revision'. WPNR 5503 (1980).

W. Snijders. 'Vers un nouveau Code Civil néerlandais. Etat des Traveaux'. *Revue de Droit International et de Droit Comparé* 56 (1979): 223–231.

'Unofficial Translation of Book 6 of the Draft of a Netherlands Civil Code'. *Netherlands International Law Review* 17 (Kluwer, 1970): 225–274, with an introduction by H. Drion and notes on some general problems of terminology by F.H. Lawson.

F.J.A. van der Velden & N.A. Florijn. 'Harmonization of Private Law Rules between Civil and Common Law Jurisdictions'. In *Netherlands Reports to the Thirteenth International Congress of Comparative Law*, eds Hondius & Steenhoff. The Hague: Montreal, 1990, 42–57.

J.B.M. Vranken. 'Einführung in das neue niederländische Schuldrecht'. Teil II, *Archiv für die Civilistische Praxis* 191 (1991): 411–432.

B. Wessels. *Civil Code Revision: System, Contents and Future.* NILR, 1994, 163 ff.

In Dutch

For all literature in Dutch, *see* the bibliographies in:

C.J. Van Zeben & G.J.L. Seesink. *Nederlandse wetgeving, Nieuw Burgerlijk Wetboek.*

R.W.E. van Leuken, M.M.C. van de Moosdijk & V. Tweehuysen. *Hartkamps Compendium van het vermogensrecht* (2017), No. 3a and *passim.*

The draft bills and all the official documents are published in:

C.J. van Zeben et al., *Parlementaire Geschiedenis van het nieuwe Burgerlijk Wetboek.*

Here, some limited literature references are made, arranged by subject matter. Law of obligations in general/law of contracts in general/law of torts and quasi-contracts:

Asser/Sieburgh 6-I, *Verbintenissenrecht*, De verbintenis in het algemeen, eerste gedeelte (2020).

Asser/Sieburgh 6-II, *Verbintenissenrecht,* De verbintenis in het algemeen, tweede gedeelte (2021).

Asser/Sieburgh 6-III, *Verbintenissenrecht,* Algemeen overeenkomstenrecht (2022).

Asser/Sieburgh 6-IV, *Verbintenissenrecht,* De verbintenis uit de wet (2023).

A.T. Bolt (ed.), *Groene Serie Schadevergoeding.*

R.J.Q. Klomp & H.N. Schelhaas (eds), *Groene Serie Verbintenissenrecht.*

Jac. Hijma (ed.), *Groene Serie Vermogensrecht.*

Special Contracts

Asser/Hijma 7-I, *Koop en ruil* (2019).

Asser/Rossel & Heisterkamp 7-II, *Huur* (2021).

Asser/Valk 7-III, *Pacht* (2020).

Asser/Tjong Tjin Tai 7-IV, *Opdracht* (2022).

Asser/Heerma van Voss 7-V, *Arbeidsovereenkomst* (2020).

Asser/Van Gulijk 7-VI, *Aanneming van werk* (2022).

Asser/Van Olffen 7-VII, *Maatschap, vennootschap onder firma en commanditaire vennootschap* (2022).

Asser/Houben & Van Schaick 7-VIII, *Bewaarneming, borgtocht, vaststellingsovereenkomst, franchise, bruikleen, altijddurende rente, spel en weddenschap* (2023).

Asser/Wansink, Van Tiggele & Salomons 7-IX, *Verzekering* (2019).

Selected Bibliography

Asser/Houben 7-X, *Onbenoemde overeenkomsten* (2019).
S.E. Bartels, A.J. Verdaas & E.F. Verheul, *Groene Serie Bijzondere overeenkomsten.*

Agency

Asser/Kortmann 3-III, *Volmacht en vertegenwoordiging* (2017).

Sale of Goods

Asser/Hijma 7-I, *mentioned above.*
B. Wessels, Koop: algemeen, Mon. BW B65a (2015).
M.B.M. Loos, Consumentenkoop, Mon. BW B65b (2019).
A.A. van Velten, Koop van onroerende zaken, Mon. BW B65c (2013).

Building Contracts

Asser/Van Gulijk 7-VI, *mentioned above.*
M.A. van Wijngaarden & M.A.B. Chao-Duivis, *Hoofdstukken Bouwrecht* (many volumes).

Lease, Commercial and Agricultural Leases

Asser/Rossel & Heisterkamp 7-II, *mentioned above.*
A.M. Kloosterman, H.J. Rossel & M.H. Rozeboom, *Hoofdlijnen in het huurrecht* (2020).
H.J. Rossel, *Huurrecht algemeen* (2011).

Compromise

A.A. van Rossum, *Vaststellingsovereenkomst*, Mon. BW B80 (2001).

Suretyship

J.W.H. Blomkwist, *Borgtocht*, Mon. BW B78 (2012).

Contracts with the Government and Other Public Administrations

M.W. Scheltema en M. Scheltema, Gemeenschappelijk recht (2013).
G. Snijders, *Overheidsprivaatrecht, algemeen deel*, Mon. BW A26a (2011).

Annex: Table of Contents of the Books 3 and 6 of the Dutch Civil Code

Annex: Table of Contents of the Books 3 and 6 of the Dutch Civil Code

Annex: Table of Contents of the Books 3 and 6 of the Dutch Civil Code

Index

The numbers here refer to paragraph numbers.